Tully Kossack

3404 Pauline Dr

Chevy Chase Md

20015

The Dial Press    New York    1973

# THE CONFESSIONS
# OF A MASTER CRIMINAL

ROBERT H.
ADLEMAN

Manufactured in the United States of America
Third printing, 1973
Design by Margaret McCutcheon Wagner


Library of Congress Cataloging in Publication Data

Adleman, Robert H      1919–
Alias Big Cherry.

1.  Scolnick, Sylvan.  I.  Title.
[HV6248.S39A4]     364.1′63′0924 [B]      73–4751

For Burgess Meredith

*The two black inmates had been slouching lazily against a wall in the prison recreation yard, but they sat up as the Fat Man approached. One of them said, "Heah he comes. Big Cherry. Big Bad Cherry from Cherry Hill," and the other joined him in giving the clenched-fist salute as the enormous white convict passed by.*

# FOREWORD

Everything in this book is true—or at least contains as much truth as I can isolate after talking with Sylvan Scolnick (also known as "Big Cherry," "Cherry Hill Fats," and "The Fat Man") for hundreds of hours and after cross-checking his remarks and descriptions with at least fifty other people who were his henchmen, adversaries and reporters.

Many of these recollections chose a form which sacrificed accurate chronology. For example, when I talked with him or an accomplice about bank swindling, the stories ranged over a period of years and I was never sure of any date other than that the "move" had taken place at a time beyond the period set by the statute of limitations for prosecution. As a result, my chapter sequence describes classes of activities rather than a chronological progression. Incidentally, the extracts heading many of these chapters originally appeared in the report of the Philadelphia County presentence investigation and have no reference to the reports involved in the federal prosecutions.

A few of the names have been changed because when Big Cherry went straight, so did some of his associates and I see no point in making it tougher for them in their present jobs. I've also disguised the identities of some of his other friends because I'd just as soon not have them feeling that they have a bone to pick with me.

A majority of those people who were the research sources for this book have asked me not to identify them—a few because they were concerned with the possibility that I might end up writing something that glorified Big Cherry, and others because they had a confidential relationship with the man but gave me their opinions and recollections because they felt he had the right to get as honest a story as possible written about him.

One more disclaimer; I should say at the outset that I like Sylvan Scolnick, but the reader should be aware also that there are many others who fear or detest him. I've tried to reflect their opinions, too. For example, in October 1971 a reporter for the *Philadelphia Magazine* wrote:

> In almost every way, Sylvan Scolnick is the epitome of the superlative. He is the most. He is undoubtedly the fattest, probably the shrewdest, unquestionably the most deceptive, perhaps the evilest and likely the most driven criminal conspirator in modern history. Ahhh, how that would hurt him. He is also one of the most sensitive of men. He is frequently given to philosophizing on life and morality and often expresses a reverence for the verities of religious ideals. When he wants to, he can have you believe that he is the gentlest and most considerate of men, an extremely likable fellow. He is a master at selling himself.

I agree that Sylvan Scolnick is a master salesman. His torrent of colorful anecdotes and recollections and the additional dimensions supplied by his friends and adversaries sold me to the point where it seemed advisable to tell as much of the story as possible in his and their own words.

—Robert H. Adleman

Alias Big Cherry

# Chapter 1

# THE $100,000 HEIST

REPORTER: *How did it feel to pull it off?*

SCOLNICK: *It was like the junkies say, a high. I can't tell you the feeling. I was high because I didn't hurt nobody and I succeeded. They wanted to go in with guns and actually stick up the bank. I told 'em no. I said you don't have to go in with guns. I said it's simple, just take it with a trick. And oh—what a feeling! The guy that was with us in the insurance business, at the time when he heard it on the car radio and read it in the paper, he told me that he knew I done it. He didn't know how I done it, but he said he knew it was only me that could have done it.*

REPORTER: *Was it a feeling of power?*

SCOLNICK: *Absolutely! There's millions and millions of dollars in safe deposit boxes all over the country and I could rob any box I wanted without them knowing. Man, what a high!*

No question about it, it was a brilliantly planned heist. The bank was crowded with customers and employees and yet no one realized that the $100,000 had been stolen from the locked and federally sealed safe deposit box until a secretary noticed the federal impound notice lying on the floor.

Four men did this to the Philadelphia Savings Fund Society bank in northeast Philadelphia on December 30, 1965. They were Sydney Brooks, Harry Cohen, Tom Mitchell and Sylvan Scolnick, known at that time as "The Fat Man," and who was once described as having the mind of a souped-up computer.

The reporters covering the story found the robbery even more interesting after it became generally known that the safe deposit box was registered in the name of Sydney Brooks and that its contents were suspected by the police as representing his share of the loot from a series of burglaries.

Sydney Brooks must be introduced first to explain how the money in the box came to the attention of the police a few weeks before the heist took place.

Even in the trade, he is accepted as a very hard citizen. "I knowed Brooks before," said one man, "and I knowed him in prison and I never seen him in any way but as a guy you'd feed with a very long spoon. It never paid nobody to get too close to him."

"Sydney done everything," said another ex-associate. "There are damn few better burglars in the country than him. He was also a first-class torch. Every joint he was connected with would sooner or later burn down for the insurance company to pay out on.

"And, starting with the Blaney murder, the Philly cops automatically used to pull him in for questioning when anything heavy happened. It was like it said in the book that that was the thing for them to do.

4

"And tough? Man!" A long whistle. "He got a name as a street brawler when he was running the bust-out joints. You know, the bars where they'd have the girl shows and the hookers sitting around waiting for the tide to come in. I remember one night when he mixed it with Charley Cigar, the shylock.

"He owed Charley Cigar, but the one thing Sydney hates more than anything else is to pay out money. After he stalled Charley Cigar five or six times, the shylock laid for him outside of a joint Sydney was running at the time. When Sydney came out, he tells Sydney to pay up or else. Sydney don't even wait to find out what 'or else,' he just decks him with one punch. Charley Cigar gets up and there's a razor blade in his hand. He takes a swipe at Sydney and cuts his face so bad that later on I understand they had to take almost a hundred stitches to put it together. But that don't stop Sydney. With his face hanging in pieces, he beats up the Cigar so unmerciful the guy ain't back in action for a couple of months.

"Anyways, Sydney is tough and so tight it'd take a tractor to pull a needle out of his ass. In fact, that's how come the cops picked him up and found out in the first place about the box with the hundred grand in it. One time he took Herman Kutsher with him to put some money in the box, and when Herman found out he had so much there, he figured that Sydney had been oontzing him; so when the cops pulled Herman in, he gave up Sydney after very little heat."

Brooks is also a very arrogant man. Although he had no respect whatsoever for Herman Kutsher, he should never have permitted Kutsher to know about his safe deposit box. He should have realized that Kutsher, who never held on to a dime, would certainly suspect that the presence of so much money was the final proof that Brooks had given him a short count after their Park City West job, a simple burglary of an apartment house which later grew into a comedy of errors involving

5

subornation of perjury on the part of several of Philadelphia's criminal lawyers, bail bondsmen, city hall hangers-on and a crazy artist.

Kutsher, in the words of one of the detectives who arrested him, "is one of the best key men in the business. He'll take you past any lock, but after that, get rid of him. He's a lightweight who'll screw up any job where they let him inside. And he can't take no heat."

The heat, applied by the detectives who picked him up for questioning in connection with the Park City West burglary, combined with his belief that he had gotten the short end in the division of the loot, was the reason that Kutsher mentioned the name of Sydney Brooks in the very early stages of the interrogation.

After Brooks was arrested, they found a key to a safe deposit box on his key ring. Within a few hours, the key was tracked down to the proper bank and branch and a search-and-seizure warrant was secured which permitted the opening of the box. When the box was found to be crammed with fifty- and one-hundred-dollar bills, one of the more enterprising policemen suggested that since the warrant only permitted them to pick up jewelry, the way to keep the money on ice would be to contact the Internal Revenue Service. Before three more hours had passed, the cash had been inventoried and locked back up in the box which was then sealed with a notice stating that the contents had been impounded by the federal government under a tax lien filed against one Sydney Brooks.

Next morning Brooks's lawyer had him out on bail. His first call was not to his current wife, who wasn't devious enough to help him solve his problems, but to the Fat Man, who was. "I gotta see you," he said. "Right away."

"I'm here."

"Well, stay there. Don't move."

6

"Maybe you never noticed, but I don't move very often. You in trouble, Sydney?"

"You might say that. I'm also saying again, don't move. I'll be there in a half an hour."

The Fat Man's office was sixty-three city blocks from Philadelphia's City Hall, but long before the thirty minutes had passed, Brooks was asking the girl in the front room, "He back there?"

She nodded, not showing that she knew who Brooks was and that she was afraid of him.

He walked into the back room and said, "Buddy, I'm in trouble."

"What else is new?"

"Joke later. They nailed me last night and, like a jerk, I had the key to my bank box on me."

"Do they know what bank?."

"Nah. It'll take them a day to check out the banks to find out which one and in what branch. I got another key, but I'm afraid to go down there myself. You got to get me somebody."

The other man, who was thirty-six years old and weighed 642 pounds, pushed his chair away from his desk, got up and walked with difficulty to the window. Looking out on Broad Street he said, "Sydney, you're coming in like a shortstop. It was already in the papers this morning."

"Oh, Jesus, no! They found it?"

"Yep. They found the bank, they opened the box, they counted up the hundred thousand bucks that was in it, and they put it back with a nice bright seal which says that the box is impounded, I thinks it's by the federal government. Didn't you know this, Sydney?"

"No. Honest to God. I just got out."

When the Fat Man didn't answer, Brooks said, "Look, Syl,

7

it don't matter whether you believe me or not. But you gotta help me get that dough."

"Why?"

"Because I need it for my lawyer. I'm only out on bail, or did you forget?"

"I meant, why do I have to help you? As of now I don't even know you."

The thin edge of gravel always present in Sydney's voice became flat and very noticeable as he said, "You know me, Syl. You goddamned well know me. If I go down the drain, I'm taking you with me."

In addition to his fast brain, another of the Fat Man's strengths is the ability to forecast most of the next moves of an opponent in almost every given situation. He knew Brooks was quite serious about the threat, so he took only a moment before answering, "Well, of course, that makes it different."

"Sydney had a lock on me," the Fat Man explains, "ever since I used him as the torch on the $700,000 Frankford and Bridge streets burn. That was a home remodeling outfit I had which wasn't doing too good. So when he says it to me so cold like that, I thought maybe I'd better reconsider about helping him out.

"I told him to shut the door because I didn't want my bookkeeper to hear . . . you know, I was stalling for time because this was pretty heavy. Up till then I never had been in nothing like this before and I said, 'Sydney, run it down for me.'

"So he tells me about where the box is and what's in it and that as soon as I give him the okay, he'll get some guys down from New York and we'll go in and do it in whatever way I say.

"I told him to wait a minute. 'We don't need no pistols from New York,' I told him. 'We can do it by trick.'

"He says, 'I knew I came to the right guy. How?'

" 'Stop pushing, will you? Let me think,' and I swiveled

8

my chair around and looked at the back wall, figuring to let him get real impatient. For a long time I'd had a theory on how to pull something like this, but there was no point in letting him think it was easy. It was going to be hard enough to get Sydney to pay me my end, and if I had let him know how simple it could be, he'd a paid me like he paid Kutsher; like a shortstop.

"Finally, I turned around and I said, 'Do you know Tommy Mitchell and Harry Cohen?'

" 'I seen 'em around. They work for you, don't they?'

"As a matter of fact, they did. I mean, I let them hang around the insurance company I was also running at the time. I think I had Tommy on the payroll for a few bucks, maybe a hundred a week. I let Tom talk to the people who came in with claims, which is as much action as they ever got, and I let Harry do odd jobs. Of course, at that time I didn't know them very well. I didn't know that they were both stone crazy. They were working for me during the day and at night they'd be out sticking up houses.

"When I found out about it, I told them I'd break their necks if they did any more of that crap. And you know what Harry says to me? I swear, he says, 'What are you trying to do, keep us from making a living?' The son of a bitch, it was like he figured he pays social security on what he sticks people up for. Stone nuts.

"Let me tell you about these guys. Harry was a real little skinny guy, weighed in at about ninety pounds, about five feet two, big protruding ears and a very bony face. His whole ambition in life was to be a killer, a big-time hood. His hero is the other guy, Tommy, who was tall, way over six feet, and very bright. An educated man, I think he was also a registered pharmacist who used to work in his father's drug store before the old man got onto that Tommy was stealing from him and threw him out.

9

"Anyway, I got these two guys, Mopey and Dopey. One guy, Tommy, is on the payroll and the other guy hangs around because he wants to be near me, the big-time Fat Man, the boss. He really loved that racket crap."

At this early stage in their relationship, the Fat Man regarded both Harry Cohen and Tommy Mitchell as expendable, which is why he settled on them for the job of helping Sydney Brooks out of his dilemma. He told Brooks to return later that night and at that time the four of them would begin planning the robbery. He further sharpened Brooks's appetite by telling him before he left that there might be a way to not only recover his money, he might also be able to sue the bank for permitting it to be stolen. "You might get two for one, Sydney. You'd like that, wouldn't you?"

On the night of December 23, 1965, Brooks and Cohen met with the Fat Man in the back room of the offices at 6335 North Broad Street where he told them: "Look, there's got to be two keys to every safe deposit box. The guy who owns the box has one and the bank has a bunch of master keys. You need both keys to unlock the box. . . ."

Cohen butted in, "That's very interesting."

Brooks, glaring, said, "Will you shut up, Harry? Come on, Syl, everybody knows this but Harry. Skip the song and dance."

The Fat Man said patiently, "Harry and Tom has got to know it too. I been studying banks for some years now, and in a branch bank like the PSFS, they probably have no more than five master keys. Now the people in banks get very lax, like the tellers who, if they would take the time to check the signature and call the bookkeeping and this and that, they wouldn't be paying out so much on bad checks, the banks would lose a lot less money. But they don't care, it isn't their money, in fact it even stops being money to them, it's only paper and some of them get very lax when they handle it.

10

"Same way with the master keys. They handle them too often to respect them. A lot of times they just leave them laying around on the desk or in their middle drawer or something.

"So what we do is this. Sydney, there's a guy down on Market Street who won't ask any questions about making a duplicate of the extra key you still got to your box, so in case anything happens you can show you still got your key and they can't trace nothing to you. After you get it made, give the duplicate to Harry."

Cohen was so excited by the fact that he was going in partners in a job with big-time Sydney Brooks that he failed to notice that this arrangement indicated that he was going to be left squarely in the middle, nor did he interpret the quick glance of understanding that passed between Brooks and the Fat Man.

"All right," said the Fat Man, "now let's get Tommy Mitchell in here." Mitchell had been kept waiting in the outer office. When he came in and sat down beside Cohen, he wondered at the air of importance his sidekick was projecting. All of a sudden, it didn't seem like Harry.

But the alienated feeling left after Brooks told him that they were going to knock over the PSFS bank and that he and Harry were going to be the key figures. "You're moving up," he said to them.

The Fat Man took over. "Here's how it goes down. You, Tommy, I want you every day to go into the bank and rent another safe deposit box. Nobody'll say anything about it, they're in business to rent boxes. Maybe you go in there every day to make change or put something in one of the boxes or take something out so they get used to you.

"As soon as you get a box near Sydney's, you let us know. Then, the next day, you go in with Harry. There'll be some confusion or something we'll cause, maybe we'll stage an accident outside the bank, and everybody will run to the front window to see what happens. Then, Tommy, you grab the

11

master keys off of the girl's desk or maybe they'll be in her drawer, and you open up your box and Sydney's. The same master will work them both. You and Harry then switch boxes, understand? Don't take nothing with you, just take Sydney's box and put it in yours and your box and put it in Sydney's. Then lock both boxes and walk out. A week later Tommy can go take the money out without anybody asking questions.

"You see how it goes down, Sydney?" he continued, turning toward Brooks. "We stage an accident or throw a brick through the window from outside and it's all over in a minute and clean with you being miles away."

"It's very good, Syl," answered Brooks. "All except one thing. It's my money and I'm going to be there watching."

"If that's what you want, okay. But if that's the case, let's also talk about the split right now. I want fifty grand for my end which I'll take care of Harry and Tommy out of."

Brooks said, "You'll take twenty. It ain't Christmas yet."

This split was finally agreed upon after it became obvious, even to Harry Cohen, that now that he had the plan, Brooks was beginning to play with the idea of digging up some lower-priced associates.

Brooks left first that night. Afterward, the Fat Man told the other two, "I got a few financial problems, I'm borrowing five off the top and then we split the other fifteen three equal ways."

Although the four men met in the insurance office for the next six nights in an effort at further refinement, the job came off substantially the way it had been outlined by the Fat Man at the first meeting.

As it turned out, Brooks threw the brick through the bank window but it didn't attract enough attention in the crowded bank to cause the excitement envisioned in the original plan. Mitchell, standing in the back, said to Cohen,

12

"That's a diversion?" and, thinking quickly, he ran to the front, yelling, "My God, what's happening. They're breaking into the bank!"

Naturally, the other customers and employees followed in his wake, leaving Cohen alone by the doorway to the safe deposit box room. At that point, Cohen picked up the ring of master keys from the desk inside the room and opened the box containing the money. But because he was not used to thinking under pressure, he disobeyed instructions and put the box under his raincoat and walked out of the bank so quickly that Brooks, who had come in and was standing by the front teller's cage, missed him in the crowd.

The first knowledge that the Fat Man had that the job had been completed came in a telephone call from Brooks. "Is he there yet?"

"Who?"

"The little guy. The little guy. Is he there yet? They took the box with them."

"When?"

"Just now. It worked just like you said."

"Hang up, Sydney. He might be trying to call me. I'll let you know."

The Fat Man hung up without waiting for an acknowledgment. After glancing at the clock on the wall, he sat quietly and expressionlessly until, after fifteen minutes, the phone rang again.

It was Cohen. "I got it, I got it," he said, and began giggling because he was completely turned on by the coup. "A piece of cake! The guard on the front door even opened it up for me when he saw I was carrying a heavy package under my raincoat. Politest goddamned bank you ever saw."

The Fat Man was aware that a dangerous element had been introduced into the plan by taking the box rather than

13

switching it, but he only asked, "I thought you was going to meet them at the diner?"

"I wanted to talk to you first. Let's cut a new deal, huh, Syl?"

"Like what?"

"Like the fifty for us and the fifty for him we first talked about."

"Listen to me, Harry. Is Tom still with Sydney?"

"I guess so. Sure."

"Is Tom your friend?"

"What are you talking about? Sure. I'd like to see anybody say he wasn't!"

"And he's still with Sydney?"

There was silence on the other side for a few moments. Then, "I see what you mean, Syl. I'll be right down."

"Come in the back way. And, Harry—"

"Yeah, Syl?"

"Don't stop anywhere before you get here. You wouldn't want to have to worry about both Sydney and me, would you?"

There was genuine hurt in Harry's voice. "Hey, Syl, what kind of a dirty guy you think I am? I'll be right down."

The Fat Man recalls Cohen's trip to the office. "He come in the side door and put the box on my desk like he was a little pup that just fetched me the newspaper. I said, 'Very good, Harry,' and I opened it up and dumped all them fifties and hundreds on my desk. They smelled awful . . . old and musty, but that didn't bother me too much. I just cut out my twenty and put it away. The rest of it I swept into the top drawer. Then I told Harry to go back to his motel until I called him.

"I didn't make no more calls. I just sat there. About half an hour later, Brooks comes in and he's a nervous wreck. The sweat is running down his face. He looked at me without saying nothing and I said, 'Yeah, I got it,' and a smile came over him

14

from ear to ear. I took out the money and put it on the desk in front of him. He was wearing a trench coat with the most enormous pocket I ever seen, and he just dumped all the money in that pocket and threw his arms around me and kissed me and he said, 'You're the greatest! You're absolutely the greatest!' and then he walked out and that was the last I ever saw of that eighty grand.

"I understand that when the news of it got out, there was a run of people taking their things out of their safe deposit boxes. Up until then it was considered the safest place that could be, that they never could be entered, but of course that turned out to be the simplest thing to do."

Apart from the inclusion of Cohen and Mitchell, the plan was created and put together with a masterful hand. But the Fat Man has made a career out of putting schemes together with a maximum efficiency. Some law officers and reporters have estimated that the amounts involved in his illegal activities total somewhere between $25 million and $50 million.

He has taken down sizable scores in almost a hundred major fraudulent bankruptcies and there have been those who came to him from all over the country to buy large lots of his astonishingly accurate forgeries of American Express checks, passports, driver's licenses and other official documents, and, inevitably, credit cards.

Some people came to him for money and if the proposition was promising enough, he arranged the financing after taking his "vig" off the top.

He quarterbacked holdups, teams of bank swindles and other group crimes, and through it all lived like a prince off the proceeds. He spent $75,000 during one weekend in Las Vegas, and has given away as many as six expensive cars to friends within a single week.

He was known as the Fat Man before he went to prison.

15

While within the walls he was called Big Cherry, although sometimes the other inmates, and even the guards, used the term "The Big Man" to describe his position in the subculture in which he moved.

He is big. Right now he weighs in excess of 600 pounds although a strict diet regime in jail brought him down to 515.

Most of the time the expression on his face is that of a brooding Buddha, but it can swing between icy menace and so much benevolence that aggressively heterosexual men have kissed him in affection.

In the words of a girl friend of one of his former associates, "Sylvan's an awful interesting guy."

# Chapter 2
# WHY DO THEY KEEP PICKING ON MY KID?

*The Subject has lived all of his life in white, middle-class communities. None of the environments in which he has lived could be said to have a high incidence of crime. All, however, would be environments in which the dyssocial behavior noted in the psychiatric evaluation would be common. They are environments in which there is considerable emphasis placed on financial success, with a considerably lesser emphasis on achieving such success by ethical means.*

—An extract from the
presentence report ordered
by the sentencing judge.

Late in 1971 his mother asked a reporter assigned to do a newspaper feature on Sylvan Scolnick, "Why do they keep picking on my kid?" and this is as good a statement as any to indicate her lifelong attitude toward her son.

Most of the people who knew them agree that he is a spectacular example of the "mama's boy."

17

He married his first wife in 1951 and they separated within a year. "We were just kids of about twenty," she recalls, "and Ida, his mother, moved in with us right from the first. It used to burn me up to watch her helping him put on his socks."

Twenty years later a young district attorney who had been brought in to help prepare one of the cases against him said, "I'll bet Scolnick had a strong mother—a very strong mother." When asked why, he answered, "Most of the Jewish males with pronounced self-destructive tendencies that I've come across seem to have that kind of background."

A man who had been his friend for most of those twenty years said, "Sylvan loved his mother with all his heart. She was never out of his mind. If he bought Ruth [his second and present wife] a fur coat, he bought his mother one, too. I don't think he ever did anything in his life without thinking of her."

But Irwin Paul, the attorney who represented him until just shortly before his first trial, qualified this by saying, "Sure Sylvan loves his mother. But she never made up his mind for him. His mother does not control him at all—I don't think she ever did. *Nobody* controls him! He's the most independent person you'd ever meet. No one can ever change him once his mind is made up, not even his mother. But I've never had any question about the great love and affection the woman had for that boy. She will excuse him under all circumstances. No question about it, she's the classic Jewish Mother."

When his parole officer, Eugene Kelly, was asked for his estimate of the effect of this attachment on Scolnick's criminal career, he answered, "Well, it's only a guess, but if you have a person who has been cultivated by a mother or older sisters, this person learns from his earliest years that there are ways of 'getting by' the person who is their mentor. That's fine within the family and no one outside the family suffers any great damage by whatever rule-breaking goes on.

18

"But the external society has its own rules. These rules are objective, they aren't personal. They aren't related to 'well, I hurt you, dear, and I'm sorry.' If you hurt society, then society reacts. If you hurt [external] people severely, then they react severely. But the person who has been cultivated in such home circumstances over a long period of time is almost brainwashed into believing that everyone is going to accept and forgive what they do.

"When they discover (and this usually takes a while) that people aren't as apt to forgive them as their families, they're in trouble. You see, one of the difficulties is that they have learned so many personality tricks that it takes a long while for the people with whom they are associating to discover that they are tricky. So, a person with an overprotective mother is likely to get into trouble in those areas. These are usually nonviolent areas, but they keep expecting that they'll get their mother's treatment from the external world."

It was totally unpremeditated, but once during an angry flare-up, Scolnick delivered his own private explanation of the bond. He and a guest in their home had been sitting at the lunch table when his present wife, Ruth, volunteered that Sylvan had been heavy, even as a young man. His mother, hearing this in the kitchen where she had been preparing the meal, called out, "He wasn't so heavy, don't kid yourself."

Scolnick threw his napkin on the table and turned to his visitor: "Do you hear that? That's my mother's dream! She says I was never really that heavy. I was only as heavy as an elephant, but my mother says I was really never that heavy. She believes her dream. She doesn't see an ugly fat guy sitting here and neither does my wife. My wife sees her husband as a guy who's stronger, mentally, than the average man. She sees a guy who can stand on his own two feet and take all the gaff and never complain about it and she respects me for it.

19

"But with my mother, it has nothing to do with respect! She loves me! She feels it's part of her fault; because she's got fat legs, I got fat legs. Because she's fat, I'm fat. She's takin' the blame. And she's going to scrub floors and sew at the sewing machine all her life and give me everything she's got to try and pay me back for the suffering that she brought me by bringing me into the world."

His mention of the sewing machine referred to the fact that Ida Scolnick began as a young girl and then worked all her life in the needle trades as a sewing machine operator. She was still in her teens when she married a quiet, unaggressive carpenter, but she continued to work because her husband did not earn enough to support the three sons who came along in the early years of their marriage.

"It got damn tough for a while," she once told a reporter. "In 1934 in the middle of the depression there was a time when both me and my husband lost our jobs."

"What did you do then?"

"What did I do? What the hell could I do? I went out and got another job. I got dressed as a man and got hired as a sheet metal worker. But that job only lasted a couple of months. When the guy that ran the place found out about it, he come up to me and said, 'Lady, you're a good worker. You're one of the best men I got in the place, but I never had no women working here before and the other men are complaining.' "

"Did he fire you?"

She shifted her heavy body restlessly and stared over the head of her son's visitor. "Well. I just couldn't let it happen. I told him how bad I needed the job what with a husband out of work and three kids and all. I said, 'I'm putting out as much work as anybody here in the shop,' and he had to agree that was true; so he let me stay on until my old job opened up again and they took me back. Then my husband got a job as a milkman, and it got easier."

Her "old job" was with a Philadelphia plant that manufactured tuxedos. She worked there for almost forty-five years, refusing to retire even during the years when her son Sylvan operated a string of crooked enterprises involving millions of dollars. But when he went penniless to jail, Ida Scolnick took her life's savings, borrowed a few thousand more from friends and relatives, and gave the money to him for his legal expenses.

He was born in Philadelphia on June 27, 1930. His mother and her brothers were all unusually heavy, but he weighed only seven pounds at birth.

Although the family was poor, their life wasn't impoverished. Ida Scolnick got up at five each morning to prepare a substantial breakfast for her husband and sons, and they wore scrupulously washed and ironed clothes when they left the house for school and work. After she had seen them off, she went to her own job.

But Sylvan, her favorite and youngest son, was also her especial burden. The intelligence tests that he took in school showed him to be far above average, but his grades were invariably bad. One teacher was so interested in the boy that she brought his father in to tell him, "Your son is a mathematical genius. . . . We've got to find some way to get him into the right channels."

But he continued to play hookey in order to gamble and shoot pool at the neighborhood billiard parlor.

"I liked mathematics," he recalls. "I even designed my own system when I was a kid. I figured out how to operate with tenths and round off numbers, the way the kids are doing it today. But I hated school. I didn't want to do it their way. I even taught myself how to use a slide rule. I knew every theory,

21

algebra, plane and solid geometry from the books I used to buy at Leary's secondhand store. I knew trigonometry before I went into tenth grade.

"It didn't do me no good in school, but knowing mathematics has helped me in almost everything else I ever went into. In businesses I could always figure percentages and project them. I could look at any company and see where they were going. I can do it in a flash. Just look at their statement and I know how much should go for advertising, commissions, expenses, and how much they should be making or losing.

"I can do it with cards, too. I play gin, poker, pinochle, and I can tell you every card out on a deck. After the third or fourth play, I know what all the hands are. In gin rummy, after five or six throws I know the cards people are holding or what they should be holding."

One of the judges whom Scolnick faced later in life was so puzzled by the gap between his capabilities and his legitimate achievements that he sent an investigator to dig up his school records. The investigator reported:

> [Scolnick] dropped out of Northeast High School while in grade 12B. He states that he left this close to graduation because of his father's death and that since both of his older brothers were married and living away from home, he felt an obligation to go to work and help to support his mother and himself. It should be noted, however, that his father did not actually die until some time after the Subject quit school. It appears, therefore, that the Subject was primarily interested in achieving a measure of financial independence from his family. There are also indications that his school work was slipping and that he was becoming increasingly unhappy in school.

"When I was a kid," Scolnick said, "the first thing in my mind was to get the hell out of school. I guess I hated anything

22

where someone told me what to do. And I was awful heavy. I didn't go out with girls until after I was sixteen. I used to fight a lot, too.

"And gamble? Man, that's all we ever did. Sometimes I used to knock dough down from the restaurant my mom and dad ran for a while and I'd head for the firehouse where me and my friends used to shoot crap.

"It's a shame the way I bagged school. I should have graduated high school when I was about fourteen and a half. I know when I graduated ninth grade, I wasn't twelve yet, but I just didn't like it. I remember during that time I took an intelligence test and got a grade of one forty-one. One of the teachers said that put me in the genius class but I figured she was just crapping me up so I'd stay in school.

"My dad and my mother, they really loved each other. My dad was like a boyfriend to me. He'd beat the hell out of me when I'd come home with bad marks, but most of the time he was the nicest, quietest guy you'd ever want to meet.

"He knew what it was all about. He used to tell me, 'Don't ever lie to me. Tell me the truth and take your medicine.' And, although I could con Mom, I never could con him. He was a quiet guy, but in his own way he was a stone tough candidate. I was only eighteen when he died, but I never forgot him."

This facet of his father's character left its mark on Sylvan Scolnick. Although he has devoted most of his adult life to scheming, trickery, fraud and theft, he has the paradoxical, continuing compulsion to tell the truth about himself.

"He's everything bad, but he's not a hypocrite," said one man who knew him well. "He's got some kind of need to tell anybody he's with just who he is and what he is and what he's done. And he always tells the truth, at least whatever he believes is the truth at that given time."

Probably much of his unhappiness in school was due to his

weight. When he was sixteen, he was five and a half feet tall and weighed 250 pounds, which is exactly twice the amount of weight that the insurance tables suggest for that height.

"I was always big," he says. "I was heavier than the other kids and I couldn't run and play ball like they did. Maybe that's why I spent so much time gambling. My weight has always gone up and down. When I was thirteen, I wore a size forty-three suit. I weighed four hundred nine pounds when I was twenty. They weighed me in at seven forty-one when I went to jail, and I weighed about five hundred when I came out.

"One thing used to strike me funny was when one of my friends would fix me up with a blind date. I used to laugh before I went into the girl's house because I knew what would happen. I used to want to see the different expressions on their mom's and dad's faces when I walked in to pick the girl up and they saw how heavy I was. Or when we'd go to a show, you know, and when all the eyes would do that double-take, I would laugh to myself."

His first wife still refuses to be publicly identified as the former Mrs. Sylvan Scolnick and it isn't certain whether this is due to his notoriety or to the fact that she detests him as strongly today as she did when she left him twenty years ago.

She was a pretty, big-eyed youngster, not quite out of her teens and, according to a friend of theirs in those days, quite unworldly. And, although he was heavy, in her words, "He was big but not a freak. He was sort of built like Jackie Gleason.

"When I married him I didn't know where I was going or what I was doing. And he came along like gangbusters, like he was wealthy, which he was not. When he showed me a diamond watch, I thought he was. He told me how much he loved me and how much he would do for me, how good it would be, and being only a kid, I said, 'Well. . . .'"

24

"The trouble with his mother started almost immediately. Although she didn't discourage the marriage, she didn't want to let go. She wanted it to be a threesome.

"In the beginning we lived in an apartment on the first floor and she lived upstairs on the third. When it was time for him to go to work she'd yell out the window at seven thirty in the morning, 'Sylvan, it's time to get up!' No matter how many times I told her that I had an alarm clock and that I was capable of getting him up, she'd never stop doing it. So when Sylvan got up, the whole neighborhood got up.

"Up until then, I had never heard a woman use the profanity that she did. One time while I was pregnant I walked into the neighborhood butcher shop and she was standing there talking to a group of women. Seeing me, she yelled out, 'Here comes the son of a bitch, now!' Maybe she didn't mean anything by it, it might have been just her way of talking.

"She and I were always fighting but instead of taking my side, he'd always try to stay on the wire, in the middle. He'd say to me, 'She's my mother, what do you want from me?' She'd be screaming at me and I'd be crying and he'd keep running back and forth.

"And whenever things got tough, he'd go to her for sympathy because he knew he wasn't going to get it from me. I remember one time when he was working for IT Circuit Breaker. He was a machinist. It was a hard job; he used to come home filthy dirty and he would look for sympathy from me which I would not give him because this is what a man is supposed to do—however you make a living for your family, just go to it, baby. Whatever way you do it, you have to bring it home, it's your responsibility.

"Once, when I had gone out somewhere, I came home and she had already cooked up some steaks for dinner that were so huge they were hanging over the plate. I really think that in her

25

heart she thought she was doing a nice thing by making dinner, but it was really a destructive thing to do.

"I walked in and I sat down and said, 'I don't think I can eat, I don't feel so good.' And there he is, throwing food in his mouth and she is also packing it away. After watching them for a while, I said, 'Would you do me a favor, Sylvan? Whistle just before you explode so I can get the hell out of the room.' You know, I can be a bitch when I want to.

"He was always a terrible liar. He'd say he was working when he'd be out shooting pool or hanging around and gambling with his friends. And he was lazy, not mentally, but physically. In those days he really wasn't much of a bargain.

"I left him a couple of times and he'd get me to come back by promising that he would keep his mother out of our lives, but he never kept his word. So I finally left him for good during the time I was pregnant with our son. He had just taken a bath and I went in to straighten up the bathroom and I saw that he hadn't cleaned the tub. I was furious and I came out to where they were sitting and said, 'There's going to be trouble if you don't get back in there and clean out that tub!' She butted in, 'I always cleaned out my husband's tub. I even used to cut his toenails for him.'

"I was furious. I said, 'I'd die before I'd do that. It might have been fine for you, but don't say it's fine for me.' And I ended up arguing with both of them.

"So I went in and started cleaning the tub and getting madder with each rub. Finally I threw the rag down and went in and got dressed and when I came out again I said, 'Give me a dollar for the cab, I'm leaving you for good.' And they let me go.

"I've only seen him once or twice since then. Sylvan agreed to let our son be adopted by my next husband, and he didn't see him either until just a year or so ago.

26

"The last time I saw Sylvan, it was about five or six years ago. I had to talk with him about my son's affairs, but I didn't want any discussions in front of the boy. So when I called him, we fixed a date to meet in his car which would be parked at Broad and Locust streets in center Philadelphia.

"I pulled up behind his Cadillac and went over and got in the back seat with him, and when I tried to put my handbag down on the seat, there was no room. He took up the other two seats in the back. He had no lap! I was shocked that human skin could stretch that much!"

The records show that they were married in 1951, lived together for less than a year, and that the marriage ended in divorce after a separation of two more years. He rarely discusses this marriage, telling one court investigator that it was so insignificant and happened so long ago that he had forgotten all about it.

However, he did make one comment to a friend. "It was at one of my court trials," he said, "and they had her as a witness for something, I forget what. Anyway, she showed up with her big sunglasses stuck in her dyed blond hair, and she had her fat legs jammed into these long plastic boots. I was so embarrassed that people would connect me to her that I didn't know where to look. I just kept my eyes down on the table in front of me all the time she was in the courtroom."

A few months after his divorce in 1953, he met and married Ruth Stein, a tall, buxom, but attractive woman whose shy manner generally masks her perception and considerable intelligence. With the exception of a two-year spree that occurred while he was riding high, he has always returned her devotion and love. They have no children.

27

## Chapter 3

# HOW FAR DO YOU GO FOR A WATCH SPRING?

*The large number of jobs the Subject has held and their
extreme variety precludes any detailed evaluation of the Subject's
employment history. He states that he has been in the mortgage
business, in the loan business, a short-order cook, a machinist and
a machine operator. In short, the Subject has engaged in many
enterprises, some licit, and some rather less so.*

—An extract from the
presentence report ordered
by the sentencing judge.

Throughout the years the swindles and thefts that have
given him the greatest pleasure were those directed against
banks, bankers and insurance companies. "I boffed 'em out for
millions," he says, "and it always felt good."

This animosity dates back to the period shortly after his
father died when he was eighteen. After the funeral his mother
said to him, "You know, Daddy had a balance on his bank loan
of a few hundred dollars and you have to go down and pay it

28

off because I wouldn't want your father to have a bad name."

A few days after he had paid the note, the family received a letter from the insurance company saying that the loan had been insured and that they required official notification so that they might make the final payments on it.

"So I go back to the bank," he recalls, "and I started to raise hell about them not telling us that the loan was insured and that they ought to give me the money back and then they should notify the insurance company.

"The guy at the bank tells me they can't do that . . . that it'd be too much trouble to recast the loan because the papers were already all marked up.

"What was I going to do? A kid of eighteen go sue a bank for a couple of hundred bucks? So I got indignant and started to holler and it wound up they called the police who came and threw me out of the place. That was my first time with the bank.

"Then, about six months or a year later, my brother and I went into partners and bought a luncheonette. The guy who sold us the place had a whole set of phony books that made it look like he was doing eight or nine hundred a week. But he was only doing less than four.

"But we bought it. We took a loan of four thousand dollars from the bank; the collateral on it was my car and my brother's car and the fixtures in the place.

"When we saw we wasn't going to be able to make the payments on the loan, I told my brother that I'd step out and get another job and that he would run it until we sold it for at least enough to pay off our note so we wouldn't have credit problems.

"He agreed, and I went to work at IT Circuit Breaker, cleaning up garbage pits and things like that at a dollar twenty-two an hour, and after a few months I worked my way up to being a machinist.

"Six months later I walk by our luncheonette and it's closed. When I call up my brother, he says, 'Syl, I'm sorry. I just couldn't bring enough money home to live.'

"So I said, 'Well, I'll go over to the bank and give them a check for the payments you skipped and then I'll try running the place.'

"But when I go to the bank, they tell me they're foreclosing. Going to sell us out. So I go down to the bank's main office and I see the guy who's head of all the consumer loans. I told him about me and my brother and that my wife was pregnant and that I really wanted to go in and work if he'd recast the loan, let me pay the interest or something, I'd work night and day to make the place good.

"He said, 'Nah. This account has never been anything but a problem. I'm going to foreclose so we can clean it off the books. We can't be bothered with all this petty stuff.' I pleaded and begged him to give me a chance but he turned me down stone cold."

Because the luncheonette was a partnership rather than a corporation, the brothers were held personally responsible for the business debts. Their cars were sold off and his brother, to keep from losing his home in the bargain, filed a petition in bankruptcy.

"It came as a shock to me," Scolnick said, "to realize that when my brother went bankrupt, I had to go that way, too. Otherwise I would still have been responsible for the rest of the bills. I didn't know that the law looks at a corporation as if it is a separate entity and that means you're one guy and your corporation is another. And when your corporation goes down, that doesn't mean you have to go down with it like I had to with my brother.

"Anyway, on the day they told me, I go to the court of the referee, who is really a judge in bankruptcy matters, and I sit there. Nobody else shows up.

30

"After the referee asks me a couple of questions like do I have any money in safe deposit boxes, he announces that the case is adjudicated a bankruptcy. I asked my lawyer, 'What does he mean?' and my lawyer says that it means 'you don't owe anybody any money anymore.'

"I says, 'You mean nobody can come to me now and ask me to pay the bills we owe and my personal bills and everything else?' and he says, 'Right. The law provides when a man borrows money or goes into business and he's not successful, not due to anything crooked, then the burden of payment shouldn't rest on his children or children's children after they hound him to death. If it's an honest loss, and a man just can't meet his debts, we don't send him to debtor's prison like they used to, we give him a chance to start fresh in life.'

"So I said, 'Boy, this is something,' and it laid in my head from then on."

His dislike of insurance companies also stems from these years. He is convinced that the payment on the $5000 policy that his father took out for the benefit of his mother was unjustly withheld. The company's position was that the policy contained a two-year "contestable" provision and since the policy was only twenty-three months old when Irving Scolnick died, there was no obligation on their part to pay the claim.

This, too, "laid in his head from then on" because his mother, not wanting to ask anything of her sons who were struggling to keep their new families afloat, worked even longer hours at her sewing machine in order to pay off her husband's funeral bills.

The separation from his first wife and the discharge in bankruptcy left him with a rootless feeling. Although he had become a skilled machinist, he was depressed by his slow advancement at work; so he quit and, for a period, drifted from job to job as a sandwich man and short-order cook.

31

While working in one delicatessen, he came under the influence of the owner whom he describes as a fantastic but stupid businessman. "I learned two things from him. The first thing, I learned how you can go into business with no money at all. Before this guy even had a lease on a place, he'd get money from the meat man, the milkman, the bread man—they'd all ante up to back him in order to get his business. They all felt he really knew how to run a place. And he did. He'd run it like a dream. He'd have crowds standing in line to get a table. And then he'd take all this money he was making and gamble it away. That's the second thing I learned; you're a jerk if you gamble."

He learned quickly enough to leave the delicatessen operator within a year and open his own shop. It was successful, but he disliked the confining life. After turning it over to his backers, he took a job with a direct sales company selling housewares and silverware door to door. This job became the setting for his first illegal act.

"I was doing pretty good," he said, "but I got bored with the dollar-down and dollar-a-week kind of stuff and I went into mass selling. Instead of following my route, I'd go into restaurants during lunch hours and I'd end up selling twenty or thirty sets of silver at a time, and I was getting something like twelve or fifteen dollars commission on every one.

"Then, once, I was short of money, so I loaded up a car with silverware and I sold it off for whatever I could get. Then I parked it somewhere and put in a claim that it all got stolen. I got about a grand from the insurance company for that. That worked so good that a few months later I done it again. That was my first shot back at the insurance company."

He left the direct sales company, but he had so enjoyed the career of salesman that he went into the business of selling portable typewriters. "We made a fortune," he said. "We were selling so many typewriters the dollar-down way that the Remington Company had to close one of their factories down to retool.

"Me and this friend of mine were getting the typewriters from Remington and L. C. Smith and these companies would do the financing themselves. So I hired a couple of guys and I started running training programs teaching them how to sell. You know, 'Change your kid's *C*'s and *D*'s into *A*'s and *B*'s' . . . things like that.

"I end up with a field corporation with some four hundred men working for me and I was only twenty-two or twenty-three years old at the time. The money was just pouring in and me and my friend were doing things like buying each other Cadillacs. His was a baby blue convertible and mine was a pink and white sedan.

"I used to have pep meetings for my sales force. I remember one time I'm up on the platform really pouring it to them, firing 'em up, you know: 'Believe in yourself! Anything man's mind can conceive and believe, he can accomplish!' and so on and so forth. I'm telling 'em that I've handpicked 'em and they're the cream of the crop—and as I'm talking the stage breaks and I start falling through, but I keep on talking and firing. I don't stop talking for one minute and I don't break down.

"I'm hollerin', 'We got the Forward Look!' and I start going right through the stage until only my head is sticking out over the top and I'm still pitching. I didn't leave up for a minute and it took about ten guys to pull me out. I'll never forget it.

"After the typewriter thing played itself out because the companies didn't want to go with no more financing, I get a call from some guy up in north Jersey. He's married to one of the Du Ponts, I think, and he's heard about me being such a genius at door-to-door selling. It turns out he's got a hundred or so

33

thousand ivory alabaster statuettes of St. Peter he had from some deal with the Vatican and he wants me to unload them; that he'd give them to me for sixty-seven cents and whatever I got for them was mine.

"Well I got a crew together and we started working the area. I'd have them going door to door while I walked down the middle of the street with my collar turned around and singing the Lord's Prayer. The guys would knock on the door, and the people who'd be coming out to see what all the noise was would buy them for ten dollars apiece because my guys would be telling them it'd be a way of bringing religion into their hearts. We got rid of all them statuettes in no time.

"But after a while I got tired of the monkey business and I got an interview for a job as a salesman for some outfit that was manufacturing rivets. At first, the guy didn't want to hire me because I pulled up in front of his place with a pink and white cadillac. He says, 'The best I can give you is seventy-five dollars a week against a commission.' I told him I don't want no salary just a commission and he says that would be great. At the same time, I took two more jobs with other companies in the same line so I ended up working three shifts and doing such a good job for all of them that two of the companies made me sales manager.

"The third company was run by two partners that didn't like each other, even though they were brothers-in-law. Then, one day I came in to them with this order for a million rivets to be used on some display material for RCA Whirlpool washing machines. The display had a wheel on it with a disc with about ten pictures and it set into a sleeve which was held together with one of those brass fasteners that you push through a hole and then spread out the sides. I told the display company that they could turn them out cheaper and faster if they used rivets instead of brass fasteners.

34

"I saw the partners look at each other when I brought the order in. And when I told them there was another order of twenty million more waiting, besides the work I could get on the stuff the Ford Company was doing for the Edsel, their wheels really started turning.

"Finally, one partner got ahold of me in the back room. After telling me how crooked and useless the other guy was, he asked if he broke up the partnership with the other guy, would I go in with him?

"I saw which way it was going down, so I said sure and what's more, I was working on inventing a machine that could turn out these rivets twice as fast as the way they were doing it now, and at this he got so excited he couldn't control himself. Finally, he said that he would put up the money and that I wouldn't have to work on a commission anymore, that he and me would be partners.

"I could see he was a thief, going behind his brother-in-law's back that way, so I said that I didn't want to be partners, but that I'd sell him the machine, and this was something he wanted with all his heart.

"Well, I went to some electrician I knew and had him make the machine that I designed. It looked beautiful. I had different colored electric lights flashing on and things were turning and pumping and it was making all kinds of noise like a train going through a tunnel. Only thing, it didn't make any rivets. But this guy was kind of lazy and he didn't feel like hanging around to see it in production. So I charged him fifteen or twenty grand for it, and we both went our separate ways."

He tells the stories of the days before he became a professional criminal with enormous gusto, but becomes almost wistful when he is asked why he did not diet away the weight that handicapped his business career.

35

"During my life, I've gone up and back down to almost normal about five or six times, but I finally decided that I just can't pay the price. I had one doctor tell me that it was glandular and that I could correct it with an operation, but they're afraid to do it since I had that heart attack in 1958. Anyway, it's not all food. I used to eat a lot when I was a kid . . . Mom was always watching over me . . . But it's not the food alone. My body just seems to retain liquids. Since I got out of prison, I been watching myself and even though I don't eat most of the day and just eat a steak at night, my weight stays around seven hundred pounds.

"If I wanted to pay the price, go on a starvation diet like I did in prison, I could get back down. But I guess I just don't want it bad enough. I want to be able to think about important things, not spend all my time thinking about how good food would taste and when I was going to get my next decent meal. Whenever you go on those kind of diets, you end up doing nothing but thinking about food.

"I can explain it with a story: There was an old prospector, about seventy, and he'd never found gold. But one day he struck what he thought was gold and he was so happy he jumped right on his mule and rode into town to take it to the assayer's office.

"The assayer, a young guy, said, 'I'm sorry, Pop, but it's not gold, it's iron,' and at this the old man just busted down and started to cry, he wanted to hit gold so bad.

"But the young guy says, 'Look, you can go across the street and there's some guy there who makes shovels and he'll give you three dollars for your iron.' But the old man kept crying.

"So the young guy goes on, 'In the next town there's a guy who'll give you thirty dollars for it. He makes pocket knives.' And when the old man still doesn't quit, the young guy adds, 'And if you go to St. Louis to where they make springs for watches, you could get maybe three thousand for your iron.'

36

"At this, the old guy got happy and took off for St. Louis with his iron.

"That's the end of the story. And it's the same thing with the weight. How far are you gonna go to get what you want? Or do you scale what you want down to how far you're willing to go? My answer is, I'm not going to go to St. Louis. I can't pay the price. It's too strong for me and I recognize it. I only want to get the pocket knives. I can't handle the trip for the watch springs."

In discussing his obesity problem, his doctor, William Block, a general practitioner in Cherry Hill, New Jersey, would not offer an opinion on whether Scolnick's weight was due to gluttony or was a glandular or genetic defect. "It's hard to say. The medical profession isn't all that certain of the causes of obesity. But this is a man whose body demands a great deal of food. He has habitualized himself throughout his entire life to eat great quantities because he needed it for the amount of energy he puts out. Not only physically, but mentally. This man's mind is working overtime at all times and he's burning up enormous amounts of energy. He needs this replacement.

"While he was in prison, and practically at rest, he was able to take off some weight. But now, in his full activity schedule, he gets terribly exhausted after a week or so on a diet. He can't do his work properly. If he went through a long period of rigorous diet, he wouldn't be Sylvan Scolnick any more. He wouldn't be able to produce."

When Dr. Block was asked about Scolnick's mortality expectations, he shrugged and answered, "How can I comment on that? He's forty-one now [this was in 1971] and all I can do is tell you that I worry about him all the time. I can't see how he can continue to function with this tremendous load he carries. I can't even begin to guess how long his heart can continue to function under the demands of his life-style. His mother is in her sixties and she works hard, so maybe he is a genetic phenomenon. But, looking at him as a physician, I fear for him. I really do."

"Doesn't he recognize the danger?"

"He uses the excuse of being busy as a way of avoiding hospitalization I think he needs in order to get a complete evaluation."

"Do you think he is obsessed by the fear that he has very little time left?"

"He has never mentioned it. Never. In all the times, I've attempted to throw a fright into him, to slow him down, to diet or take his medication properly, he never once used this as a force to follow my instructions. I think he feels he's just going to go on and be what he wants to be. I think he has to prove something to himself and to the world so all these complications are just incidental details to him. He knows that he has them but they are just in his way."

His heart attack seems to have been one of the reasons for the almost manic urgency he shows in attacking any problem. His criminal career began shortly after it occurred.

"It was in 1958," Scolnick recalls, "the day following Labor Day. I had just landed a job with Illinois Lock and it was one of the best hardware jobs in the country and they picked me over two or three hundred other men.

"Because I was so fat, that they didn't even want to talk to me at first, but I went to the house of the guy who was doing the interviewing. I said, 'Pal, you're making the biggest mistake you ever made. You just lost the best man you could have for the job.'

"So he calls me back and I started to talk to him and after a while he gives me the opportunity. After a couple of weeks he tells me that I can go with him to the hardware show in New York.

"But the day before the hardware show I start getting

terrible pains in my chest. I thought it was indigestion but they made me go to the hospital. I said I would, providing I could take my good suit along with me because that Thursday I had to be up at the show.

"They take me to the hospital and, oh, the pain was fantastic, like an elephant treading on my chest; and they're giving me shots of morphine like every few hours and I got these blood clots developing in my legs and they're shooting me full of penicillin and my arms are blowing up.

"Because I weighed about six hundred pounds then, I couldn't fit into the bed, so they got me strapped up on these boards and I look out the door and I see a family I haven't seen for years.

"I can't understand it. What are all these people? Aunts and uncles that don't even talk to my mother. And all these other friends. So I call the doctor and when he comes I say, 'Doc, what's going on here?'

"He tells me, 'Well, you're a pretty sick boy. Just take it easy and we'll see what we can do.' I said, 'That's not good enough, Doc. I see relatives out there in the hall that I haven't seen for years.'

"He starts to hem and haw with me, so I said, 'Look, Doc, you got to tell me the truth.' He says, 'Are you sure you want the truth?' 'Yeah.' 'Well, you're going to die. Maybe less than a day. Two days at the most.' I said, 'You sure?' and he answers, 'I wouldn't give a tin nickel for your chances.'

"After the doctor left, I realized that I'd better make up my mind about things. I started thinking about everything I'd done, not that I had ever done anything really wrong up until that point, but I didn't have no insurance and my wife, Ruth, is a bad diabetic and my mother isn't well and I don't figure to depend on my brothers to help them out.

"So I said to myself, 'This is really something.' I look out

39

in the hall and I see Ruth sitting in the hall and crying and in a flash I knew what I was going to do, so I holler for her to come in.

"When she comes in, I say, 'Close that door and push that chair against it so nobody can come in.' I said, 'Come on, we're going to ball!' She started to scream and holler, 'You're crazy.'

"I says, 'I don't want to know about nothing. If I'm going, then sex is the way I want to go.' So she says. . . . Well, anyway, we did it and I got out of bed and went to the bathroom and the nurse came in as I was getting back into bed. She was going to give me my morphine shot.

"Well, I told her what to do with that morphine. I said, 'No more morphine, no more of that stuff. I ain't dying and there's nothing going to happen to me and get the hell out." And I picked up a book and settled back and started to read it. Six weeks later I went home in an ambulance.

"But that ain't even the end. When I get home, they're carrying me in on a stretcher and the thing snaps in half, doubling me up. It was the first time I seen my feet in years. I tell you, it was the funniest thing you'd ever see in your life. Me screaming and hollering and the four guys holding on, not wanting to let me go, struggling up them steps with the stretcher in half. It was wild, I mean wild!"

His wife Ruth, a quiet woman, had been sitting by as he told the story. After he had finished roaring at his own description of being taken up the steps she said, "It's a good story, Sylvan, but you only think something happened in that hospital room. The morphine wasn't telling you the truth."

"Well," he said, "you'll never convince me different." He turned back to his visitor. "But I learned something in that hospital. I knew I was never going to be in that spot again. Next time I came that close, I was going to be ready for it. I made up my mind that when I got better I was going to make a lot of dough any way I could. I wasn't ever gonna take the chance again of leaving Mom and Ruth without nothing."

He thought for a moment and then said sadly, "It's the weight. It's always been the weight. They judge an ordinary man on his ability, but the first reflection that a man gets from me is that this guy is so fat he won't be able to handle the job. I always had to be smarter than anyone else. I always had to outthink them. Nobody wanted me to work for them, they'd worry that people would think they had a clown representing them. They'd think I'd bust all the chairs in their office, just by sitting in them. I had to do it my way, there was never no other way I could keep up. To keep up, I had to be ahead of everybody else. All because I was so fat."

He thought for a moment, his veiled eyes accenting his strong resemblance to a brooding Buddha. Then he shrugged and said, "And maybe this is all a lot of crap. Maybe I just always wanted to be a thief, anyway."

41

# Chapter 4

# THE FRAUDULENT
# BANKRUPTCIES

*The Subject claims to have no financial assets whatsoever.*
*The home in Cherry Hill, New Jersey, is owned by his mother.*

—An extract from the
presentence report ordered
by the sentencing judge.

Scolnick is convinced that his entry into the field of fraudulent bankruptcies was based upon necessity. "Every time I went to see the doctor after my heart attack, he used to tell me it was a miracle I was still living. He'd say, 'It's only a question of time. I don't see how you're ever going to make it!'

"So, suppose I was only going to last another three months? That wouldn't have been time to do anything legitimately. I didn't figure I had a lifetime in front of me to build a business and save money, you know, do it the right way. And so I took my shot and the first shot I took I scored over a half a million dollars for myself in nine months.

"What happened was this: after I got back home from the

hospital, I stayed there for a few weeks and then I met this guy, Sam Koff. I had known him from before and he was in this guy's store, a guy name Carlucci, down at Second and Market streets near the Philly waterfront. This Carlucci was selling the stuff so cheap, I asked Koff, 'How in hell is he selling it at these prices?' and Koff said, 'He's running a BR.' 'A what?' 'A BR, a bankruptcy. It ain't reached the stage yet of him going to court, but as soon as he takes down his score, that's where he'll go.'

"Well, I bought a load of goods from this Carlucci and I sold them off at a good profit. So then I figured, what the hell, I might as well set up my own BR.

"This was the M. Stein bankruptcy. My father-in-law was living with me and Ruth because his wife had just died. This was early in 1959 and up until then he had just been a small upholsterer and he owed a lot of money. So I took him in with me as a front. He's a nice quiet little guy and he didn't know from nothing. So I turned his upholstery place into a store that sold general merchandise: jewelry, furniture, appliances and things like that. We even ordered and got in such things as candy, fruitcakes and, one time, five grand worth of cookies.

"And we sold them out the back door to everybody. One time a Benrus salesman filled my order for thousands of dollars' worth of watches and then I told this legitimate retailer that I knew that he could have them for twenty-five percent off their wholesale cost. 'The only thing,' I says, 'don't start selling 'em for a few weeks because in case there's a comeback, like if Benrus wanted to check on me, I oughta have 'em on hand for a while.' And he says okay. I wanted this margin of safety because it was the first time I had been dealing with watches.

"Sure enough, a few days later, I got a phone call from the Benrus salesman. The distributor I had taken the retailer away from had beefed to the salesman because the retailer had told

43

him he was buying them from me cheaper than they cost. He says to this salesman that if he wanted to prove it, all he'd have to do is come up and see me and he'd find out that the watches were already gone.

"So I get on the phone and tell the guy I sold 'em to to get the watches back up to me, which he did in an hour or so. I piled them on my desk and got the bills out so it would look like I'm checking off the numbers and kinds and waited.

"When the salesman came walking in, he takes one look and curses out the distributor, and says, 'Boy, aren't some people something? They'll do anything to get a guy in trouble because he's hurting 'em in business.' After that, he recommended about fifty salesmen to come see me and I banged every one of them."

Hundreds of manufacturers and distributors were left holding the bag when M. Stein & Co. was declared bankrupt on December 14, 1959. The company's liabilities were shown to be $623,757.35 and in answer to the questions about what happened to the merchandise, M. Stein answered that he couldn't remember. He recalled that he had lost about $12,000 in Las Vegas and that in order to pay some of the creditors who were pressing him, he had to borrow large amounts from loan sharks who charged him 100 per cent interest. Stein said that he was now flat broke and besides, he really didn't have much to do with the operation of the business. His job had been to help with the unloading of the trucks at the delivery platform and that the books and records had been kept by his son-in-law, Sylvan Scolnick.

Unfortunately, Scolnick wasn't available at the time of the hearing. He was in the hospital and the referee was told that he was there because he was overweight and had such high blood pressure that he couldn't safely be subjected to questioning.

44

After that he was on his way.

Although he changed many of the members of his ring from deal to deal, a few of them proved so efficient that he kept them with him as mainstays in almost every succeeding venture. Sam Koff became his spotter to bird-dog promising situations. "Big Murray" Farber was his chauffeur, companion and, since he was tall, heavy and stupid looking, the truck driver who picked up the goods at the manufacturer's warehouse whenever the gang felt they had to get merchandise as quickly as possible.

An expert in ordering goods over the phone is a key figure in a fraudulent BR operation because this avoids mail fraud, an offense that can bring another federal investigatory agency into the picture. So, "Little Murray" Packer, described as the best phone man in the business, held the job of convincing hesitant sales managers to ship them large quantities of merchandise before a thorough credit check could be completed.

And, finally, there was Big Cherry's longtime friend, the slim, smooth and totally engaging con artist, Billy Somerville. Billy first saw jail from the inside when he was thirteen years old. He and two other boys had discovered that their teacher kept the income from the school's sale of bus tickets in a drawer in her desk. Shortly afterward the trio broke into the building one night and got away with the entire semester's proceeds, which totaled six hundred dollars.

They used the money to treat everyone they knew to beer, pinball games and nightly trips to the local movie house, a spree which lasted for about two weeks, which was the time it took for news of their affluence to reach the policeman investigating the theft. Within another month the three boys were on their way to reform school.

There were other offenses and other penal sentences before Billy enlisted in the navy in 1956 when he was eighteen years old. His father, a former numbers writer who left the rackets to become a taproom operator, thought the enlistment might "straighten the boy out," but it didn't work that way. Billy found the discipline so irritating that he spent most of his hitch in the brig for fighting.

"Most of the time after that and before I met Sylvan," he recalls, "I just floated around. I worked amusement parks as a steerer and a barker and then I got into the blue suede by selling aluminum siding and storm windows and the rest of the home improvement stuff.

"I turned out to be a first-class salesman because I always honestly believed in what I was pushing. I might be selling you aluminum siding at a buck a square foot when it was worth maybe twenty cents but I knew it would do the job I claimed it would do. You never had to paint it, it was waterproof and it was going to last you up until the day you got tired of it. That's the most important thing you can do in business; believe in yourself and what you're doing.

"That, in a way, is what I felt about Sylvan. I met him when I was partners in a home-mod business with a guy named Sy. What happened was that I catch this Sy keeping money for himself that he should of been splitting with me. I nailed him on a six-hundred-dollar check that was coming to me on the completion of a job that the people had paid him but he never turned over to me.

"Well, all of a sudden Sy disappeared. I couldn't raise him anywhere. So I went over to his house one night and he had a wife who was very very nervous. A real screamer. I asked her if Sy was home and she yelled, 'No!' So instead of giving her my story, I left.

"While I was walking away from his house, I saw his car parked around the corner. Now I had the keys to his car and he had mine. So I just took his car. Actually stole and hid it.

46

Then I went back and left a note for Sy which said, 'I want to talk to you. Don't bother driving over, just call me on the phone.'

"Next thing I know, I get a visit from the Fifteenth Police Precinct. They wanted to know about the car and they grilled me for a couple of hours, but I clammed up tight. Finally, what they did, they charged me with failing to register as a criminal, which was ridiculous, so I'm really hot now. Spending a night in jail for something like that.

"Next morning, after I got discharged and I got home my wife told me that she had got a very bad message that I was to get in touch with Joe Arm, which isn't his real name, but it's the one he got for being an organizer; an arm for the union. He was a very tough guy. Vicious. He was supposed to be also in heroin and things like that.

"So what do I do? I know that Sy has given Joe Arm his song and dance and that Joe was out to collect the car in exchange for a price. Then I remember that a friend of mine had introduced me to Big Cherry a little while ago and that this friend said that any kind of a problem I ever got, he'd be the guy to go to.

"So I go over to see Sylvan in Cherry Hill and told him that Joe Arm had said to my wife that he was going to break both of my kneecaps if I didn't come down to see him and straighten out the deal about Sy's car. Sylvan said, 'Billy, are you leveling with me about the six *C*'s?' and after I said I really was, he just stared at me for a while and then kind of shook his head. He writes down a telephone number on a piece of paper and says, 'You take this. You go down there and listen to Joe Arm while he gives you all the tough talk he knows. He is going to threaten you and everything. You just shut up and be quiet. And when he is done, you politely ask him to call this number. Okay? And then everything will be all right.'

47

"So I said okay, put the number in my pocket and drove over to the place where Joe Arm was. I walk in and Sy is sitting there with him but he doesn't say anything. Not that the Arm even gave him the chance. As soon as I walk in he started hollering; 'I don't want to know about you and Sy; you guys work out your own problem. But I want that frigging car back right away or I'm gonna. . . .' And he goes on to tell me all the things he'll do to me if I don't come up with the car.

"Like Sylvan said, I didn't answer him back. I just waited until he got finished and then I said, 'Joe, before I go, I stopped to talk with some people on the way over here. They could probably straighten this whole thing out if you just call this number.'

"He picks up the number, dials it, all the time repeating his threats and mumbling that nobody is going to straighten this thing out. Then he growls into the phone, 'This is Joe Arm. Yeah. Uh huh. Sure. Okay, don't worry, no problem. Don't worry . . . okay . . . don't get excited. Please calm down.'

"He hangs up the phone and without even looking at me, he turns right to Sy and says, 'Where is this kid's frigging money?' Sy, seeing what had happened, started to stutter, saying that he didn't have it right then but that he would get it.

"Then Joe gets up and goes from the room. He comes back in a few minutes with his own check for six hundred dollars which he gives to me, saying over his shoulder to Sy, 'Now it's me you owe the money to, which you'd better not forget.'

"To me, he says, 'Now do me a favor, please. Give him his car back because he needs it and there's some stuff in the trunk. What did you do with the car?'

"I couldn't resist acting smart. I said as seriously as I could, 'Gee, I hope it's not all wet,' and he sort of moans, 'Oh, no. You didn't. . . .'

"Then I thought I better not push a good thing too far so

48

I told him where I had parked it and got out of there and went back to Sylvan's where I found out how he had done it."

The about-face was brought about by Scolnick's friendship with Cappy Hoffman, which began during this period.

For most of the four decades preceding his death in 1967, Samuel "Cappy" Hoffman was considered one of the most potent racket bosses on the East Coast. Reputed to be the lieutenant and chief enforcer for several gang leaders during the Prohibition era, Hoffman was regularly suspected by the police in New York and his native city of Philadelphia to possess at least intimate awareness of almost all the important murders and protection and robbery operations in both areas. At one time he was alleged to be a key figure in the traffic in dope but the charge was never proven.

"I called him Sam, I never called him Cappy," says Scolnick, "because he didn't like the name. I think he got it because he had a big hole in his forehead dating back to some fight and he always used to wear a cap to hide it. But to me he was a good friend. I remember one time I gave him a surprise birthday party and when he came in to my house and saw all his friends standing around singing "Happy Birthday" to him, he just broke down and cried. He may have been a tough egg to everybody else, but to me he was a nice man.

"So when Billy got jammed up I went to Sam and told him that Joe Arm was threatening to break both his kneecaps. I said that the kid was stone in the right and the guy was pushing muscle that he had no right to use. I said, 'Look, Sam, I'm tired of this punk going with the tough-guy crap, threatening to kill the kid and everything just because he's looking to make a couple of hundred out of that Sy. Now this kid has got a problem and I'd appreciate it if you'd take care of it. I already give him your number this morning.'

"So we sat there for a while talking about this and that

until the phone rings. He picks it up and I hear him say to Joe Arm, 'Listen, you junked-up son of a bitch, if I hear one more time that you're threatening any friend of Sylvan's, you won't have to worry about breaking somebody's kneecaps, they just won't find you no more. Now you make sure that kid gets his money back and I don't want no more phone calls because I don't like phone calls and the next one I get, you are going to have a problem'; and then he hangs up without waiting for an answer."

This episode left Billy Somerville with the almost mystical belief that Sylvan Scolnick could do anything, a conviction that has never wavered during the ten years of their friendship. "Nobody can ever drive a wedge between me and Sylvan," he says. "I'd jump off any bridge he told me to.

"I remember one time when I was working for one of his BR outfits in one of those big shlock farmer's market operations over in Jersey, and a guy who was also in there came to me. His name was Jackie and he wanted me to leave Sylvan and go to work for him. So naturally I tell Sylvan about it.

"Sylvan said, 'I was going to close this operation down in a few weeks anyway,' but I answered, 'I don't care, I want to be with you guys in whatever you do next.' 'Well,' he said, 'we got something planned for next month, so, in the meantime, what I'll do is sell you. We aren't just going to give you away to Jackie.'

"That was fine with me so I went back to Jackie and told him that I was willing to go with him, but first he had to check it out with Sylvan. The next time Sylvan comes over, Jackie gets ahold of him and Sylvan tells him, 'You can have Billy but it'll cost you a thousand dollars.'

"The guy screams, 'What the hell do you think you are, the Yankees or something? What am I getting, a ballplayer?' Sylvan listens very quietly and then he answers, 'I trained him to where he is one of the best guys going now. If you think I put in all that time and effort just so I can turn him over to you, Jackie, you are just plain simple. I am just asking you to compensate me for my time and effort.'

"Well, the guy did some more moaning and muttering about how he wasn't dealing with the Yankees, but he finally says okay. He turns over the money in cash to Sylvan and tells me to be there at nine next morning. After he leaves, Sylvan strokes me five hundred dollars and I asked him how long I should stay. 'Stay at least a week with him,' Sylvan says. 'That ought to be enough to teach him a lesson not to go stealing salesmen from people.' And that's what I did."

Big Murray Farber also became a loyal member of the Fat Man's ring because of a favor that Scolnick did for him. He had been running a bucket-shop BR in association with three other men until it became evident that the venture was going to flop because of insufficient working capital. One of them had heard that the Fat Man had been known to supply money and advice in situations like these, so the approach was made through an intermediary.

"I could see right from the get-go," said Scolnick, "that this wasn't for me. Penny-ante stuff operated by a bunch of losers including Joe Arm who was in the deal with them. However, I took a liking to Big Murray so I went in.

"But after a while I realized it was hopeless. They just didn't have good sense and they wouldn't take my advice. So I went over to the Merion Bank to draw out the eighteen thousand dollars I put in. It was a small bank and they didn't have that much on hand, so I waited until next morning and then I got my money.

"After that, I contacted these guys and told them what I done. I said, 'I'm finished, but I'll get you enough money to pay off your bouncing checks and to pay off the money you invested

51

when you thought it was a legitimate business going in and then I'll walk away and leave you on your own. But the only way I'll do this is if you cut Big Murray loose. I don't want him going bankrupt with you so I want you to all sign a paper saying you bought out his share of the company and that he doesn't have anything more to do with it.'

"They went along with the deal, of course, so that's what I done. I took Big Murray out of it because he was honest with me. He'd called me up and told me the truth, see?

"So I put him on my payroll to drive me. First thing off, I asked him how much he owed. You see, he was a high roller. Loved to gamble, and outside of his heart, all of his brains are in his pants. Loved the broads. Anyway, he listed all his bills and how much he was behind in his mortgage and I paid it all off. It only came to a few grand. Now he doesn't have any pressure on him and I paid him a hundred or a hundred and a half a week so he had enough to live on and from then on he was able to pay attention to business and do what I told him to."

He met Little Murray under substantially the same circumstances; Packer and two others were unsuccessfully running a BR and they had to seek the Fat Man's help to keep them all from being criminally prosecuted. There was a badge of fraud fastened to almost every step they took, and the Fat Man pulled Little Murray out just before the wagon came. Little Murray once said, "Sylvan taught me all I know. When he talks I listen because he's never been wrong."

Very few men remained with the gang as continuing members. Only the two Murrays, Billy Somerville, Sam Koff and a dealer named Hotsy were the key figures in the ring which sometimes numbered as many as twenty operators. But all were united in the firm conviction that it was them against the whole outside world.

52

To almost everyone else, "bankruptcy" is a partially understood state that ranges between an unfamiliar experience and, sometimes, a frightening ordeal. So, a closer focus on the subject can be helpful before going on with the description of the Scolnick gang's operation in this field.

For example:

She was only a secretary, but she had charged almost $7000 worth of clothing and incidentals in stores all over town. She didn't use cash anywhere. Almost every cent she spent was listed on her charge account and credit card bills.

She did not pay one bill, nor did she have the financial means to satisfy the demands of her creditors. When their pressure became too intense, she filed a petition in bankruptcy.

Since she had only a few dollars in her checking account, lived in a rented apartment and had either worn or used up all of her purchases, none of the creditors felt like sending good money after bad. Not one of the stores, banks or credit card companies to whom she owed money was represented at the hearing which took place within five weeks from the time she had filed her petition.

In reply to his questions about her actions she said, "I don't know, Judge. I guess I just went haywire." After a probe into her current cash position followed by a lecture upon the evils of extravagance, the referee granted her absolution from her debts. She walked out of the courtroom, not legally owing anything to anyone.

The story is not apocryphal. It happened and continues to be repeated in varying degrees in almost every one of the eighty-nine bankruptcy districts in this country. In the fiscal year ending June 30, 1971, the government's figures show that approximately seven hundred nonbusiness bankruptcy filings occurred every working day of every week in the year.

53

In the same period, business bankruptcies totaled a bit more than 10 percent of that figure, meaning that each day seventy businessmen closed their doors and asked the courts to please excuse them from paying their debts. The permission was granted in almost every one of these cases because, under our laws, the primary reason for refusal of the petition is the provable presence of fraud.

There is a popular misconception that the referee in bankruptcy is supposd to represent the interests of the unsecured creditor. He does not. He is a neutral arbiter, a judge with all the powers of a federal district judge except the power to jail someone for contempt of court. He sits without a jury and when, as in most of the cases, the debtor doesn't have enough assets left to make it worthwhile for the creditors to pay the legal expenses involved in investigating his situation, it is left to the referee to determine the facts. Most of the time, it is just the referee, the debtor and his attorney talking with each other.

If the referee feels that there is no fraud involved, he grants the petition. If he thinks that there is, he can refer it to the United States attorney and the FBI for investigation.

Besides fraud, which generally takes the form of concealment of assets, the only other major roadblock is that the debtor must not have looked for bankruptcy relief in the preceding six years.

Actually, bankruptcy can be voluntary or involuntary; that is, if a debtor doesn't declare himself bankrupt, then three or more creditors can get together and force him into the referee's court. This is generally done when the creditors either feel that the debtor is hiding some assets, or want to see him punished for stealing from them.

Obviously, the above is only a simple description of the maze of laws and decisions which fill many volumes. But it is essentially the situation that Sylvan Scolnick and his gang exploited for so many years. They capitalized on the fact that it is no crime to run a business badly or to kill it by squandering its income in any one of a dozen irresponsible ways.

Swindlers rarely file a voluntary petition in bankruptcy. They simply operate until there is no one left willing to give them credit or when the creditors, in an attempt to preserve whatever assets are left, have their attorney file the involuntary petition so that the court can immediately appoint a receiver to take over and control the operation of the business. This is rarely an easy task; although it is a violation of the federal bankruptcy acts to falsify, conceal or destroy records, there is nothing illegal about keeping poor records or not keeping any records at all.

H. Kent Presson, the principal staff attorney of the Bankruptcy Division of the United States Courts, said:

"I am unable to tell you the number of bankruptcies *proven* [italics his] fraudulent . . . [and] I am unable to estimate the amount of money involved in fraudulent bankruptcies.

"I am sure you realize that many businesses fold up with substantial losses to creditors without the assets being administered by the federal bankruptcy courts, i.e., without the business being involved in a federal bankruptcy proceeding."

Emil Goldhaber, a referee in bankruptcy for the Eastern District of Pennsylvania—the district which had jurisdiction over many of the operations of the Fat Man's gang—added, "When I first came to the Bar, it was considered a scar, a blot on your record, to have been declared a bankrupt. I think that is now completely eliminated from the minds of most people."

The fact that legal insolvency is no longer a situation of disgrace deepens the fog that hides the fraudulent bankrupt. It has become relatively easy for the crook to lose himself in the crowd that passes through the referee's chambers, because, contrary to popular opinion, bankruptcies increase when business is good. During "up" periods, shippers are more prone to extend credit—they seem to go with the spirit of the times.

"To find the truth," says Judge Goldhaber, "you must rely on the integrity of counsel [the creditor's attorney]. Some counsel are thorough and there are those who are not. But the bankruptcy court is not of itself an investigative agency. If the facts are not brought out then we don't hear them and we wouldn't even know about them. For the most part, it's largely confined to a questioning of the bankrupt, mostly in the absence of any creditors and therefore he has no hesitation in making any kind of statements that he wants without fear of contradiction.

"We don't have our own investigative agencies so the court is stymied in its efforts to prove fraud when there is an absence of creditor participation.

"The facts generally come out only when the creditors file claims through their attorneys and then the attorneys get interested enough to investigate on behalf of their clients or the receiver or trustee. Short of that, we are almost impotent in our efforts to get at the truth because it is difficult to appoint a receiver and expect him to conduct a thorough investigation when it is obvious to everyone that there aren't enough assets left to assure him that he is going to get paid for his work.

"If there is nothing left, you can't get anyone who is altruistic enough to want to go into it just for the sake of uncovering crookedness. So, unless the creditors are interested enough to finance the search [for the bankrupt's assets], then the referee has to go to the United States attorney and ask him to bring in the FBI.

"But, frankly, the US attorney and the FBI are overworked. The FBI has very little time to go out and make searches on their own. So you make sure you have the real McCoy, real suspicion of fraud, before you ask them to make an investigation."

The obvious projection of Judge Goldhaber's comments is that the professional crook leaves no assets in an insolvent company. He knows that anyone attempting an investigation is going to meet with creditor resistance because there are few creditors willing to invest additional money in a bad debt. They take their loss and that is the end of it.

And, until Congress is convinced that a large segment of the business population is suffering from this crime, no one contemplates giving the referees in bankruptcy an investigative force of their own. Although as long ago as 1964 the Delaware Valley Credit Management Association estimated that honest businesses were losing more than $2 million every working day of the year to fraudulent bankrupts, no one in authority seems to think that the situation represents a national problem—not even the consumer who pays off this debt through higher prices.

A spokesman for the United States Justice Department said that they had no separate force dealing with the situation and that since their interest in the situation was only a "supervisory" one, they simply referred suspicions of criminal acts of bankruptcy to the FBI.

Judge Goldhaber had voiced the suspicion that the situation represented an open invitation to organized crime but there is no indication that the FBI shares this opinion. "We have no strike force specifically on the lookout for bankruptcy cases as opposed to anything else," said a bureau executive, "We conduct investigations of allegations of violations that are referred to us, and these sources are usually the US attorney through the referees or trustees and sometimes the principals. If anyone makes a complaint to us, we will determine the facts and discuss it with the US attorney to see if he wants to prosecute. All bankruptcy cases, in their final analyses, are reviewed by the criminal division of the department—which has the final say. But we don't have any special forces, all of our agents are capable of investigating anything."

57

Meyer Mauer is an attorney with many years of experience representing creditors in bankruptcy actions; he became known to the Scolnick gang as The Bald Eagle. This refers as much to his ferocity in going after a debtor he suspects of fraud as it does to the lack of hair on top of his head. In discussing bankruptcy frauds in general and Scolnick in particular, he said, "In order to perpetrate a real fraudulent bankruptcy—one that pays—you have to be able to get goods on credit. The big suppliers who could trust you with enormous quantities of goods simply won't do it with a person whom they don't know.

"The way the racket used to be worked before an organized group like Scolnick's came on the scene was that a gang would buy no more than three hundred dollars worth of goods from four to five hundred suppliers. If the bankruptcy was going to take place in Philadelphia, the goods would be bought in St. Louis, Chicago and other remote places. Maybe they would actually start off with a token order of fifty dollars which would be paid as soon as the bill came in.

"Then their next order would be one hundred and fifty dollars and then they would send a repeat order worth, say, three hundred dollars, while the hundred-fifty-dollar order was in transit. Well, if you multiply that by three or four hundred creditors, you run up to several hundred thousand dollars.

"Now, the advantage of buying goods in small quantities was that no businessman would be interested enough to come from Chicago or St. Louis or Atlanta in order to testify in a criminal prosecution on behalf of the government. The witness might be asked to wait around for three or four days before he was called; so, the result in most cases was that the government was not able to prosecute successfully because most of the businessmen were willing to take a small loss and forget about it."

He was asked, "Is it true that Scolnick took bankruptcy

out of the bucket shops and refined it into a highly sophisticated technique?"

"I think so. His first big enterprise involved his father-in-law, Morris Stein. In that situation he was able to get a total of $1,200,000 on credit . . . and these were all goods he was able to get rid of out the back door for as much as seventy-five percent of their wholesale cost. He was a very convincing operator because he was willing to wait for extended periods of time before he hit. Salesmen have told me that when their firm sent them up to M. Stein and Company to find out why they hadn't been paid, Scolnick would say, 'Oh hell, pal, there's no problem,' and then this fat colossus would pull out a big roll of bills and pay the salesman. That made a terrific impression and they not only received the money, they also received an additional order which would then be filled.

"He had a flair and he got away with murder. What he did was to take the old techniques, but he put them on a much larger scale. Instead of getting small orders from a large number of people, he got larger orders from a smaller number of suppliers which made it more effective and a lot less work. In the thirty years that I've been practicing, I don't think anyone else in the country has ever come up to his standards. To my knowledge, there hasn't been anyone else so unafraid to operate on the grand scale."

The M. Stein bankruptcy was the first in almost a hundred similar projects. The gang never changed the formula and the money poured in. Once, when pressed for the total amount of the "take," Scolnick answered, "Man, that's a hard one. Naturally, we never kept no records, but it had to involve way over ten million dollars.

"Let's see now: There was the Cape May Drug bankruptcy for a little over $100,000; the Levak Sales deal which was

$397,000; we got over $600,000 or so out of M. Stein; and then there was the Grendel deal for between $400,000 and $500,000. The Del Rey deal went for between $350,000 and $400,000, and we took about $400,000 out of Savoy Waste. Kaniff was $350,000 and Steinbrecher, where we come up short, was good only for a little over $150,000.

"It's hard to say. There was so many places and so much money going out as fast as it rolled in that I'd have to sit down and figure for a month before I could work out an accurate total.

"Of course, you got to remember that it wasn't all gravy. In a bankruptcy you usually wind up with approximately fifty percent of what the outstanding bills are. In other words, if you owe out $300,000, you usually make $150,000. But, also, a lot of it gets ploughed back into other deals which you sometimes lose. And then, of course, there's your partners and other people involved—everybody gets a piece of the action. My own share generally ended up pretty healthy; like in one deal where we cut up a quarter of a million, I got $75,000 which I would use for other deals. And that's about the way we always cut it."

Although the formula didn't vary from deal to deal, the various fronts used in the operations generally fell into two categories; either the gang would operate behind the name of a respectable old firm that they had taken over, or they began from scratch and sometimes waited, as with Levak Sales, for a few years before blowing it. During this period they would pay all bills on time, take whatever trade discounts were offered for punctual payments and generally conduct the business in a highly responsible manner.

A typical example of this latter operation was the Kaniff deal. It began when they took in a young jewelry salesman named Herbert Kaniff who had been selling his merchandise from his home and a car route he had built up. They opened a store for him, bearing his name, in one of the crowded, lower-income neighborhoods in Philadelphia. This was in August 1962. Less than a year later his creditors brought him into the bankruptcy court where it was discovered that he had assets of less than $4500 against debts of $256,824. He claimed that most of this money had been lost in floating crap games and two trips to Las Vegas. He also stated that his brother had sold off large quantities of merchandise at a loss in order to finance his drinking and women-chasing. Kaniff's brother wasn't around to deny this allegation because he had died a few months earlier.

In explaining how such a small and newly established retail outlet obtained so much credit from so many companies in such a short space of time, Scolnick said, "They want to be blind. Like one time we bought six portable televisions and six table radios from a salesman we didn't know. He was from an outfit, I think its name was Weststorm, and it turns out to be a subsidiary of a big national conglomerate.

"We sell off the radios and TVs and I tell Herbie I'm going to send out a check right away so that we'll be paying the bill for them within ten days.

"Not two more days go by before the salesman comes back in and we tell him that the radios and TVs were tremendous and we want two more dozen of each. The very next day the stuff comes in and, like before, I send out a check right away.

"Now I tell Herbie, 'This outfit is pretty good to do business with, I'm going to find out what they're all about. So I get on the phone and tell them that this is Mr. Kaniff calling and that I'm interested in buying larger quantities of their radios and televisions, but first I wanted some more information about the company. I asked them about the availability of filling large orders from their current stock and what arrangements they had for repairs and could we get a better price because we wanted to run a big advertising promotion.

61

"This sales manager started to get excited and wanted to know how much was it we were interested in. I said, 'Well, do you carry ten, fifteen thousand dollars' worth of inventory in these goods?' He said so fast that he does that I said, 'Well, I might want twenty-five, fifty thousand dollars' worth,' and he says that it's no problem, they can handle it.

"Then since he was biting so good, I asked him if he had any other numbers we could use and he told me that he had a portable TV that worked on batteries and was turning out to be a fast mover. So I said that we could use a couple of hundred thousand dollars' worth of them, but that now we were getting into figures where I should know more about the company before trusting them with such a big order.

" 'I'll tell you what I'll do,' I said, 'I'll send one of my men up to New York to see you and I'll appreciate it if you give him a financial statement on your company to bring back to me. I really have to see what kind of a company you've got before I make this kind of an investment with you.' And he said that would be very fine with him.

"So I send Little Murray up to New York the next day and they can't do enough for him. They show him all through their warehouses and their production figures and everything else. Then they go to lunch and when the sales manager tries to pick up the check, Little Murray says, 'Oh, no. Mr. Kaniff would be very upset if you bought me anything. I'm paying for the lunch and it goes right on my expense account. Mr. Kaniff would want it that way.'

"Then he excuses himself and calls me. 'It's a piece of cake,' he says. 'Shall I sign the order?' I told him 'No. Get the statement and get back here.' He goes back to the table and tells them, 'I just called Mr. Kaniff and I told him I was very satisfied and he's agreed to give you the order which he'll sign as soon as he sees your financial statement.'

62

"When Little Murray comes back and tells me that their warehouse is a city block square and when I see that the company is really a subsidiary of the conglomerate, I call up the sales manager and place an order for fifty thousand.

"Next day the shipment comes in. No credit check, no nothing. Here my own statement only shows twelve thousand and the guy ships me without even thinking about it. I realized that because of the size of the company they must have a big credit department away from the warehouse and the sales department, and that it's going to take a couple of weeks for the paperwork to go through between the two places. So the guy ships me without checking and within a week I sold off all the stuff to dealers all over the city for twenty-five percent below cost.

"Now, I figure to really bang him. I call up and give him an order for $250,000 worth of the battery operated TVs and an order for $60,000 worth of the radios and regular TVs. But this time the guy says, 'Well, gee, Mr. Kaniff, you've already reached your credit limit. I'm going to have to refer this to one of our credit managers,' and I answered, 'Well, that will be fine, suppose you just transfer me over to him and I'll arrange the payment.'

"So I talk to this credit manager on the phone and told him who I was and how big operators we were and then I said, '. . . and now, suppose I have my accountant, Mr. Bruderson, call you back,' and I hung up. Bruderson was the name of a house painter my dad worked for for a while when I was a kid.

"Then I stuffed some paper in both my cheeks and called the guy back and told him I was Mr. Bruderson. He says, 'Oh yes, Mr. Kaniff told me to expect your call,' and I said, 'Well, we won't ask you to ship the merchandise, I'll send up one of the company's trucks or trailers to pick it up and we'll give the driver a note of trade acceptance for the previous bill and you can, in addition, bill us for whatever the discount cost is at the bank.

"So they done it. They took the note I sent them and discounted it at their bank which means that they were liable on the note, not me, and they loaded up Big Melvin's truck with the radios and some of the TVs, the rest being held up by the shipping strike and he come back with the stuff which we got rid of in a few days.

"A week later they must have finally checked our record because two US marshals come with a writ of replevy and two vans to pick up the radios and TVs. Kaniff calls me on the phone and asks what he should do. I answer, 'Why, give them back to the man, of course. It's his merchandise.' And since we only had two busted TVs left, the marshals put one set in each van and drove away. And that's how we beat them for $110,-000."

The S. Steinbrecher bankruptcy is typical of the other kind of situation, where the gang bought out an established business for use as a front. Mrs. Jean Bromberg, the daughter of the founder of the company, described the take-over:

"My father was S. Steinbrecher and he had a small furniture store in northeast Philadelphia for forty-five years. After he died in 1962, my mother gave the building to a real estate man to sell. In September he brought in this man who said he wanted to buy the store's name as well as the building. My mother didn't want him to use Daddy's name because he had always been so proud of his good reputation, but the real estate man and the lawyer convinced her that it would be all right.

"The man gave my mother a small deposit and said he would make final settlement a few months later, in December, but that he wanted to take possession right away.

"My mother agreed and moved from her apartment in the back across the street to a second-floor apartment in a building that Daddy had also owned.

64

"From her front window in this apartment my mother began to notice that almost immediately there was a long line of trucks that came every day to make deliveries. But then, at night, she'd see more trucks pulling up and taking merchandise away. This went on for a while until finally my mother notified the FBI. Of course, the man never paid the rest of the money. After the FBI came, he and the rest of the men in the place just sort of disappeared."

Scolnick had used a bald-headed man, nicknamed Curly, as the front in this operation. His intention was to move fast by rushing big orders in during the Christmas shopping season on the strength of the Steinbrecher name, pay no one, and abruptly fold the day before settlement was to be made.

"Curly got worried," he recalls. "He got the idea that the FBI had the place staked out. So he came over to the warehouse where I had my office and tells me how he feels. I told him, 'If you can't hold up, just go away and forget about it, I don't need you.' He says, 'I want to stay but I'm working over at Kaniff's, too. Suppose some salesman sees me in both places?' I could see where that was a problem, so I told him to wear his toupee in one place and go bald in another.

"So it worked out pretty good. One time a salesman came in to Steinbrecher's who had just seen Curly that morning over at Kaniff's. The salesman says to him, 'Gee, you look familiar,' and Curly said, 'Well, I got a familiar kind of a face,' and placed twice the order he had put in with the guy earlier that morning at the other joint."

According to the schedules filed with the referee in bankruptcy, during the months of October and November S. Steinbrecher & Co. ordered $150,000 worth of merchandise. Included in these shipments were such items as $4200 worth of clocks, $4300 worth of soldering guns, $2100 worth of flashlights, $1500 worth of gold cigarette lighters, $10,000 worth of percolators, $5000 worth of sealed beam lights, $9300 worth of Prestone antifreeze and ten tons of Luden's candy worth $7400.

Presumably competent national sales managers authorized all these shipments to a nondescript little furniture store which had just been poking along for the preceding forty-five years. Scolnick explains why:

"I went at it like a professional. With me, stealing was a business. I wasn't like the guy who, if he didn't have any food at home or shoes for the baby, he'd go in and stick up a candy store or something. Instead, I picked my spots. I didn't go every day or every month or even every six months. I always waited until I found the right place at the right time and then me and the boys would go in.

"Before I went into the field, the bucket shops used to operate on a get-in-and-get-out basis. They'd take one shot; order a lot of goods from a lot of people and sell it out the back door as fast as it came in the front. Then they'd disappear.

"I thought that was a stupid way to operate. I made my companies solid. I paid bills, parlaying one to the other, meaning I'd use one guy's money to pay the next. We'd go for six or eight months paying our bills on time, maintaining a respectable bank account and keeping a list of fifty or seventy-five solid creditors happy because we always had a float of forty or fifty thousand dollars coming in and out. Then, when I am ready to blow, everybody would be breaking my doors down to ship me goods. It was the first time anybody had set up a fraudulent BR operation that paid over a half a million dollars in bills before busting out."

And, although his gang worked these places like a swarm of termites, Scolnick rarely remained visible for any length of time during the daily operations. He stayed in the back rooms where the decisions were made or in his warehouses where deals were negotiated with the reputable distributors and merchants who, after parking their cars a few blocks away, would scurry

66

in to buy what was on hand or to describe the goods they would like to have.

Big Murray would drive him from place to place and, in most cases, would actually go in and make the collections while Scolnick sat in the car. It was only when Big Murray came back to report an interesting situation or the beginnings of a problem that the Fat Man went in, generally through the rear door, to take over the situation.

On one occasion, the trip inside cost him $2800. His operator of one stand, a man named Hotsy, told Big Murray that the Fat Man ought to come in and hear the colorful pitch being made by a salesman who was a small, elderly Frenchman desperate to sell them an order. He had heard on the street that these people were fantastic customers; the kind of people that could save the failing little manufacturing business that he and his wife operated.

"I had only gone in for the laughs," the Fat Man recalled, "so I took over while Hotsy went into the back. But the little guy really got ahold of me. He was crying real tears, he needed the order so bad. But I wasn't about to take him because I only believed in boffing out the big guys. What did I need to jam a little fella like this?

"Hotsy was listening from in the back and when he saw I wasn't about to give in, he dials me on the intercom. I picked up the phone and I hear him say, 'They all go when the wagon comes,' and I realized that I'd be setting a bad example for the rest of the guys if I let the Frenchman get away. So I placed the order. But after the place blows, I sent Big Murray up to New York to pay off the little guy with my own money. He later made a special trip back down here to thank me. He said he would of gone under if I had hurt him for the twenty-eight. What the hell. I never needed no gun and I never needed to jam the little guys in order to take down a sting."

He would also come in to "move the phone" when there

67

was a potentially big order to be wangled, but this became an infrequent gesture after his protégé, Little Murray Packer, became a graduate master in the technique of buying over the long-distance wire.

"To be a good phone man," says Little Murray, "first of all you talk quietly and with confidence. You act so sure of yourself that the other guy knows that if he presses too hard, you're going to tell him to take his merchandise and go home with it. You're letting him know that you don't need him, you can buy anywhere.

"Once you're on the offensive, then you look for the chance to get indignant . . . and that makes him sit up because people don't want to lose customers, especially customers that are talking the big figures that I'm throwing around. You tell a guy that you only want to buy fifty dollars worth of fountain pens and he don't even listen to you. But tell him you want ten thousand dollars' worth of antifreeze and he falls all over you.

"Can you believe it? They send us ten thousand dollars' worth of antifreeze! In September, yet! I told him we're breaking in to the automotive market and I had big crews of men on the street where they could each sell five or six gallons on the installment plan and I would also run a promotion to give a couple of gallons away with every set of furniture. And, being a salesman himself, he believes every word.

"All you got to do is study the catalogues so you sound like you know everything about them and their competitor's product, act confident, put 'em on the defensive, get indignant once in a while, and then bargain about a price for a big load. Then it comes down to what Sylvan always said—their greed."

Scolnick, who had been sitting by, broke into the conversation with every appearance of righteous indignation: "Greed! It's always greed! Man is greedy! I got a store that looks like a little basement and they come in to me and I order three

68

thousand electric frying pans and they send 'em to me. But Macy's only orders three dozen. Gimbels orders a dozen. But me they send three thousand. It's just sheer hunger! They're looking for the money, not at the size of my store. Who the hell ever heard of a furniture store ordering ten thousand bucks' worth of antifreeze? Or five thousand boxes of Hershey chocolate bars?

"And the credit managers are even dumber than the salesmen. They don't know what they're looking for. You send them a financial statement, whether it's real or unreal, and they'll ship you ten percent of what the statement says is your net worth. Without the credit managers you couldn't go bankrupt."

The law firm of Meyer Mauer, the Bald Eagle mentioned before, represents many of the country's largest manufacturers and credit insurance companies in the defaulting debtor cases, so he is in an expert position to comment on the weaknesses of sales and credit managers in this situation:

"Well, imagine that you're a salesman and you're trying to sell a carload of antifreeze to this customer. You are asking, say, a buck and a half a unit and he tells you he wants it for a dollar twenty-five. This goes on on the telephone for five or ten minutes and finally you compromise at a dollar thirty-five. You're elated. You've just sold a carload in ten minutes!

"Then you look up S. Steinbrecher in Dun and Bradstreet. You see the firm is rated as good pay, they discount their bills and although their credit line is only ten or fifteen thousand dollars, they've got a good history. How do you know that at the same time the exact same spiel is being given to ten other companies?

"Now if you are Union Carbide or Hershey, the chocolate company, ten thousand dollars isn't a lot of money. And, you see, the competition for business is so keen. If a sales manager gets a better year than the year before, he becomes a big shot in the eyes of his boss.

"Now the deal comes to the credit manager who, in most cases, is a sophisticated man. But there is always an internecine battle going on between the credit and sales departments. I am quite sure that when the order for the Prestone came in, the sales manager was for it and the credit manager was against it. But since most emphasis is placed on sales, the sales manager prevailed. This is the situation that makes fraudulent bankruptcies so profitable."

The fraudulent bankrupt's next step after "buying" his goods, is to dispose of them. Scolnick's cynical estimate of the morals of most businessmen colors his description of the process: "Man's greed is also how you get rid of it. Every legitimate businessman is a thief. It's part of the system. His job when he goes in business and puts that sign up on his window is to buy merchandise cheaper than anybody else so he can sell it cheaper than anybody else. So, when you're dealing in merchandise and not in threats, he doesn't feel he's doing anything wrong in getting together with you.

"I had one guy, a distributor with a very fine name in the community, come in to me, and I said, 'You're buying Sony Tape Recorders wholesale for a hundred bucks. I'll give 'em to you for seventy. He didn't ask me where I was getting 'em. He only asked, 'Can I get a bill?' I said, 'Sure, why not? Your check is good, isn't it?'

"See my point? He didn't care about anything as long as he had a paid bill for the Sonys in his files. That meant as far as he was concerned, he bought legitimate and paid by check.

"Now, after you do business with these kind of guys for a while, they get really greedy. Now they start to realize how you're doing it, so they're not satisfied with just buying the stuff

70

I have on hand, they want to teach me about their line of merchandise so I can set up a flow of the kind of goods they need. In other words, they want to get to where they're preordering and I'm preselling.

"So that's what I do. Next thing, they want to turn it into a system and they make me up a card with a couple of hundred suppliers they deal with; their names, addresses, type of goods, price breaks and what they want to pay for it. And that's what we used to do all day long; do nothing but dial out on the phone and order merchandise.

"They were guiltier than me because without them I couldn't operate the fraudulent BR. It's impossible to operate without the 'ethical' businessman because you'd have nowhere to distribute so much goods. What the hell, I can't put an ad in the paper saying I got a hundred hot Sonys for sale!

"And as I got deeper into it, I got to the point where I could call buyers in Chicago, Florida, Los Angeles, anywhere and they'd come in with trucks, trailers, and loaded with cash.

"Like, for example, I done business with a guy in New York whose company does about ten million dollars a year. Once every two or three weeks he'd come to one of our warehouses and he'd buy thirty or forty thousand at the discount. Then he'd tell me who to order from. Once he gave me the name of one of his best friends and he had me order thousands of dollars' worth from this guy. This manufacturer was his good friend! Their families used to take vacations together.

"So, you talk about me being the Fat Man, or the Big Cherry who is such a criminal mastermind. Well, I could go through the yellow pages in the phone book and pick out a hatful of reputable retailers and distributors who taught me how to be a mastermind. I didn't know who to call for goods, I didn't know how much to order and who to sell 'em to; *they showed me!* But I have a talent; you don't have to tell me more

71

than once, and sometimes you don't even have to finish the sentence for me to get the message. You start to talk and I'll get the feeling of what you are looking for. And that's how it was with me and them yellow-page beauties."

Most of the money that came in to the gang was funneled through a maze of distribution companies that had been set up for the purpose of hiding the origin and the distribution of their funds. But, obviously, some red-herring indication of expenditures had to be left for the day that the affairs of any of their operations was put before a referee in bankruptcy. Scolnick's henchman, Hotsy, described how the gang used the frenetic Las Vegas atmosphere as a smoke screen:

"In the Kaniff deal, Sylvan told me that I should start drawing big checks out of the company and go out to Las Vegas and make with the wine, women and song. He said I should be very conspicuous, that I should carry on so they would remember me when the FBI came out to investigate the story that it's where the money from the business went. So that's what I did. I'd buy big stacks of chips and holler and carry on at the crap table, and then, every once in a while, I'd go into a men's room and meet one of our guys and give him most of my chips. Then when I went back to the table, he'd go around to the different cashier windows and cash them in. But there was plenty of testimony at the hearing that people remembered me losing a big bundle in Vegas after I told the referee that that's where the money went."

Judge Goldhaber was asked if there wasn't some way for the honest businessman to protect himself against the operations of the fraudulent operator. He said, "It's a tough situation. When you look at the classic case of a man who takes in money, deposits it in his bank account and then takes it out again in a large lump sum, you have to get suspicious. You call on him for an explanation and he answers that he gambled it away. But what can you say? What proof can there be that a man hasn't foolishly lost his money? You don't get receipts at the gaming table, you don't charge your losses on your Diner's or American Express card.

"There is only the man's bald statement before you and you can either accept his story or disbelieve it on your own instinctive reaction to the individual.

"Obviously, you can claim only so often that you lost your money in gambling and the repetition of the excuse becomes a warning flag. Or if a business has been operating very modestly for many years and then suddenly, for no ostensible reason, it begins to buy in large quantities and, at the same time, stop paying bills, then this too becomes a signal.

"But I would believe that most of the fraudulent operators are too smart to go on using the same old excuses. They are too sophisticated. So, here again, in the absence of the participation of creditors in an investigation, I must admit that the court is just about stymied in its attempt to prove fraud."

Since most other authorities agreed that one of the hardest crimes in the book to prove is that a man has opened and operated a business with the specific intent to steal from his suppliers, it was logical to ask the most proficient crook in the country how he would protect himself if he were a manufacturer or distributor.

"It's simple," Scolnick answered. "Just do the job you're getting paid to do. I can smell a fraudulent BR even if it's a couple of thousand miles away. All I got to do is draw a Dun and Brad or a consumer's report and study it. It's their way of opening accounts. It's the type of merchandise they order and how they pay their bills. What was their original investment in the company. When they made up their financial statement, what portion of it was in cash, what portion is receivables and what portion is inventory?

73

"It's even easier if I can walk in and see the operation. I can tell by the prices they are charging, by the type of goods they buy and the way they keep their merchandise. You see, in a bankruptcy, you buy only stuff you can sell, not stuff you're going to take a lacing on. In a legitimate business you buy goods that fill everybody's needs; you buy a line of watches that go for one thousand, five hundred, one hundred, thirty, ten and even down to three dollars. But, if you go into a BR joint you won't find no middle-of-the-road stuff. Everything is either high or low because the operator wants to sell it off in bulk and he don't want to be saddled with an inventory. The BR operator don't have the room to set up twenty or thirty different numbers, but the legitimate businessman wants to give everybody a choice.

"Hell, in two weeks I could train anybody to walk into a BR and see the flags that are sticking out all over the joint. The salesmen that come in don't see it because they don't want to see it."

As for a defense against the operator who orders over the phone, Little Murray Packer said, with elaborate scorn, "Jeez, all it is is common sense! If somebody would call me up and tell me they want to buy ten thousand dollars worth of antifreeze from me for their furniture store, I would tell them one thing: 'That's my game, pal. Come up with another story. This one is very weak.'"

74

# Chapter 5

# THE BIG TIME RACKET GUYS

*The Subject belongs to no lodges, fraternal organizations, clubs or other recreational organizations. His friends and associates appear to have been generally undesirable.*

—An extract from the
presentence report ordered
by the sentencing judge.

He was riding high. The inside people told each other stories about the Fat Man and his gang and whistled at the size of their scores. When he moved with Ruth and his mother across the Delaware River to expensive suburban Cherry Hill in 1963, the wise guys in the know expanded his participation in crime and his massive bulk into a form of folklore. Now he was Big Cherry, the man you went to with a really important illegal problem.

He loved every minute of it. He was no longer the grossly fat kid in the school yard or Sylvan the sandwich maker waddling behind the delicatessen counter; he was the important shadowy figure in the background who pulled strings and directed men and could afford any foolish extravagance because there was a lot more where that came from: all he had to do was use his brains.

As his reputation grew, so did the circle of his friends. But now the friendship of people like Billy Somerville, Hotsy and the two Murrays was no longer enough. Syndicate chiefs and the other men who ran the rackets accepted him as an equal: in fact, sought him out because he was colorful and funny and, above all, highly successful. He found that the qualifications for social membership in these sets could be put in one sentence; if you make a lot of money in your racket, you are a big shot, and big shots like to be with big shots. His sponsor in most of these associations was Cappy Hoffman whom he met as an indirect result of a partnership with Harry Karafin.

Most newspapermen agree that Harry Karafin represents one of the real lows in American journalism. After many years as a reporter for the Philadelphia *Inquirer,* he was finally unmasked as a shakedown artist whose victims believed that he could put any story he wanted in the *Inquirer,* and that he was so close to M. L. Annenberg (then publisher) that he was provided for in the old man's will. He was a feared figure in the city and even one of the largest banks in the country, the Pennsylvania Company, was willing to pay him $1000 a month for five years in exchange for his services as a "public relations counsel." At Karafin's subsequent trial for extortion, most of the bank executives found it difficult to define these services which, in the opinion of many observers, really consisted of not writing about the bank's financial backing of some fairly tough home remodeling and loan companies.

After he was indicted, *The New York Times* described

Karafin's career in a lengthy article in its editorial pages which said, in part:

> Harry Karafin was a figure out of *The Front Page,* a hard-knuckled, gum-shoed reporter who seemed to be everywhere scooping everybody.
>
> Not just for the fun of it, either. The cocky little star for the Philadelphia *Inquirer* was a crusader out of the old school, exposing, during the last fifteen years, corrupt magistrates, poor nursing homes, auto accident rackets and even a baby photo racket.
>
> "For years," a Philadelphia weekly said recently, "lawyers cringed, city officials winced and politicians prayed when Harry Karafin walked into their offices."
>
> Last week, the man who made his reputation by shaking people up was accused of shaking people down.

The Karafin episode was considered one of the worst black eyes that the newspaper profession had suffered since Jake Lingle, the reporter who was killed back in Prohibition days for his complicity with Chicago racketeers. *Time* magazine devoted its "Press" section to it in one issue and the executive committee of the Newspaper Guild of Greater Philadelphia issued a statement which said, in part: "We are shocked and angered by revelations concerning Harry Karafin who, according to published articles, used his job as a reporter for the Philadelphia *Inquirer* to betray his employer, his co-workers and decent newspapermen everywhere."

The Philadelphia *Inquirer,* itself, ran a ten-column story expressing its disgust with his perfidious conduct using such strong descriptions as: "An ailing company attracted Karafin as much as the stench of rotting flesh attracts buzzards. Karafin's fee schedule was simple: Whatever he could gouge."

And what seemed to be the most upsetting aspect of the

77

Karafin mess was that it was finally brought to light that his instructor in extortion turned out to be Sylvan Scolnick. As the *Inquirer* said: "Scolnick was one of the initial victims Harry Karafin preyed upon when he chose shakedown as a way of life. Scolnick was the partner who in self-defense taught Karafin how to broaden his scope; to stop mooching clock radios and cut-rate watches and to strive for a six-figure annual income."

"There wasn't a chance that Harry wouldn't hear about my BRs," Scolnick recalls, "so I was locked in when he came around and started leaning on me. However, he got real bad, like when he'd come over for dinner and his wife would say, 'Harry, that little table radio is just what we need,' and I'd have to stand by and watch Ruth steam as they walked out the door with it under their arm.

"So I figured, what the hell, I'll make an older boy out of him, and I showed him how he could get real money instead of nickels and dimes.

"One of the things that came out of it was our partnership in shaking down the home remodeling guys. All of them were scared to death of a newspaper story showing how they operate. So they put Harry on as a public relations man and my cut was that they'd subcontract a lot of their small work out to a home-mod outfit I had going at the time.

"I didn't have to do anything. I would send out a one-lung mechanic or a carpenter or a stone man and let him go through some motions and the price would be one hundred twenty-five dollars on their tab. I was grabbing myself about a grand a week out of it.

"Well, one of these guys was in the water softener business and he called me to come over and talk about handling his work. When I get there, he introduces me to Cappy Hoffman who was associated with him in some way. Cappy says, 'I hear you got all these guys on your payroll; why not include me in?' I did it and that's when I started getting friendly with him.

"Like a jerk, I really admired the reputation of guys like him in those days. I see now that I put him on the payroll so I could hobnob with him. I was fantasizing. I wanted to be a big shot, a big-time racketeer, and I thought that was the way to do it, you know, being with a guy like that who was supposedly the banger for all the top guys. I mean, he was supposed to have killed so many men, and I was fascinated just being around him. I really dramatized myself into the situation."

Something else happened during this period that drew Scolnick even closer to Cappy Hoffman. *Philadelphia Magazine,* one of the hardest-hitting muckraking magazines in the country, published a story entitled "Bankruptcy for Fun and Profit." It was a roundup story which alleged the possibility that a gang of thieves were operating fraudulent bankruptcies throughout the east. The story mentioned Sylvan Scolnick as the possible supply of brains for the gang, although a major portion of the article was concerned with the description of a series of fishy blow-outs and stopped just short of actual accusations. The story inspired no immediate legal action, but it was so painfully accurate that Scolnick decided that he had better start operating from a position that was even deeper into the shadows.

"I figured I better watch out," he said. "So , instead of fronting deals, I began to act as a buyer in the BRs that other guys were running. That worked out okay, too. The minute I walked in, everybody knew who I was, so I got whatever I wanted at the kind of prices that let me turn the stuff over at a hell of a profit.

"One of the deals we came across was a big grocery store that was going out because they didn't know how to run it. It looked good, so me and Sam Koff and Cappy put in thirteen and a half grand apiece and took it over and we started a company called Fresh Foods.

"After we took it over, I met Ben Jones, who is president

of B-J's Markets, which is a multimillion-dollar chain of grocery supermarkets. I didn't let Ben know I was one of the owners, I just held myself out as the manager. He was a pretty sharp customer and at first he didn't want to do anything with us because he couldn't see anybody connected with the operation who knew anything about the grocery business.

"But after I spoke with him a few times, I was able to hammer out a solid deal with him. I bought five thousand dollars' worth of stock in his company and he gave Fresh Foods the right to buy from his warehouse on an open account. I guess he thought he was just dealing with an average grocer and how much could such a guy order?

"Well, instead of ordering directly from him, I'd order direct from the big guys like General Foods and Hormel's and the other national food processors. They'd ship it direct to me and, because we were an open account with him, they'd send him the bill and before he could turn around, I had him in for eighty or one hundred thousand dollars. I did that because I wanted to make sure that if Fresh Foods wasn't successful, then I could take my investment out of the first sales that came into the company.

Jones got scared when he found out about this, but what could he do? We had already resold the bulk shipments to other food distributors. He came down from North Jersey to get us to sign a note for what we owed him and to get maybe thirty or forty grand in front.

"Well, he didn't get no front money and he didn't get no check for anything. I told him we would pay him out. I said, 'What's the difference if it's a note or not? Why should we have our signatures on a note?'

"Now he was in the hands of the Philistines. There was nothing he could do about it. We had him over a barrel and all he could do was hope we'd stay in business long enough to pay him out. Worst of all from his standpoint, he had to keep shipping us to make sure that we would stay in business long enough to pay him off.

"But he was no dope. While I wasn't around one day, he got Sam Koff to sign the note for him. So, the next time he come in, I gave him around thirty grand out of our receipts, which meant that instead of that money going into our pockets to cover our investment, he got it as front money.

"That Koff was really a madman when it came to running the business. All of a sudden he started to figure he was a grocery tycoon. And the funny part of it is we were really doing big business at first. Koff, he'd pitch right in. But he'd get sore when people would come in and only buy the specials we advertised as leaders. He'd stand by the checkout counter and curse the people out. One time he got so mad at somebody who came in to return a couple of cases of empty soda bottles, he picked them up so violently that he popped himself square in the eyes. He walked around for about a week after that with two big shiners. He bawled the living hell out of Billy Somerville once after he caught him making himself a steak-tartare patty out of some hamburger meat we had in the cooler. It took Cappy Hoffman to pry him off of Billy's back.

"Can't you just picture it? Straight out of Damon Runyon! Harry the Horse and Louie the Lug and all their buddies operating a big, complicated grocery supermarket. And then the word got out that Cappy was in the deal and all his friends started to congregate in our back room in the morning. Just to say hello and drink some coffee and eat doughnuts.

"There wasn't one big racketeer that didn't come in to say hello. Then they would spend maybe a hundred fifty or two hundred dollars for about fifteen cartfuls of groceries. Just to show Cappy they were his friends.

"I thought that was really something. I was really im-

81

pressed that his friends would spend a couple of hundred bucks on groceries every time they'd come in and really not need any groceries at all because they lived in a hotel or a two-room apartment. Man, I wanted to get into this kind of a high level, you know, this leadership of crime. It was just ridiculous!

"And all of them took a liking to me. Skinny Razor, who's dead now but used to be pretty high up in the mob, once put his arm around me and said, 'Sylvan, you're my man, you're my cousin.' But Willie Weissberg, who was on a par with Cappy Hoffman, said, 'Listen, you Dago bastard, he ain't your cousin and he ain't nothing. Cherry is with the Jews, see, and you keep the hell away from him!' Willie was so mad he was wild.

"I didn't understand what was going on, so I kept quiet. But after a while, I realized that this was the first step for Skinny and his guys to get in with me. You know, back a BR for me to run so they could then be in my line of business. But Willie saw what was going on and he didn't want me in with them.

"There was all kinds of guys that used to come in there. I won't mention no names because some of them are still around, but they used to get together and sometimes they had meetings in my office in the back."

Scolnick was asked about the agenda of these meetings, but in answer he simply said, incredulously, "How the hell would I know? Do you think I hung around to hear? God only knows, because I don't. A guy can get himself buried knowing them kind of things. I used to sit outside the door and all I can say is that I can't see them getting together to talk about a game of golf.

"After I got to know them, these guys really scared me. One time they asked me if I wanted to go into the loan-shark business with them, so I said okay and all of us put up ten grand apiece. So we had eighty going in.

"In less than a month, we had doubled the eighty. But then I got out. What happened was I hear them talking about one guy who hadn't paid up, and one of my partners says, 'Well, let's put him up on a meat hook for a while.' At that I took Willie and Cappy aside and said, 'Hey, this ain't my shtick. Boy, this is pretty strong—way too strong for me.'

"Put a guy on a hook! There ain't no way you exactly come out of that alive! I remember once when I was a little kid climbing a fence a nail went through my arm, and when they said that, I remembered that flesh tearing and, man, the whole thing just dug at me. So, since Sam wanted to be with me on other things, he went into the back office and, after an awful loud argument with the other guys, he got me back my ten, and after that I never knew about no loan business or nothing else. From then on, it was: 'Good morning,' 'Hiyah, pal,' and 'Have some coffee,' but nothing that ever came close to having business dealings with them."

The loan company venture was worrisome, but he was still too pleased with the emerging picture of himself as a major underworld figure to give it more than a passing thought. Harrry Karafin, as a surprise gift for his new partner, got him a gun permit and a shiny, nickel-plated revolver. Scolnick had a special shoulder holster made and cultivated the habit of allowing his coat to fall open so that the shoulder strap and the holster would be revealed. "Dumb son of a bitch," he says of himself. "I thought I was Bat Masterson."

He expanded his partnership with Hoffman into other fields. They went into the heating and air conditioning business and bought and operated several manufacturing concerns. These were all run legitimately, but the gangland chief turned out to be an extremely demanding associate. "If you had an appointment with Cappy for ten o'clock and you come in one minute late, you were in trouble. You had to hear a whole song and dance about how time cost money and all that crap. But if he was your friend, he went all the way. If somebody said anything about you, he'd call them in and make them repeat it in front of your face.

"And it got more and more exciting. I remember one time the head guy himself dropped by to say hello. Phew, what a charge I got! *There goes the boss!* I said to myself. It was out of sight, just out of sight. I couldn't of gotten a bigger charge out of meeting the President."

Occasionally, the "charges" were more tangible. A man named Albert held out $2000 from him on a business deal, but the circumstances made it the kind of situation in which ordinarily he might have taken the loss and charged it to experience. But he happened to mention it to Hoffman one day in their office.

"What are you going to do about it?" Hoffman asked.

The Fat Man shrugged. "Nothing. I'll wait. I'll get him someday and it won't be for nickels and dimes. And if I don't, the hell with it."

"Sylvan, that's no way to do. You let a punk like Albert take you and they'll all be standing in line to take their shots. I'll handle it."

Hoffman skipped the preliminary gesture of calling Albert and demanding the money. He sent his car for him.

Albert walked in and found an angry Cappy Hoffman waiting in the middle of the room. Then, when he noticed the Fat Man sitting impassively in the corner, he understood what the meeting was going to be about, so he became really frightened.

"Sit down."

"Look, Cappy, I can straighten . . . "

"Did you hear me?"

Albert sat down in the empty chair near the desk, which

left him with his back to Scolnick, a seating arrangement which caused him even more concern. Hoffman took another chair, placed it directly in front of him, and straddling it, sat down as that his face was just a few inches away from Albert's.

Hoffman gave him no opportunity for an explanation. "Listen, you son of a bitch, you think you can get this straightened out? Well, King Kong can't straighten it out for you. Are you trying to spit in my face and tell me it's raining outside?"

Albert began to cry. Tears streaming down his face, he tried to tell his story—he had used the money to pay for his sister's operation, but Hoffman cut him off. "You take that kind of crap out to the curb where maybe it'll do you some good cause it ain't doing nothing for you in here. You be at Sylvan's house by the end of the week with two grand in cash, or else nobody's gonna hear from you again, and that includes your sister who better start learning how to pay for her own operations. Get me?"

Albert got it. He walked into Scolnick's home the following Friday, still so frightened that he could not look directly at the Fat Man as he turned over the cash. Scolnick was impressed. The next time he met Hoffman, he asked, "What would you of done, Sam, if he hadn't paid?" Hoffman said quite seriously, "Why, Sylvan, it never even crossed my mind that he wouldn't be there."

It is not copping a plea to point out that idealizing gangsters is not a trait peculiar to men like Sylvan Scolnick. The libraries are full of books about the outlaws of the Old West who lived by their guns and wits and there were few Prohibition gangsters who haven't been re-created in a motion picture. Obviously, a large segment of the law-abiding public has always been fascinated by the activities of the historic hoodlums who became "stars."

85

It is still true. Cosa Nostra or Mafia leaders become folk-lore figures long before they die or are deported. The death of an honest community leader gets only a few lines in the newspapers outside of his own city, but almost any congressional sub-committee can share national television coverage for its interrogation of a gangland chief.

We fantasize. We don't see these hoods as a menace because we are rarely aware that their activities touch any part of our own lives. They are entertainment. And they were especially attractive to Sylvan Scolnick. Although his family was poor, it wasn't the kind of grinding poverty that makes crime the only doorway out. He was grossly fat, but other men have had physical handicaps and managed to live comfortably within the pale. His considerable intelligence could have brought success in many legitimate fields. But he chose crime and the company of criminals, probably because after he had slipped into the field, he found it so easy to turn his childish fantasies into fact.

He was able to act out these adolescent dreams because there were no holds on him after he had once gone beyond the law. The weak spots in our economic system seemed to thrust themselves at him. His qualities as a leader quickly attracted a gang willing to trust in his judgment and he had the nerve necessary to use them to carry out his plans.

And, after he was in operation, he looked around and saw respect in the eyes of the other thieves. In this milieu he was admired and liked. Once the chips began rolling in, his weight became only another colorful aspect of a charismatic personality. He turned out to be a man who knew how to plan and bring off good projects, which was all that counted in his circle. His word was good, he was trusted and he had guts and brains—in other words, he was becoming the kind of hood that people fantasize about.

Take the way he wound up the Fresh Foods situation. Once it started turning sour, a Cappy Hoffman would have simply let it cave in and then threaten anyone who wanted to ask questions about it. People like Sam Koff or Billy Somerville would have quietly vanished, leaving others to clean up the mess. But under Scolnick's direction, the gang walked out with a fat profit in their pockets.

After their bill with the supermarket chain that had bankrolled them reached $150,000, he called in B-J's president, Ben Jones. "Ben," he said, "we're all over a barrel, but mostly you. Almost everything we bought was through you, so if we blow, you still got to pay the bills. So what I'll do is this; you pay off the creditors and you can have the place."

Jones had no other choice. He realized that the gang was wholesaling off the entire inventory at far below the market price and stuffing the money away. He hastily signed the agreement because the place would have been stripped bare within a week.

"Over and above the profit," says Scolnick, "I had to do it that way. I couldn't afford to be involved in an open bankruptcy after *Philadelphia Magazine* ran that story about 'Bankruptcy for Fun and Profit,' and what with Cappy Hoffman being in it and all, I just had to figure a way to go out face up. So, I gradually worked Jones into a corner. It's impossible to beat a planned attack and it took a while for him to realize what was going on. So, once I drove him into a corner, it was all over, there was nothing he could do about it. B-J's took it over and three months later, they closed it up and moved out all the equipment. Cappy was just thrilled the way it all went down."

The Fresh Foods episode contributed to his growing reputation as a leader of criminals. Now he says, "I should of discouraged it. What the hell did I need all that kind of crap for? But I was getting a kick out of it. I used to read comic books about gangsters when I was a kid and I used to watch Elliot Ness on television and go to see Edward G. Robinson and James Cagney in the gangster movies and I always thought that was the real thing. So I let it rub off on me, which is only an excuse, of course, because only a jerk mixes up movies and television with real life.

"But , it always happened that I turned out to be the guy that called the shots, no matter if there was three or thirty-three people involved. Sooner or later, in every transaction, people always lay it in front of me to make the final decision. I guess it's because I'm always sure of what I'm doing after I think things through. At least, I learned to act sure.

"For example, a guy comes in to me. Some little fella who don't know too much; all he does is read the newspapers or hears of me through some friends. Say he's got trouble, some-body is threatening him or crowding him, something like that. He wants me to help him and I can't turn him down as long as he thinks I'm that big. So, I make a call. While he's standing there I say on the phone that he's my friend and the heat better be taken off him. I hang up and he's thrilled. He's so happy, he wants to cry, and he leaves with his mind all at ease because Sylvan Scolnick, the criminal mastermind made a call for him. He feels better because he heard me say that if anybody gives him a problem, the guy I'm talking to should take care of it. It's that kind of thing that used to put me on people's payrolls. But what did I do? I dialed the weather bureau, that's what I done!

"It was fantastic. It was Disneyland. People putting me on their payroll for a hundred a week because they think I'm protection. The more stories they printed about me being Big Cherry and the Fat Man, the more people wanted to be with me and respect me. I'm no criminal mastermind. I'm just Syl-van Scolnick. But nobody believed that, least of all the guys in

88

organized crime. To them, I was just as real as they was to me. All you got to do is do things with a straight face. Like one time I gave a party which people still talk about. Here's how it happens:

"I'm sitting one night in Tony Spaggs's bar and a character comes in that they called The Maestro. He was an old guy whose real name was Joseph Fisher. He liked to sing, only he was tone deaf. He'd travel down Locust Street where the bars were and he'd come in and sing parts of operas and the guys would give him a buck or so to encourage him. When I see him, the idea comes to me: I'll have a big party in his honor.

"So, I buy a piano and print up invitations inviting people to the house to hear 'The Atomic Basso Unique—The Maestro Joseph Fisher.' And I invite all the high-class racketeers, but I don't tell them nothing. Then I go to a place I know where they rent costumes and I rent him a devil's outfit for *Faust* and also a real fancy matador's outfit. He's going to sing a few numbers from *Faust* and *Carmen,* right? Then I hire a piano player and a violinist to accompany him.

"I take my pool table out of the basement so we would have plenty of room and I rent chairs and everything to make it look like a theater. I even had Mom cook up all kinds of food, like she was a caterer. We had a sweet table and a table full of knishes and kishke and sweet and sour meatballs; the whole deal. It really looked like—boy, we're going to hear *some* opera singer, all right.

"Then the people come. At least fifty of them, with the diamonds and the jewelry and the evening clothes. The women are made-up, with their hair and their fur coats and everything. Everybody's coming to hear this opera star, this frigging seventy-two-year-old bum, Maestro Joseph Fisher.

"Now, it starts. Everybody lines up and sits down and the violin and piano is going on and out comes Fisher, dressed like

89

a devil, with a big pitchfork in his hand and he starts singing.

"Only, he can't sing even a little bit. I tell you, the son of a bitch is absolutely tone deaf. But he keeps croaking on and everybody is looking at everybody else and they don't know what to do. And I'm standing in the back, laughing my ass off. What the hell do these bums know about opera? They never been in an opera house in their whole frigging life.

"Willie is looking, Charley is looking, Cappy is looking, and none of them know whether it's supposed to be this way or not!

"Then, all of a sudden, in the middle, the Maestro stops. He says in his broken English, 'Mon woice, mon woice,' meaning his throat is getting sore. So, he goes over to the sweet table and gets himself a big grape and starts to eat it.

"At this, everybody got it and started to bust up laughing. The chairs were falling all over the place. One woman peed all over the carpet because she was laughing so hard.

"It was the greatest thing you ever saw. We all got drunk and kept him singing until four in the morning. It turned out to be a hell of a party. Cost me three or four grand, but it was worth every nickel of it."

For a while, it was all funny and colorful, but then he began to realize that there was another, more serious side to these relationships. He became aware that his headquarters at Fourth and Fairmount streets in Philadelphia had come under surveillance by the F.B.I. and other law enforcement agencies interested in the activities of his friends. "And," he recalls, "I also started to realize that they had their own moral codes. Their code of ethics is: 'You are a rat if we say you are a rat. And you're a goodie only when we say you're a goodie.' In other words, the rules and regulations aren't made for them, they're made for you and you never know when they're going to be changed.

"I let too much of it rub off on me and I got scared. So I disengaged. Whenever they started to hint that they'd like to come in with me on a BR or they wanted me in on something they were running, I'd tell them it wouldn't work because I was being watched by the F.B.I. I let them know that my place was under surveillance and that's the way I got them to drift away.

"Later on, at one of my trials, the prosecutor asked me about my association with them. I wasn't about to lie, and besides it was past the statute of limitations, so I told them about the loan business I was in with them for a few weeks. But I didn't tell them about anything else, because I made it my business not to know about anything else. I went right down the line with Maggie Kline, but that was it. When I saw what they was, I backed off and I'm glad that it was before I had the chance to ever get in with them for anything besides coffee in the morning or drinks at night.

"Listen. When you talk about hanging people up on meat hooks, you're not talking about the normal stealing of money. This has nothing to do with money. You're talking about killing people, and there's a big difference.

"I finally realized that there's something wrong about a guy who takes a gun in his hand. You know, I might take twenty dollars out of your pocket, but I'm not going to cut your arm off. I'll never need money that bad."

## Chapter 6
# RAIDING THE BANKS

*The Subject has a propensity or a talent for listening to underlying messages and not attending to the verbal content when someone speaks to him. This is usually true of individuals who are highly creative and who have the ability to read messages or hear communications which others miss, and in addition, these communications give them insight and tend to give them solutions that other people would not consider.*

—From the psychiatric evaluation
summary prepared for the Philadelphia
County Court of Common Pleas,
April 11, 1969.

While Scolnick was still in Fresh Foods, Big Murray walked in to his office one day and handed him $500 in cash. "What's this for?"

Murray stood back and grinned. He seemed very proud of himself. "Don't ask no questions, Syl. It's your end. Just put it in your pocket."

"Nothing goes in my pocket that I don't know how it got there." The Fat Man tossed the five notes back across the desk. "Murray," he said, "I don't like games."

"Don't worry about it. I scored and it's your split."

"Now I *am* worried, Murray. I worry every time you go off and do something by yourself. Where did you get the five?"

"It wasn't five, it was a grand. The five is your end."

When there was no answer, Murray suddenly remembered that he had heard his boss say on many occasions, "*I hate to get hit from the blind side,*" and he realized he'd better stop smiling and explain.

"I found a turkey, that's all. Remember the guy that was in here this morning trying to get your account for that branch of the North Jersey bank? Well, I had an idea. . . . "

Now Murray noticed that his boss's silence had become stony, so he hurried on, " . . . I go up there about an hour ago, and it turns out this guy, his name is Anthony Smith, he's the vice-president in charge of the branch."

"I know his name, Murray."

"Well, anyway, I figured I'd test him, you know, try to move him around a little. So, I go up and introduce myself, tell him I wanted to open an account and. . . . "

"What name did you use?"

"Bruce Casino."

"And you got a loan?"

"Like cream. He only asked me a couple of light things and then did I want the money in cash or deposited to my account. It wasn't more than ten minutes before I took the grand."

He grinned again, expecting praise. Instead, the Fat Man looked thoughtfully at him. "Murray," he said, "you're a real jerk. You stumble over a genuine turkey in the straw and you want to blow after taking down only a little sting. You're gonna pay him back the grand and I'm going to make a loan and pay him back, and then, if my feeling about Mr. Smith being extra hungry for business is right, we're gonna really move him."

Next day, Scolnick called and made an appointment with Mr. Smith at the branch bank. To help him make his first stand, he tucked four $500 bills in an envelope before he left to meet the banker.

At the meeting, he passed over the envelope, saying that he wanted to open an account and start doing business with Smith's organization. He explained that although he couldn't immediately open an account on behalf of Fresh Foods, he had been thinking about going into the second mortgage business for some time now, and if Smith could finance these loans for him, it was just possible that he might turn into a million-dollar account for the bank within a relatively short time.

Smith was impressed with Scolnick's casual manner in turning over the $2000 to him. It was obvious that his new depositor was used to large sums of money and regarded this initial deposit as only a gesture. Calculating rapidly, he came to the conclusion that if he could nail down the business that Scolnick offered, he might even be able to accomplish a very rare feat for a new branch bank; to turn in a profit in its first year of operation. But, there was a large stumbling block in his way. One, he was delighted to find, that Mr. Scolnick had anticipated.

"Now, I know that national banks aren't allowed to lend on second mortgage paper," said Scolnick, "but I think I know how we might get past that little technical problem." He went on to explain that there wasn't anything to keep Mr. Smith from financing his mortgage company so long as it had sufficient collateral to cover the loans. What he was willing to do was to put all of his second mortgage loans into one portfolio and the bank could simply increase the amount of the financing for Scolnick's company each time a new mortgage loan was added to the portfolio. Of course, Scolnick assured him, the bank could charge its largest legitimate interest rate in advance, each time.

Smith was so excited by this solution that he chose to ignore its obvious violation of the spirit if not the fact of a federal law. The large profit potential was enough to make him willing to accept the proposal at this first meeting.

But the Fat Man was thinking ahead. Instead of jumping into the deal, he said, "Let's try on a small scale for a while to see how it goes. In that way, we both have minimum exposure." He was sure that this kind of approach would result in Smith making a maximum service effort in order to secure the balance of the proposed account.

"And that's the way it went down," Scolnick recalls. "I looked around and met a guy who was really in the second mortgage business, and I started putting his paper through my bank. Everybody was happy, only, after a little while, this guy with the company got annoyed because everybody in his outfit was looking to me for decisions, rather than him. You know, they was acting like I was the boss instead of him.

"So after a while, he decided to sell out to me. I bought his company, which was J. J. Patterson, for twenty or twenty-five grand, and I opened an office at Fourth and Cooper streets in Camden, New Jersey. Then I started doing business with the bank on my own and, within two or three months, we were into them for a couple of hundred thousand.

"At first, we got our second mortgages by advertising in the paper—you know the ads, 'If You Need Money We'll Consolidate Your Debts'; that kind of thing. Then I went around to all the other mortgage companies and if they couldn't get their paper through their own banks, I'd buy the piece from them for fifty or one hundred dollars and I got so much of that kind of paper that I stopped advertising.

"The bank was making money and we were making a fortune. The profit margin in this kind of paper is fantastic. You get a forty-five percent hit every time you lend out $3000. I'd break up the hit into settlement costs, filing charges, brokerage fees, preparation and recording of instruments, appraisals, and all that phony-baloney stuff, so what you get is $4350 and that's what the people was paying interest on. Then, instead of them paying six percent simple interest, they get charged six percent add-on, although I was only paying the bank six percent simple. This is very complicated to the average man. He's got no idea at all about what's involved in his interest payments. And that's what makes the banks the biggest thieves going.

"For example. They tell a man they're charging him nine percent interest. But, instead of giving him nine percent interest, they charge him nine percent discounted. All this means is that they deduct his interest off the top before they give him the money for the loan. The man borrows one thousand dollars for a year, but they only give him nine hundred and ten dollars. But since he's paying interest on the full one thousand dollars, he's really paying interest on money he never received.

"Then they'll make a loan at an add-on rate. They say they're charging you six percent interest over a five-year period for a five-thousand-dollar loan, but it doesn't come out to six percent, it comes out to eleven point nine or twelve percent because on the last year you're still paying interest on the full five thousand dollars, even though you only have a thousand left on the loan. In other words, they don't amortize the interest. You're paying on the full amount instead of just the unpaid balance. Man, they can talk all they want about me, but banks are still the biggest crooks in the world!

"So, when I brought the papers into the bank, the bank would credit my account with $4350 on the $3000 loan, plus half of the interest they were charging the guy, which came to

96

around six hundred. I made almost two thousand dollars on every deal I took. Beside that, I made the people take out a life insurance policy for the amount of the loan and they paid the premiums to me. I used to place these policies with any of the big insurance companies and after I turned in the first month's premium, they'd annualize it, which means they'd give me back the whole amount of the first year's premium. On that part of it, I was earning over a hundred percent.

"And beside that, I took three payments in front off the people—to be applied at any later date, in case they fell behind.

"The bank knew what I was doing and they didn't object when I recorded all these mortgages in the name of my company. They were satisfied with just my company's promissory note instead of actually having any collateral."

He laughed in derision and added, "They were satisfied because they were making money every step of the way. They knew I was jamming deadbeats and tombstones in, but they didn't care because of that figure on their monthly profit sheet. As long as I kept the payments reasonably current on every account, they just looked the other way.

"And, to keep myself in the background, I added a couple of stroke companies between me and the bank. So nobody could ever blame my company, J. J. Patterson, if the thing should blow up because, by the time it got to me, I was just what the law calls an innocent holder in due course.

"Here's how the stroke companies worked. The first company I set up was a broker company. The second was a placement company, and the last one was the holder. But actually, I owned all three of them, so I was able to put on the books charges for a brokerage fee, charges for the placement costs and then I was the holder in due course—the third party that nobody could ever sue. I know this sounds as crooked as all hell, but it happens all the time with some of the most reputable real

97

estate outfits you ever heard of. They clip the guy every way they can who comes in for his mortgage, and it don't have to be a second, either.

"Anyway, after a while we were doing so great that Mr. Smith got scared. By that time, they had loaned me $450,000 on my tombstones and deadbeats and, since *Philadelphia Magazine* had just come out telling those things about me in their story, 'Bankruptcy for Fun and Profit,' I figured the smart thing was to go in and grab the bull by the horns. A lot of times it's smart to make the first move.

"I go in to see Mr. Smith at the bank and I'm looking very worried and unhappy. He asked me what the trouble was and I told him that this unfair story had just come out about me and that, yes, I had been involved in a bankruptcy, but that wasn't my fault, I had just been trying to help out my father-in-law.

"I said, 'Naturally this kind of thing would worry you and your superiors, so I thought that what I ought to do is give you some better collateral. Now, Mr. Smith, I've been involved in some other business deals which have made me a lot of money, which I got in cash because I don't want to show it on my income tax. But if it would make you feel better, I'd be glad to put a half million in cash in one of your safe deposit boxes and we'll let that stand as collateral.'

"This really took a load off him. He don't lose five seconds in agreeing this would be a very fine way to relieve everybody's mind. So, what I did was go out and buy ten thousand dollars in brand new hundred-dollar bills and five thousand dollars in brand new ones.

"Then, I got a load of wrappers from a Philadelphia bank, the kind they use to put around ten-thousand-dollar stacks. Me and Murray then sit down and we make up stacks with a brand new hundred-dollar bill in front and a brand new hundred in back and a load of brand new ones in between. We made up fifty stacks like this and they were all supposed to be ten-thousand-dollar packages. Then we went back to the bank.

"This fella Smith was a sort of a Caspar Milquetoast type; quiet, reserved, very dignified, a real nice guy. The kind of guy that believes everybody in the world is wonderful. He believes in Cinderella, the Good Fairy, Porky Pig and all that.

"So I put the suitcase on his desk and open it, but when he sees all them stacks, he gets scared and slams it shut. 'It's all right,' I said. 'I'm going to leave you this half-million dollars. We'll put it in a box and the first time I go back to the box, you can stop payment on our paper. And this money will guarantee you that if any of our paper goes bad, we'll buy it back.'

"So he says, 'Gee, I can't ask for anything more than this,' and we go into the board room and he gets signature cards and we sign for the box. He goes out and comes back in with a box that was so big it looked like a coffin. But while he was out, I told Big Murray to make sure that he leaves the door to the board room open so people can see in.

"Anyway, he comes back and we start loading our bundles out of the suitcase and into the box and, just as we're getting into high gear, I raised my head and looked over at the open door. Smith follows my look and says, just as I had expected, 'I'll go out and stand on the other side of the door, to make sure nobody comes in,' which he does. And we then go into reverse and start putting the bundles back in the suitcase.

"The reason I figured he would go out is because I didn't think he'd want any of his bank employees to see him standing there while all this money was floating around. They might have gotten some funny ideas about where he stood. And even if he hadn't gone out, all I would have been out after the thing blows was the fifteen grand I had in the phony bundles.

"But he does go out, and then me and Murray, leaving our suitcase there on the table of the board room, walk out with the box, carrying it like it was heavy with the half million. Actually, at that point, there was nothing in it at all. We slide it in the vault and lock it up and I go over and offer him the key, but he wouldn't take it. He said, 'No, Mr. Scolnick, that's not necessary. It's good enough just the way we agreed on it.'

"So, I told him that it really was a pleasure to do business with him and turned as if I was getting ready to go. He says, 'Don't forget your suitcase,' and I thanked him for reminding me and then me and Murray left.

"After that, we really started cruising. I started jamming in paper like it was a snowstorm. In no time at all, I was up to a million two hundred thousand."

Scolnick often makes the statement that his criminal career was devoted to "boffing out the big guys, I would never look to hurt no little man," but his second mortgage company's cold exploitation of hapless homeowners scrambling to get a few thousand dollars to keep the roof from being taken from over their heads weakens this pious claim.

If he hadn't admittedly used "heavy collectors," the kind of men who come banging on the doors of delinquent debtors in the middle of the night, it would be easier to accept him in the role of the freebooter. The man who searches out the weaknesses in our system and uses them for his own advantage does not remain an interesting folklore figure past the point where we begin to recognize his victims.

But, as always, he has an explanation; "I had to do a certain amount of hounding to keep the bank happy. If there wasn't a few calls complaining about the tactics we used, then no banker on earth could shut his eyes to the fact we were running a scam. And you got to remember that these were people that couldn't get a loan if their life depended upon it.

"When they came to us, they were already hocked up to

100

their ears. No equity left in their houses and they'd already been to ten other loan companies who had turned them down. By the time they came to us, they were through dealing.

"But I didn't care. It wasn't my money, it was the bank's. And none of them ever paid their loan, anyway. Most of the times I ended up making their payments for them, so my account would be current up until the time I knew I had to blow.

"At least, with me, they walked out with the three thousand dollars to keep 'em going a little longer. We even used to show 'em how to fill out the credit application. We'd ask, 'Just give one credit reference where you been paying reasonably on time. Who do you pay good, we don't want to know who you pay bad.' Then my guys would fill out the rest and, as a result, nine out of ten of my loans would be acceptable to the bank.

"The banks want their paperwork to look like it's in good order. Suppose you got a loan on your signature of maybe ten or fifteen thousand dollars, and then you can't pay. Well, all you got to do is make the banker look good for his home office. If you pay him two hundred dollars a month on it, or almost any kind of payment at all, they'll let you alone. Just don't let your loan get on the delinquent sheet because once a branch manager's delinquent list goes over, say three percent, he's in trouble with his home office. You're all right so long as you keep that manager out of trouble, but once somebody starts burning his butt, he's got to start burning yours.

"So that's the way we was running the company, and the money was just pouring in. We had everybody on salary, every hanger-on that ever came around. Friday morning was the day we give out pay and expense checks and sometimes it seemed that we had more expenses than General Motors. Little Murray was in trouble, so I give him a car. Louie was in trouble, I give him a car. Curley was in trouble, so I put him on the payroll. It got ridiculous. Louie beefed about the car I got him, so I took it back and got him a bigger one. They all knew me and how soft I was better then I knew myself. Of couse, they all blew as soon as the trouble came, so I guess it's true; the slave knows the master, but the master don't know the slave.

"Worst of all was Sam Koff, who I took into this business as a partner. He was like a bull in a china shop, just like he was in the food company. You see, I wanted him to take some of this money and we'd use it to open other buisnesses while I still had the connection with the bank. These would have all been separate, legitimate businesses, and by the time the thing folded, they would have had strong financial histories of their own.

"But Koff gets scared. He sees so much coming in that he's afraid to leave the mortgage office in order to go out and do what I tell him. He doesn't understand the first thing about the mortgage business . . . but he wanted to stay there and watch. One time, the janitor who cleans up the office tells me that Mr. Koff is there every Saturday morning, going through the books. That bum, he couldn't even keep his checkbook and he's going through my books!

"Anyway, the whole thing goes about ten months later when somebody tells the FBI or the banking commission, some outfit like that, that it was me that was behind J. J. Patterson Company. A federal guy comes to the bank in November with a suitcase in which there's the biggest padlock and chain you ever saw. He was going to close down the bank.

It would have been the first time in twenty years that a national bank got closed down, but the guys on the board of directors did a lot of talking and they got twenty-four hours to take all the loans off the books and replace them with cash.

"Now, what do you think the bank does? The cutie pies that are on this board are also on the board of another bank in a nearby town. So they form another corporation and they pull out all my second mortgages and they use them as collateral for

102

a loan from this other bank. Then they take the cash and put it back into the first bank. All they did is to switch banks!

"This gives them a little breathing time, so now they start to study the mortgages that I had in there as collateral. Naturally, all they can find is promissory notes on which they got to sue in order to get a judgment. There's nobody they can sell out for nonpayment.

"So, the next thing, I get a call from this nice old man who is the president of the bank and who I'll call Henry Bunbury because that's close enough, and he's still around being nice all over North Jersey.

"Bunbury asks me to come to a meeting at the second bank, not the one I had done business with. When I showed up, I see all these big-name community leaders sitting around the table. They tell me they want me to assign these mortgage loans over to them and then go out and collect them on behalf of the bank.

"I tell them, 'I'd be willing to do it, but I don't see how I can do all this work without a fee.'

"He almost falls out of his chair. 'A fee?' he says, 'Are you telling me you want us to pay you to sign these things over?'

"I said, 'Well, I have a lot of time and money invested,' and he almost screams, 'Money? You didn't ever put anything in! You started with a five-hundred-dollar loan and you took out over a million and a half dollars!'

"Well, I explained that as far as I was concerned, everything was in order. Every note was signed and verified and all of them were recorded against the people's homes. The only thing, I reminded them, the bank don't hold the recordings, I do.

"He choked up at that and he looked around the table at his friends, only there was nobody there with any ideas, and he finally asked me what kind of a deal could we make.

"I told him, 'I'll tell ya what I'll do. You give me a letter, signed by your president of the bank I was dealing with, which says that you relieve me of all responsibilities and that you've checked out all of these accounts and they're legitimate and I'll sign you a blank assignment of all the mortgages.

"They did it, and I was out clear. They had to do it. It was only a question of time before the bank examiners would have caught up with the second bank where they had put up the phony collateral in order to get the cash out for the bank I was doing business with. I won't say they were as crooked as me, but I will say that I came away from the meeting pretty sure this wasn't the first time they had done some dancing in order to take care of themselves. And even if it wasn't, they sure showed what their potential was.

"Then, naturally, they fired Mr. Smith. Up until the thing blew, they had been patting him on the back and telling him what a genius he was by turning in such profits in his first year, but every one of those guys had been around long enough to know that something had to be going on. They didn't want to see it until they had to."

The participation of Anthony Smith in this scheme results in an almost classic "How to do it" study of the seduction of a financial officer.

He had just been promoted to branch manager when he met Scolnick. Understandably anxious for success, he heard only what he wanted to hear. It didn't matter that this customer was an odd six hundred-pound behemoth, nor did the stories about the man's background worry him, so long as his superiors kept complimenting him on the health of his monthly profit-and-loss sheet. And, besides, didn't he have a half million dollars of the man's money safely tucked away in his own vaults?

It didn't take Scolnick too long to introduce a personal note into their business relationship. One of the base rules for

104

a con man about to make a move is that he must become a familiar sight at the bank. As quickly as possible, he gets on a first-name basis with the key personnel and, thereafter, without apparently going out of his way, engages them in informal conversations whenever possible. Familiarity, in the banking world, almost always breeds trust.

Within five weeks of their initial meeting, Smith, during one of their chats, mentioned that he was leaving the following weekend for a banking convention in Atlantic City.

"So I get a hold of a real sharp hooker and I tell her, 'You're going to meet a man for lunch. He's a very, very quiet man and I want you to be easy with him, although I want you to give him a lot of attention. Take care of him, but don't do it like a hooker. He's got to think you're straight, you understand, that you're doing it just for him.'

"So I take her down to Atlantic City and I take a suite at the hotel where they're having the convention and I send word down to him that I'm having a luncheon party and I want him to join us.

"When he comes up, he says, 'Gee, I'm surprised to see you. What are you doing here?' And I told him that since I had to be here on other business, I thought it would be nice to have a lunch together.

"The girl had given me a funny look when she saw him come walking in with his drab suit and topcoat and his little hat and spectacles, but I let her know with my eyes that she'd better attend to business.

"He sits down for lunch with me and a couple of guys I know and I make sure the girl is sitting next to him. While the lunch goes on, she puts her hand on his knee and is acting like she is really hot to learn all there is to know about banking and before I know it, the two of them are in the next bedroom.

"She told me later that this must have been the first time

105

he was ever with a strange girl because he kept chasing her, wouldn't leave her alone. She says that she never seen anything like it, that he was like a bunny rabbit. It seems like he was knocking her off every two minutes. Really wild.

"Next Monday when I come into the bank, I walk over to his desk and he looks over his glasses at me and makes a tsk-tsk and says, 'Mr. Scolnick, you really are something else,' and what it meant was that we had done something together.

"Then I sent some luggage over to his house which he thanked me for, and then, from then on, whenever he had bad loans, no matter where they come from, I'd pay them off because I wanted him to keep on having a good record with his bosses. I took many a bad loan off his books and swallowed them.

"Finally, he took money. One day we bring in a bunch of credit apps and, when he looked inside the portfolio, he saw a couple of hundred-dollar bills. He slams it shut real quick and says, 'Oh, no.' But I said to Billy Somerville who was with me, 'Come on, Billy, let's go,' and we walked out of the bank leaving him sitting there with the money.

"Now, if he was legitimate he would have credited that money to our account. But he didn't. He stuck it in his pocket and then he was done. It's the same with all these guys who take because they work in a bank. They want it better than you want to give it to them."

Scolnick's answer to the question of how to spot a man who will "take" was, "Well, first you got to talk to him. You can't just look at a guy and know how susceptible he is to you. You got to know how badly he wants business. But you just don't come in and offer a guy a hundred bucks. That's too brutal. You wait a couple of weeks and then, say it's Thanksgiving. You ask him how many kids he has and is he going to have a Thanksgiving dinner. Then you go out and buy a big turkey and send it to his house.

106

"The first thing he does is accepts the turkey and says all that crap like, 'Gee, thanks. You didn't have to do it,' and then you know you got something going. A week or so later, he gets a half dozen bottles of whiskey, the kind he can't afford because he only makes ten or fifteen grand a year. When he goes on vacation, you make sure a set of luggage goes to his house. And once he starts taking, you know you can move him any way you want."

When Scolnick was told that the regional vice-president of one of the largest banks in America had said that his organization guarded against this kind of corruption by creating an exceptionally strong screening apparatus headed by one of the highest paid personnel managers in the country, his reaction was:

"That's a large load of crap. He takes a donkey out of college that has a couple of years of training and he pays him eight grand to start off. What kind of money is that for a guy who okays a loan of three to five grand an individual? You got to give such a guy fifteen or twenty grand and then he don't have to worry about his wife spending an extra ten dollars for a dress. When you hold a man close to you with no money, he can't help himself. He's got to become a turkey.

"These big banks claim that they delegate responsibility to lower echelon officers, but they really never do. They always keep the lower guys tied to them with an umbilical cord, so they never really know what's going on because all the guy lower down on the ladder wants to do is to keep his record clean.

"In any bank, the manager knows what's going on in the desks around him, but he don't know what's going on behind the tellers' cages. The head teller is the boss in any bank. Whatever she says—and it's usually a she—is what happens. She'll do anything for you if she likes you . . . cash any kind of checks, anything, just as long as she doesn't figure you're throwing a gun on her.

107

"A woman will be as quick to take as a man, but she takes in smaller quantities. You don't do anything big because you'll scare her half to death. You give her a box of candy to start with, maybe because she made up a payroll for you. Then the small things she likes; perfume, hosiery, and things like that.

"Pretty soon she'll ask you, whatever kind of business you're in, to do something for her. Like if you're in appliances, she'll ask if she can get a break on a new iron. So you pick her up an iron. She wants to know how much it is, but you say not to worry about it, just sort of wave it off. After that, you can bring in corporation checks and cash them without proper endorsement, do anything you want and she'll go along. She's on your team and you're on hers.

"I met very few men in my life who wouldn't take. Sooner or later everybody tells you their price. I rarely been in a financing deal that I didn't find crooks with straight collars. It's tough to say, but it's true. Once you find how to reach them— what their dream is—the rest is easy. I'm not happy about saying this. I'm not happy about saying that everybody has the capacity of being a thief.

"Now that I'm straight myself, I think it's sad that the banks take a guy with the ability to manage a national bank and pay him just enough to get by on.

"A guy like me comes along and talks to him and starts telling him what he wants to hear because he's unhappy at home. He's wearing an old suit, driving an old car, and here he is, executive vice-president of a bank or maybe even five branch banks.

"A guy like me gets his ear and starts telling him how much more he should be making and that he ought to leave the bank and come work for me, only he won't. He's afraid because he's had his job for fifteen or sixteen years and the people in the community respect him. He's afraid, but still he listens when

I tell him that he's worth more and, the first thing you know, you're close to him and he's bending the rules. And when you start bending the rules, it's only a question of time before you start breaking them.

"It was just the same in prison. In the beginning, the guards are taught that they can't believe a prisoner, that anything they say is a lie. And that's the way they function. But, after you're with a guard for a while, you talk and eat and drink with him, you help him with one of his jobs . . . then you can start telling him how big a man he is. You tell him what he wants to hear, and that's building on his weaknesses. I never known anybody to go rob somebody and trade on their strong points. I wouldn't go to open an armored car with a can opener, I'd use a bomb.

"You can use this technique anytime and anywhere. I used to send Big Murray out to spot turkeys for me. One time he turns up a loan company in Washington and, before they could turn around, we jammed enough phony paper through to take down close to fifty thousand dollars. And this was just a loan company.

"All I did was put the manager on our payroll. He was only earning a hundred fifty dollars a week, and we used to tell him that he ought to be getting twice as much. You know, the old routine: 'A guy like you, responsible for okaying so many thousands of dollars, it's just criminal the way they underpay you,' and so we got under his wing.

"Next we got him over to our office and we opened a bottle and started sitting around drinking and we got this turkey drunk. First thing you know, he's shooting his mouth off about what a bum his boss was, that he was the only guy in the outfit that knew anything about the finance business. He don't know we got a tape recorder going. When he sobered up, he was ours and we boffed him out with all kinds of paper for about six

109

months and he was happy being on our payroll every step of the way.

Are banks really the easy targets that Scolnick says they are? Some answers came from two bankers who asked not to be identified because they thought their organizations might worry about their inclusion in a story about a bank thief. However, each is an executive vice-president with over twenty years' experience. "Walter" is an executive vice-president of one of the largest banking institutions in the world, who presently supervises the operations of approximately fifty branch banks. The other man, "Bob," is a vice-president in the home office of a strong, middle-sized bank with thirty-two branches.

Bob began by discussing Scolnick's success in stealing $100,000 from the sealed safe deposit box:

"I suppose the plan could work in certain types of banks and I don't even know if we would be immune, but our people are under absolute instructions never to leave the keys on their desk or anywhere where they would be easily available to others. Another problem is that there are as many as five guard [the bank's master] keys and the robber might have to fiddle around for quite a while before he found the right guard key to go with the depositor's key. It's a tough one to engineer, but I don't say that it's impossible.

"I seriously doubt that you could go through many robberies like this before you were caught. In my opinion, Scolnick was lucky to have gotten such efficient execution of the PSFS job. This kind of an operation would have tough going in our banks; although, of course, I'm sure not all banks have our type of controls."

In commenting upon the inference that banks contribute to the vulnerability of their key employees by underpaying them, Walter said, "It's a stereotyped concept, and it may have

110

been true in the past, but I don't think it's true today. There is too much competition for good managerial talent. But anyone can be vulnerable, not because they are underpaid, but because of their own weaknesses. If someone has a way of getting to them, these people will succumb.

"But by the time we promote people into the area where they have lending authority or managerial responsibility, we've been observing their conduct and performance for a long time. But, of course, even then some of them go sour.

"Much of it depends on the ability of the sharp operator to evaluate his target. If he is really good, he can conceivably build up a story or approach that's plausible enough to get to an individual who has weaknesses that he has been able to hide from us. At that point, in spite of the size of our organization, we become quite vulnerable.

"We try to guard against this by having credit review teams that review all of the loans made by our branch managers. Twice a year, all loans are reviewed by the national bank examiners and, of course, we set lending limits for all managers. When a loan is made under a certain dollar amount, they are supposed to report it to us. If it is over a certain amount, they have to ask for our approval. But, I've got to admit, if a sharp operator has done enough homework, there are ways he can get to us.

"We try to screen and watch over our people but some of them do go sour. That can't be denied. But, hell, even in spite of all the screening that the Justice Department does for President Nixon, they still discovered that he had some illegal immigrants working as housekeepers at his California White House!"

Bob interposed: "Before you get off this subject of underpaying managers and loan officers, it just isn't totally accurate. I'm not disagreeing with you, but you must admit that some

111

banks pay well and some don't. And there's a big gap in the salary scales between a manager and the man and the woman who sits at a desk and does the paperwork. Those kind of people aren't apt to get the kind of salaries that make them invulnerable. Banks pay at the top for control purposes, but they don't pay it down at the bottom where the actual work is done."

"That might be so, Bob, in your type of bank," Walter said, "but how do we know how much money makes a man vulnerable? Unfortunate incidents, maybe an expensive illness occurs, and a man gets in a bind. Sure, if a man can manage his money at all, he can live very comfortably on what we pay him. But what is good managing? How can we tell if a man has too many kids or not?

"No matter how closely we try to screen our people, it's damned hard to be aware of all their weaknesses. I've been in the bank for a long time and every time I see a man go sour, I wonder whether it's booze, girl chasing, gambling, or what. And then I always realize how little I really knew about that man. We try . . . but we've got over twenty-five thousand people working for us. Did you ever stop to think how little you really know about your own son or daughter or your close friends?"

Bob ended the discussion by saying, "I'm not sure that it's always financial pressures that cause a man to go bad. Sometimes it's just as simple as slipping into the error of forgetting who you are.

"You take a man who is in a key position with a major bank. He's in intimate daily contact with customers who can make as much in a month as he makes in a year. He becomes friendly with these people, because it's part of his job to get to know them. It's awfully easy for him to make the mistake of trying to parallel his living style with the customers he serves.

"They go on cruises or to Las Vegas. Sometimes he goes with them and, at first, it's just to keep the friendship going. But if he gets to liking that life-style too much, or if any of his customers (and he knows he's as smart as they are) suggests that he go into one of their deals, it's awfully easy to get into trouble."

Walter, obviously thinking back over a lifetime of financial transactions, agreed, "Yeah, it's awfully easy for a banker to get in trouble."

When this conversation was replayed for the Fat Man, he shrugged wearily. His attitude was that of a man bone tired of explaining elementary matters. "It could be so simple for them," he said. "All they have to do is hire the right kinds of guys for the key spots.

"If it was me hiring a guy to be the manager, I'd look for a man that had business experience, not banking experience. He needs to know business so that he can understand that when a man comes in you don't just look at his financial statement and lend him ten percent of what it reads. You got to have sense enough to know what his business is all about.

"The banks never hire managers from the outside, they always promote from inside. They hire a kid out of school and maybe they put him on the phone for the collection department or some other kind of paperwork. Then, after a couple of years, they make him an assistant cashier or an assistant treasurer. He gets to know the inside of the bank and what the operations are. But he never gets involved with the one thing he's supposed to be involved with. He don't know how to make three dollars on his own.

"They teach the kids how to operate a bank, but that's all they teach them. They don't teach them how furniture is sold, or how furniture stores purchase and discount. They don't teach them about the construction business and the cost of materials and what union problems are. They don't have any involvement in those things.

113

"If a man has a hundred grand in the bank, he don't really need the bank to loan him three more. But a man whose business is getting larger, and maybe he's overextended himself because of things like too much inventory or too many sales before he can properly handle the volume, then the man at the bank ought to have the ability to distinguish between the problems that can be overcome and the ones that can't.

"Now, the average banker doesn't have that ability and, as a result, he generally denies the loan. But what's he done? He's pushed the businessman into a consumer discount company at a much higher rate of interest. And, since they're generally financing the discount company, they end up actually making the loan anyway. Only they've caused the businessman a lot of grief in the process and saddled him with a backbreaker of a debt that can send him under when he might have had the chance to survive.

"The banks don't want the kind of men who know how to handle these situations. That isn't as important to them as a donkey who'll follow orders and who they can pressure. Take Anthony Smith. They put him in a new branch and, right away, they keep asking him how come he don't get more deposits, how come he's not getting out more loans, how come this guy or that guy is late with his payments. They're passing out pressure that they couldn't take themselves. That's a lot of crap about being financially vulnerable. It's the pressure that causes more men to crack than anything else.

"When Anthony Smith first came to my place, I see a man with a coat that's maybe ten years old, a beat-up felt hat, and an old briefcase that's got scuff marks all over it. From his first words and the way he gives money so quick to Big Murray how can I help but understand that I got a turkey?

"Then I get to talking to him and I can see that leaving the desk and his paperwork and going out to hustle up business is really contrary to his nature. When they pushed Anthony Smith out into the field, they were really pushing him into my arms.

"And I'll tell you something. After I got into him for a while and learned what was really going down in the banking business, I actually changed my mind about blowing the whole thing out. I saw where if I owned the bank, I wouldn't have to do things crooked. I could of made all the money legitimately that I'd ever want.

"So I started buying up stock in that bank. One man was willing to sell me four hundred shares at twenty-one and I only needed eight hundred shares to be the largest single stockholder. Once I was in that position, I could have gotten enough proxies from all the smaller shareholders to have control.

"So I bought the four hundred and was buying up whatever else I could, and that wasn't hard because nobody owned a really large block of the stock. I got up to six hundred and then the blowup came and I was done dealing.

"But, if I had gotten it, I would have made Anthony Smith the president and I would have been watching everything he did. He'd of been my inside man because he knew how to run the administration . . . but, I would of been the one bringing in and passing on business. My God, there's so much business waiting to be developed by a banker who knows about something besides paperwork!

"What strength I would have had. I could have made a legitimate fortune. Do you realize the strength you got when you control a bank? Just putting your money out honestly, in the proper places, and there's no way in the world you ever have to be tempted to do crooked things!"

His firm commitment to middle-class morality standards seeps through and colors almost every conversation with Sylvan Scolnick. When he talks about being tempted to do crooked

115

things or describes himself (as he frequently does) as a thief, it is easy to see that his pride in his accomplishments never quite outweighs his realization that the nature of his career has closed out his chances of being respected by the people he'd like to be like.

He says quite often, "I've broken man's laws, but I never broke God's," meaning that he never held a gun on anyone while lifting their wallet. And yet, it is ironic that so little space separates many of his earlier capers from respectability. With just a slight correction in direction, he could have had the same amount of success without the need to breach any of "man's laws."

A random sampling of any batch of current newspapers confirms that there is no scarcity of "respectable" businessmen and community leaders who break the spirit of the law as willingly as Scolnick did. We rarely hear of them until the law claims they broke the letter, too, and proceeds to indict them.

We read of the Penn Central Railroad mess and we find the strong inference that some highly placed community pillars made a lot of money by ruining that once-great corporation. One of the principals, a retired air force general, is alleged to have supplied girls for those who could help him loot one of the railroad's subsidiaries.

On December 9, 1971, the Los Angeles *Times* carried a story which led off: "The Wall Street firm of Dun & Bradstreet was criticized in a Congressional hearing, Wednesday, for accrediting a charitable organization which investigators claimed bilked businesses and individuals of millions of dollars." The organization referred to was the Baptist Foundation of America, Inc. After admitting that his company did not audit financial statements submitted for listing in its reports, Paul Foss of D & B, explained, "We believe, basically, that people are honest," and it was obvious that he believed this was enough to excuse his company for issuing a report that helped cause hundreds of people to lose their savings.

Will R. Wilson, an assistant attorney general of the United States, was permitted to resign under fire after it became known that he was involved in a Texas banking scandal. After he had left his job as chief of the Justice Department's criminal division, he issued a statement claiming that the charges were only a political conspiracy and that "the only way to clear the decks and try to stop these political attacks seemed to be for me to resign." But he also admitted that he had borrowed over $300,000 from a fellow Texan whose real estate empire had just collapsed. This man was later quoted as testifying before a federal grand jury that Wilson advised him how to get around the state banking laws to make quick profits.

Sylvan Scolnick reads the newspapers, too. He says, "Maybe if I had stole differently, I could have been as legitimate as those guys."

# Chapter 7
# HOW TO STEAL
# A MILLION A MONTH

*The other interesting aspect of Sylvan's personality is that, on the one hand, he has a very high moral code which is somewhat egocentrically oriented, and on the other hand, this moral code is walled off when he becomes involved in business dealings of a dyssocial nature.*

—From the psychiatric evaluation
summary prepared for the Philadelphia
County Court of Common Pleas,
April 11, 1969.

The eminently profitable seduction of Anthony Smith left the Fat Man and his gang with the belief that, unlike most people, they had no need to go through life worrying whether a bank would extend or shut off their credit. It was all right if the rest of the world thought that a diet of unpaid bills could cause a banker to swell up into an ogre; to the gang, financial officers were only a flock of turkeys gobbling away until the time they were picked and plucked.

118

"When Sylvan explained it to me," said Billy Somerville, "I finally understood why you never need a gun to take money away from a bank. And he did it in the most convincing way possible; by letting me try for myself.

"One day, right after the second mortgage company blew, he said to me, 'I been thinking things through, Billy, and I'm at the point where I see that the way to steal is never to move out of the normal way of doing things. In other words, most people have set procedures and it doesn't matter if it's an insurance company or a bank or the district attorney's office. It's got to be easy to steal from them because they all have set patterns . . . and if you inject yourself into that pattern, then you've got them working for you.'

"I told him that made sense, but what did that have to do with me. He said, 'Because you're going to prove it. I've been reading this book on banking and in it they deal with money orders, and if you want a different way to take down some real easy stings, I'll show you how.' "

Naturally, Billy was interested and, even more, it sounded to him like the Fat Man was about to outline an extremely interesting adventure. Billy has a boyish appearance and manner. He likes to laugh, enjoys the sensation of running a risk, and his pleasure in stealing was always heightened when a novel approach was the base for the plan.

"I could tell, the way he was coming to it," said Billy, "that this was going to be something else. And, like all his bright ideas, it turned out to be so easy, it was great! First, he says to me, 'There must be five thousand stores and places in Philadelphia where you can buy money orders. You know, people buy them who don't have checking accounts to send in for their gas bill payments and things like that. Well, I want you to go out and go to all the stores you see that have signs outside saying that they sell them. I want you to go in and say exactly

119

this: "How much is a thirty-dollar money order?" The guy will say, "Fifteen cents," and then you say, "Okay, give me one." He'll give you a thirty-dollar money order and you hand him fifteen cents.'

"Well, I started out next morning, and I went into five places and said exactly what Sylvan told me to. And, I scored three out of five times. Just gave them the fifteen cents but never turned over the thirty dollars. Honest to God! I'd of scored in the fourth place if I had wanted to stand, but I just couldn't. The guy there asked me, as I was walking out, 'Oh, excuse me sir, I'm not sure. Did you give me the thirty dollars?' I just couldn't have kept walking with a straight face, so I told him that I thought I did but I wasn't sure, and after he looked to check the register, I gave him thirty dollars. But it works. It absolutely works. For quite a while after that whenever I was a little short on pocket money, I'd just stop and do a few pieces. There's absolutely no risk in it. If they call you, you just pay, and you're only out fifteen cents and there's no rap. But anybody doing it will hit three out of five, with no trouble."

Scolnick explains why the scheme works: "It's because the guy behind the counter is only interested in the fifteen cents. His prime concern is getting money for the service he performed.

"It's the same with a teller in a bank who handles hundreds of thousands of dollars every day, only it isn't their money. Now, why is it they can tell in a matter of seconds if they are ten cents short on their own paycheck, but you can easy slip a phony thousand-dollar deposit past them? The answer is: because the paycheck is theirs and they look it over very carefully. But a depository receipt isn't theirs, so they don't study it with the same concentration. It's only human nature. When I deal for somebody else, I don't do it as carefully as when I'm dealing for myself. But, when people check their own money . . . that's *their* money and they make sure that everything checks out solid.

120

"As a matter of fact, that was one of the main problems with Billy Somerville. He always had a lot of money that wasn't his. He's a high roller. If he's got fifty grand in his pocket, and he's in Las Vegas, he'll bet it all on one pass if they'll let him, rather than stay there all night.

"Money always came too easy to him. It had no value. His problem is the same as the teller at the bank; it isn't her money, and it isn't his money. At least, that's the way he used to be. Now that he's going straight and gets a paycheck every week, so he even buys bonds because it's money he's earned, that's his, and he wants to hold on to it."

Somerville was his chief henchman during the period in his life when he was actively raiding the banks. One of their prime moves involved fraudulent deposits which were the extensions of the pattern that had been so successfully demonstrated in the money order swindle.

The method of operation here is quite simple. The con man opens a bank account, keeps it active until it looks absolutely legitimate, and then buries a phony check among a group of honest ones in a deposit. Before the phony check is returned, he takes most of the money out of the account and disappears.

"It sounds easy, but it made a lot of money for us," he says. "I used to have guys operating all over the country. They'd collect checks, see. You have somebody operating in Alabama, and while they're working, they're also picking up blank checks for somebody else to use in Illinois. By swinging them that way, you get as much as eight days before a check is supposed to clear.

"But, in order to really pull this, or any other scam, properly, you've got to know what you're doing. Before me and Billy went into it big, we ran down everything on banks we could get hold of. We read books, we studied banks, their method of business, how they operate, where a check goes, and how it is moved around. How they borrow money from the Federal

121

Reserve, what interest they pay, and how much they keep on deposit. We knew how much of a percentage of their money has to go for municipal and federal bonds and things like that. We got to know the whole workings, from the time when someone goes in to make a deposit, until the time a check is issued."

Billy chimed in, "One important thing we learned was that a check can get lost for an extra three or four days if you switch the code numbers. That gives you all the time you need to score and get out of town. Best of all, real early in the game, one of the biggest banks in California helped me out. They didn't know it, but they really gave me a good grounding in how checks clear.

"What happened was that I was out there and I went to this bank and spoke to one of the lady tellers . . . you know, I came on like a nice young guy just getting started in, oh hell, I forgot what business I said I was in, but I told her I was going to open an account there, but that I had a big problem in that most of my checks came from out of town and I never could tell how soon it was before they cleared and I could draw on them.

"She was very obliging. She got out her *Manual of Operations* and showed me the page where it had all the code numbers of the banks all over the country, and how many working days it took for the checks of each of them to clear.

"I could see she liked my front, so I asked her if I could have a copy of that page, because then it would be easy for me to figure out how soon I could draw against a check I had deposited; but she said she couldn't because it was confidential. I told her it wasn't confidential information as far as I was concerned because I really needed that information for my business and, after we chatted back and forth for a while, she let me make a Xerox copy of the page.

"Now I had her. I know that if I deposit a phony ten-thousand dollar check coming in from North Carolina, it takes eight working days for that check to come back to the bank marked bad. But if a check comes in from some other bank nearby, it only takes twenty-four hours for it to be returned.

"So what I did is when I made up a deposit slip which would include the phony ten grand, I don't enter the North Carolina code number on the deposit slip. I use the code number of a local bank. Then, I go up and sweet-talk the girl teller to draw her attention away from the deposit I was making. All you got to do is get past the teller, because after she takes in the check and the deposit slip, she puts the check in one pile and the deposit slip for bookkeeping in another pile. Bookkeeping gets my record and the check goes to the clearing house. As far as bookkeeping is concerned, all they got is a deposit stub which says I put in a ten-thousand dollar check from a local bank.

"Now, twenty-four hours later I walk in and I say I need an eight-thousand dollar payroll. Remember, the banks are used to guys trying to move them for fifty dollars, but all I have to do is come in in a working suit and an honest face and nobody believes a guy like that is going to move them for a big score. So, anyway, I put the payroll check in and bookkeeping clears it because the deposit from the local bank more than covers it, and next day they give me the cash. Seven days later, the check comes back marked bad, but by then I'm gone.

"I never cleaned out all the money in my account. I always left them a few bucks so they didn't get suspicious right away. But I never go back because I know now there's a flag on my account."

"Excuse me, Billy," the Fat Man broke in, "but you didn't make it clear that just because the manual says it takes eight days to clear, that doesn't mean that it actually must be back in eight days. A check can get held up for a lot of reasons. All it means is that if, within eight days it hasn't come back, or if

123

they haven't been notified that it's bad, then it's automatically taken that the check is good. But they really are paying out against uncollected funds. So, as long as the check is lost somewhere, or goes to the wrong place, you have an extra two or three days to take down your money. Their weak spot is that banks keep a record of bad checks, not good ones. And there's so many more good than bad, they figure they're working on a safe percentage."

"It works," said Billy, "but there's an awful lot of places we can't go back to."

"Well, what the hell," a massive shrug, "it's part of your overhead. I still got dough laying in banks all over the country. You see, you always got to leave some money in the account so they figure they'll wait for you to come back. Here's how it goes; you first open an account with five hundred or a thousand dollars of your own money. Then, when you deposit a phony seven- or eight-thousand dollar check, you only draw out fifty-five or sixty-five hundred dollars. You always leave in a couple of grand, because then it takes them longer to get suspicious. If I could remember the names of the accounts we opened all over the country, and if I was still in the business, I'd figure out how to get that money that's still laying there. But, I think I got what they call a memory block against remembering those names.

"But, when you get right down to it, it's not a question of forgetting it. It's like a business, you know, you win some and lose some and at the end of the year you count up the split. To be honest with you, a lot of the money is hot, anyway. It came from some previous score, so it really wasn't part of your working capital. It's hard for anybody to understand except, I guess, somebody like Billy."

Billy said, "The main thing in these kinds of jobs is your face. After they've been hit, the banks and the police only have two ways of going after you. One is the *modus operandi,* that's the MO, you know; your way of pulling the job. Well, if you're unknown and they don't know your MO, they have to play hell to try and catch you. It's not a fingerprint game or anything like that. You don't leave too many telltales around. The only things they can do, after a move is to find out what this guy looked like or was there any kind of a pattern to what he did.

"So, if you're making a move against a bank and you got money invested in it [the amount of initial legitimate deposits in the account], and if the deal don't come off as planned because there is some excess heat, then you just forget about your investment. Why take a chance on going back and getting yourself caught? Once you're caught, they know your face and you are out of business completely. You're better off going for another one, starting out fresh again and make up for the one you just lost. It's just dumb to get so hungry for that money that you lose sight of the fact that there's a flag on the account."

There is no question about the efficiency of this scheme. As a matter of fact, on one occasion, it was only the failure of a henchman to follow his orders exactly that prevented Scolnick from swinging $500,000 in one bank transaction.

The henchman, George Gazzara, known to the gang as The Suit because he was always impeccably dressed, was a tall and dignified man in his middle fifties. Supposedly a builder, he opened a legitimate account in a small bank and began using it to draw cashier's checks and certified checks which, under Scolnick's instructions, he deposited to another account he had opened in a much larger bank.

After a period of a few weeks of doing business, he became known to the teller at the larger bank. On one occasion, he brought her a box of candy which she accepted with pleasure. At that point, he had a check certified for $50 and brought it to Scolnick who used it as the basis for a forged certified check for $500,000.

Gazzara then took the bad check to the friendly teller at

125

the large bank. She looked at it and said, "This is really a big one, Mr. Gazzara."

He agreed that it was, and told her that he had just gotten a mortgage on two buildings. She congratulated him as she stamped his duplicate deposit slip, saying, "It's really wonderful the way the building business is booming these days." She failed to notice that no check number had been entered on the slip against the amount of the deposit so, as far as the bookkeeping department was concerned, the item was handled as a cash transaction. Scolnick waited until late that afternoon and then called the bank. He said, "This is Mr. Gazzara. I'd like to know my balance." After identifying himself to the bookkeeper, he was told that it was $512,678.35.

"Am I able to draw on it?"

"Oh, yes, sir, That's cash."

Then came the test. Scolnick sent Gazzara to a large leather goods store, where the man ordered several pieces of luggage worth a little more than three hundred dollars. When a check was presented in payment, the clerk called the bank to verify that it was good. Of course it was.

Gazzara came back beaming. "It's set, boss."

"Okay. You can keep the bags. Now what I want you to do is to go to Caldwell's Jewelry Store. I been there and they got a diamond necklace that costs $350,000. You admire it a lot, and then say you are going to buy it. Leave the place and go to the bank and buy a cashier's check for $350,000, which they'll charge against your account. Now, do what I say because I already got that necklace sold in New York."

But evidently the closeness of the kill had overexcited Gazzara. Instead of buying a cashier's check when he went back to the bank, he wrote out a company check for $450,000 and presented it for cash payment. Scolnick could have told him that such a bank only kept about $100,000 on hand, but he didn't know this. He put up an argument when a vice-president told him that the money would not be available until it came in from the Federal Reserve on the following morning. He even refused a cashier's check made out to "cash" for the amount, saying that he was in the middle of negotiations for a large parcel of land where it would not be advisable to have on record the true price he was about to pay. When the banker looked impressed, he stepped up his insistence that he needed cash to complete the deal that night. Unfortunately for the gang, the teller who had accepted the deposit overheard the argument. When she discovered the nature of the discussion, she told the vice-president that she remembered that the deposit had been made by certified check rather than cash.

The banker said, "Oh, I'm sorry, Mr. Gazzara, but this makes it entirely different. Even though it was certified we'll have to wait until the deposit clears."

Gazzara realized that the game was up. He told the banker that he would return on the following day for the money and left to join Scolnick who was waiting for him in the bank's parking lot.

"I wanted to hit him right on the head," recalls Scolnick. "Just by trying to be smarter than anybody else, he blew $140,000 which was what I had the necklace sold for. It was a foolproof scam. All you got to do is alter the code number for the bank that's on the check. Since it takes a few weeks for all the checks to come back from the clearing house, we were in clover. We would have had that time because the check would have been lost for a while when it was sent back to the wrong bank."

In order to test the accuracy of this assertion, the matter was put before another banker who said, "It's possible that it could have worked. In our own bank, we treat some certified checks as cash and give immediate credit. In others, we don't

It all depends upon the customer and the circumstances. Tellers are supposed to have certain limits in this situation and, when a deposit goes over their limit, they are supposed to refer it to an officer. But I guess you can be set up for anything. If you consider a depositor as a big customer, and you've gotten to know him, you are generally willing to go along with him. Here I'd say that this gang did a pretty good job of setting up the deal. If someone is willing to take the time to set you up properly, there's always the possibility that they're going to get you. The problem is that you get so used to the operators who are trying for a few hundred dollars, that you forget to suspect someone who's out for a really big haul."

There is abundant proof that although Sylvan Scolnick has retired from the arena, the scheme is still producing a profit for certain operators. For example, on December 17, 1971, United Press International sent out a story which, when carried at all, was buried in the back pages of the newspapers. The article described an operation in Cornelia, Georgia, where someone took a bank in that small city for over a million dollars, using check blanks that had been stolen from a construction firm in Framingham, Massachusetts. The operator, described as ". . . speaking absolutely perfect English and a highly educated person," opened his account with three checks totalling $190,-000. He continued to make deposits which, like the first one, turned out to be phony. Before the fraud was discovered, he had taken out most of the money in cash and disappeared. The entire operation took exactly twenty-four days.

While Scolnick was in prison, Somerville executed a caper of his own, which paralleled that Georgia robbery. However, his story is more informative because he described it one day in Scolnick's presence (this was after Scolnick had been released on probation and the statute of limitations had run out on the crime), and the Fat Man professionally analyzed each step.

128

Billy said, "I got a real interesting story, if we're talking about using stolen blank checks. First of all, you got to know that a professional burglar is sure of exactly what he's doing. He'll hit ten or fifteen houses sometimes in one day, and he only takes whatever is cashable, like money and good jewelry. The professionals don't mess around with things like TV sets. He just wants what he can unload quick.

"So, I make a deal with a burglar to make a move on a Lincoln-Mercury auto dealership that had been fingered for us. I want him to take a checkbook, a cancelled check and to find out what their bank balance was.

"Now, me and this burglar goes up to the place one night to make our move. Although he knew his business, I went along because, as Sylvan will tell you, I'm a little nuts. The guy lets me go with him, because I tell him I haven't been a burglar since I was a kid, and I thought I'd like to get some kicks.

"He was a good pro. He busted in through the back of the place, got through the alarm, and it was just beautiful the way he sized the place up. I wanted to sneak into the office from the garage part where we were standing, but he said, 'No, you see that showroom out there? It only takes a second for someone going by outside to look in and see our shadows moving across that showroom. We are going to go around the back and break through the wall.' That's what we did. We went around the back and, instead of having to break through, we see a boarded up door and he says, 'Beautiful,' and he got his jimmy out and he bopped the door and we got through.

"Once inside, we ransacked the place, tore it up, to make it look like it was kids in the neighborhood that had done it. We took a few bucks they had out of the petty cash box and scattered the books and records all over so it wouldn't be any question that it was amateurs that had been there.

"Then I took a canceled check and also took the checkbook. After I read the balance, I took a check from the middle of the book and then threw the book on the pile of other records we had pulled out.

"After we finished, we go. I'm walking along, happy because we had pulled it off, but Mitch is creeping. He lifts his head up once to look at me and says, 'Goddamn you, get down. You don't live here!' and he was right. I was walking out like I owned the place.

"I filled out the blank check we stole for sixty-three hundred dollars signed it with the signature I copied off the canceled check and then, the next morning as soon as the bank opened, I had Mitch there to get it cashed. After he made the move, he came out and got in my car and we took off.

"Later, we heard what happened at the car dealer's place when they came in next morning and saw the mess. We heard it from the salesman who had fingered the job for us. When the cops came in, with them was one old detective who was just beautiful. This old cop walks to the middle of the showroom floor and just stands there, studying the place. He saw how we got in and realized we could have run right across the floor to the office, but instead we broke in through the boarded-up door, and he knew that whoever did it were pros. The other cop tried to give him an argument, saying we had broken open the cigarette machine and grabbed the petty cash box and that was nothing for a pro to do.

"But the old guy didn't pay any attention. He said to the manager, 'Where is your checkbook?' and they pick it up off the pile and hand it to him. He says, 'Are there any checks missing?' and the guy looks at the back of the book and says, 'No.' 'Go through the book,' says the old guy, and the manager did, and when he gets to the middle, he yells out, 'Hey! There's a check that's been torn out of here.'

"The old guy says, 'Call your bank right away. Find out

if anybody's been in this morning to cash one of your checks.'

"Well, he did and the bank says yes, there was a man that was here who did that, but he left about two minutes ago. Two minutes! That's how close we come, because of a cop that knows his business."

Scolnick had been listening to the recital in a totally non-committal manner, but after Somerville had finished, he shrugged and said with contempt, "Amateur night."

"Why? Where do you get that?" Somerville wanted to know.

"For three reasons. Number one, Mitch was a pro and he should have expected that the cop would be a pro. You should have taken the risk of going through the showroom rather than through the back wall. That's the kind of a move that any smart cop will pick up.

"The second is that you should have taken a page with three checks on it, rather than just one check. That way you could have gone to three different branches of the same bank on the same day and took down three stings instead of the one that you got by going to the main office.

"And finally, the whole thing was really amateurish because if you were only going to take one check, you shouldn't have taken it out where it would be noticed. You should have taken the very next one to the last they had legitimately drawn. Then you should have filled out the stub so that it would be a month before anybody found out it wasn't a legitimate transaction because nobody would have known it was missing until the day the bank calls and tells them they're way overdrawn.

"You see? If you don't plan your attack properly, you leave your flanks open. Billy, you come within an ace of gettng caught because everything was open. You even made a mistake in moving the check. You don't try and make a burglar into a check man. You pay a guy a couple of hundred bucks for the job, and then you move the check yourself. An inexperienced guy can make a lot of mistakes standing there in front of the teller's cage."

Billy grinned sheepishly. "Well, Sylvan, you were away and I had to make some kind of a move. Now that I think of it, the dumbest thing was me going along in the first place."

"Well, sure. I mean, it wouldn't have been dumb if you were getting set to clean out the whole account, because then you had to go along to verify the guy's bank balance. But you went at it like a shortstop. You was only looking to take down sixty-three hundred, and you don't have to go in yourself to be sure that a big auto agency carries that much in its checking account. You made a lot of mistakes."

On another occasion, Billy described his feelings while a "sting" was going on, and this provides another insight into the makeup of the nonviolent professional thief.

"I love it," he said with a laugh. "I get the sweats and I get scared, but that's what turns me on. You know that you're in there talking to a banker and you're getting ten, fifteen or twenty grand, whatever it is, and you gotta look calm even though you're sweating. It's really exciting and pretty soon you find yourself able to keep your cool, no matter how tight the situation gets.

"Like one time, this is an unsolved case but it don't matter because it's outside the statute [of limitations]. This colored guy and me made a move on a bank. We made the deposit with the phony out-of-town check with the local number on it, and my guy goes in on the final day to make his pickup. Now, this is a colored guy making his move, right?

"So he goes inside and I'm waiting outside for him. I couldn't go in because I was on the 'hot list' at the time. Sylvan had been arrested and they knew I was associated with him, only they weren't sure just how. Anyway, I'm waiting outside and it's taking too long and I can't stand it, because I like the excitement of being inside.

"All of a sudden, six cop cars pull up. All kinds of uniforms start going into that bank and I say to myself, 'Oh, boy. Oh, boy. He's in trouble.' But then I think, 'They don't send no six cars full of cops just for this kind of a deal . . . he must have shot somebody!' And I figured I'd go into that bank and cash a twenty dollar bill and see what was going on. I had to know and I couldn't leave him.

"Being a pro, I knew the move was to drive away, because if he was caught, he's caught. And if he wasn't caught, he could find his way home by himself. But, I go into the bank and I see him in the corner and I see the cops all standing in line to cash their checks because it was their payday. So we finish our business and we both go home.

"Now comes the funny part. Tom Keefer, the cop who almost nailed us on the Lincoln-Mercury thing, is called on this deal. From the MO he suspects it was me, and they bring me in for questioning. I said to him, 'Tom, what is it with you guys? You know Sylvan is away and I'm doing my best to stay straight. Leave me alone, I didn't have nothing to do with it.'

"He says, 'It's your MO, and the colored guy. . . .' and I butt in, 'Colored guy? What do you think, I got a good makeup man?'

"He says, 'Now you listen to me. I'm going to get this guy. And when I get him I'm going to give him a license to walk out free if he will just give you up. And when I get you, I'm going to bury you.'

"So I walk out thinking, 'Man, what am I going to do about this colored guy? He's not going to stand up once they put the pressure on him.' And I waited about three days and then I called his house. A lady gets on the phone and she's crying. The guy had gone to the hospital with food poisoning and he had just died.

"Next week, I saw Tom Keefer again. I said, 'Did you find your guy yet? I hope you do, so I can be cleared on this deal.' He says, 'No, but don't worry. We'll dig him up,' and I answered real seriously, 'That's what you're going to have to do.' "

After his release from prison, Scolnick once appeared on a Philadelphia radio talk show conducted by a conscientious interviewer named Frank Ford. In preparation for the Fat Man's appearance, Ford had amassed an impressive file of newspaper reports concerning bank robberies. Producing one of them, Ford said, "Sylvan, here's a story about a guy the New York police called Dashing Dan. He knocked off about twenty banks within a very short space of time. In each case, he just produced a note which said, 'Give me your money or I'll blow up the bank,' and in most cases he collected from the teller, said thank you, and left. By the time he was caught he had collected thirty-five thousand dollars, and it turned out that he had a steady full-time job and that there was no reason for the series of holdups. How do you explain such a guy?"

Scolnick didn't hesitate. "I'd say a man like this is just sick in the head. He wanted to be a clown and get into the newspapers. If I was in the business of sticking up banks, I'd have to get more than thirty-five thousand dollars on the first one or I wouldn't do the other nineteen. Too much risk. That guy just wanted to get caught.

"If you really want to stick up a bank properly, first of all, you got to have a crash car, that's in case a cop car comes along, and you legitimately run into it, only you're really holding them up. Then you have to have somebody watching the outside, and two men inside.

134

"And, you got to take at least fifty or sixty thousand dollars because there's a lot of expenses involved. The big man, the guy who plans it, the guy who takes the money right afterwards and goes a different way . . . all these guys have to be paid. So, a man who just comes in to lift a few bucks, he's just ridiculous. If I was really going to do it. . . ."

"Only you're not," Ford interrupted.

"You know it. No way. There's not enough money in any bank in the world to make me risk going back to prison. Only, if I *was* going to do it just once, I figured out an almost foolproof way while I was still in prison. What I would do is to take somebody who was retarded, or rumdum in some way that his word wouldn't stand up in court, and I'd shave him and get him dressed up real nice and I'd send him into a bank with a note which said to give him money or he'd blow the place up. If he got it, I'd be waiting outside and take the bag away as soon as he comes out and head in another direction. Now, he's sure to be picked up within a half a block, but what's he going to say? Who's going to put stock in a dummy's word if he says Frank Ford sent him?

"That's why you're strictly wrong when you go in with a gun. You don't have to. The man that carries a gun creates his own problems, because he's better off without it. In most cases, he don't even have the ability to use it, and by the time he gets it out—because he sure as hell can't go in with it drawn—he's already been shot three times and they still have the money. Nobody needs a gun to rob a bank!"

Of all the ways that Scolnick found to rob a bank, the one that provided the most satisfactory return for a minimum risk was in the area of borrowing money with no intention of returning it.

One of the key tools in this approach is the ubiquitous

135

"payment book" which so many banks, finance companies and stores furnish to their credit customers. This book is simply a small bound pad of slips on which the customer's account number, his payment date and the amount due are marked by perforations on each page. At one time the basement of Scolnick's home contained hundreds of cartons of these blank pads, a small printing press used to imprint the names of fictitious stores or banks on their covers, and a perforating machine to complete each page.

He explains how they are used: "First thing I do is to get them imprinted with different names, different banks, different finance companies, different furniture and appliance dealers, automobile dealers, and places like that.

"I make sure I got controlled telephone numbers listed under some of the names. Then we punch all the pages, tear out about half of them. So, now we go into the bank with a totally fictitious background. We got phony driver's licenses, owner's cards, and a phony rental agent at one of the phones.

"Now, I go into your bank. 'I need four thousand dollars.' 'What do you need it for?' 'I'm in business and I'm short. I want to buy a piece of equipment,' or something . . . any song and dance. 'Do you have credit elsewhere?' 'Yes.' 'Give me your credit sources and their phone numbers.'

"You give them all the information and they check it out. The phone numbers you give them you have previously taken out under the phony names. Here you got to be careful, because a smart banker will call Information and verify the number, but if you planned right, it's no problem.

"Now you're set. You're all checked out. You've shown him your driver's license, your payment books, he's called up and verified your employment, or that you rent such and such an apartment, and you walk out of there in twenty or thirty minutes with twenty-five hundred dollars.

"You can hit five or six banks a day like this, and nobody checks with anybody else. Banks don't work together and, as a matter of fact, there's a new federal law which says they can't tell anybody anything about you, except maybe that at the minute there's enough cash in your account to cover a check you just issued. But they don't give out credit information. They're afraid to. So, you can always give another bank as one of your credit references. They might say you got a loan outstanding, but they'll never tell another lending institution whether it's in good or bad shape.

"We used this approach to boff out so many banks and finance companies that I just lost count. At one time, I had ten guys going in for loans, working in teams, all over the country, and each one was good for twenty-five thousand dollars, or better almost every day. This was at two, three, four thousand dollars a sting. They'll give almost anybody that kind of money on their signature.

"This scam can be used to bang out anybody. When I was talking with the DA right after my trial, I told his assistant, Billy Wolfe, how this thing works and he just couldn't believe it. I said, 'If you'll let me, you just pick out any bank you want, and tell me how much you want out of it, and I'll get the money in four or five days. You know you'll give them back the money, but if you tell me it's okay to rob them, I'll do it for you, to show how simple it is to use the principles of this scam to take anything from them you want.' But after I laid out a couple of plans for him, he got scared and said that although it might be a very instructive thing to have in the file, he just didn't think the banks would like it. However, what he did do was to get a lot of the bankers together to hear my story on how easy they were, and, as a result of my talk to them, they changed quite a few of their ways of doing business.

"But you can hit anybody. Suppose I don't like IBM. I

137

don't have to go into their warehouses and steal typewriters and things like that. All I have to do is open an office, put in a couple of hundred bucks' work of furniture. Pay the month's rent and get a telephone and put up a little sign on the door.

"Then I contact IBM and while I'm at it, I also go for all the other big office equipment companies. They'll send in thirty, forty thousand dollars' worth of equipment in the next week.

"I make one phone call and I move it all out. I get twenty-five in cash for my forty grand worth of equipment. Then I close the office and move out. Who's gonna come looking for me? If they do, where they gonna find me?

"It's so simple. You can't beat a planned attack. Can I put up a defense if somebody is looking to kill me? Can they protect the President of the United States if somebody wants him bad enough to work out a good plan? How many men have been locked in a cell, twenty-four hours a day, to protect them and they still wind up dead? You can't beat a planned attack. It's an impossibility. And, here, we're not even talking about killing. We're just talking about hitting them for a few grand.

"I can tell you how easy it is to steal, maybe a million dollars in a month, if that's your plan. Hell, I could steal ten million in six months, and there's no way they could catch me.

"All I'd have to do is to go to a responsible, big stock-broker, maybe Merrill Lynch. I buy twenty thousand of AT and T stock, under whatever fictitious name I'm using, say 'Henry Jones.' Then I take the stock and print up exact copies of it by photo-offsetting it. Next, I open an insurance office or a real estate office under 'Henry Jones.' Maybe I even open up five or six offices all across the country. Finally, I take ten thousand dollars and put it in the bank.

"Now, I take my phony stock and go into a bank to borrow money on it. I'm pledging that stock as collateral and any bank in the country will give me at least sixty percent of its current value. First, they call Merrill Lynch and verify that I did buy the stock from them, then they check out my front and, after that, they give me the money. I leave them the phony stock and I even pay interest on my loan for two or three months. Then I sell the real stock and get my money back, clean out most of my account, and blow.

"If I repeat this deal with a team of men all over the country, do you know how much I can pick up? Hell, a million a month is being conservative! There's a lot of dummies that try this from the get-go, with totally counterfeit stock, but so far I haven't seen one of them go in with real stock in front. The way to do it is with the planned attack I just outlined. And, if you want to raise the ante to fifty or sixty thousand a shot after you're rolling, it's easy because now you got plenty of working capital. There's no limit on the number of banks you can hit, because you're working all across the country. It's just a matter of how many hours there is in a day. To hit a hundred banks you only need, at the most, twenty days. I've moved ten, twelve banks a day myself."

Again the attempt was made to discover whether banking institutions have defenses against the type of raid just detailed. The consensus was the same as before; a well-planned move is difficult, if not impossible, to stop. One individual, not a banker, but a federal criminologist, said, "It's bad enough under the present systems. But we're heading for a society where checks will be obsolete. I'm talking about the day when we have a central memory bank where whenever you make a purchase, it will be automatically recorded and deducted from your account. The banks are going to be almost totally computer operated. I shudder to think of that day because of the strong possibility that an operator like Scolnick is going to come along and figure out how to tap into the computers. He's going to try and loot the banks of every cent that's in them and the people who are developing this new financial technology damned well better be ready for him!"

139

# Chapter 8

# "HE'S JEKYLL AND HYDE"

REPORTER: *It was Billy Somerville who picked you up when they let you out of prison?*

SCOLNICK: *No. It was Big Murray.*

REPORTER: *As I understand it, it was quite an emotional scene.*

SCOLNICK: *Big Murray was crying.*

REPORTER: *Well, if he was crying so hard, why didn't he take care of your wife and mother while you were away?*

SCOLNICK: *'Cause a few tears is better than a few dollars.*

Your first reaction on meeting him will be to his enormous weight. He sits in an especially made easy chair and even though it is extra-large, he seems to be overflowing it in every direction. His bulk is so overpowering that literally minutes go by while you are accustoming yourself to it. Then you become aware that he is watching you.

He is deciding whether you are friendly, hostile or a turkey. The dark eyes, buried in the pale flesh of his face, never leave yours. After he has reached a decision, the eyes veil for a brief moment and then the relationship begins. If you are at

140

all sensitive, you realize that it is proceeding on his terms and this is so whether you come as friend or adversary. He is impressive emotionally as well as physically.

Suppose he likes you or, more usually, has decided to charm you. Then an alien thing occurs; after a half hour your consciousness of his weight disappears. This has become an attractive man talking to you, and the open warmth projecting from him has reached out and enveloped you.

Sometimes the speed of his thinking processes causes him to stammer or underline a verbal pause, but it is because his mind has raced extraordinarily far ahead of the sentence he is then enunciating. He is thinking of how he will take you and he is no longer concerned with the present communication.

If you interject or interpose before he has reached his point, he will pause, but you are aware that the words are still going on in his head. Later you learn that he has heard and absorbed every word you have said. You are also surprised to learn that he also understood what you really meant when you said them, and this is because he is always listening for your intent.

The stories bubble out of him. There seems to be an almost manic compulsion to tell you everything there is to him, not because you are a writer or reporter, but because you are an audience. He is assuring himself of his own existence. He is telling these stories about a man whose identity is uncertain.

If an associate has the floor, it is rare that he permits the other man to go beyond the first few minutes of the story. He takes over and finishes it because he wants every detail and every nuance to be there on the table before you.

Background conversations or a household exchange between his wife and mother will cause him to lose focus on the story that he is telling you and he flares up. He angrily demands

141

silence and he always gets it because he is always the center of a domestic or professional situation.

He speaks with an almost total disregard of grammatic rules. This is not due to ignorance because he almost completed high school and is a voracious reader. He speaks in the "dese, dose and dem" parlance because it was protective coloration in his circles and also because he is generally more anxious to communicate his thoughts than he is to communicate properly. He uses any malapropism or any argot that gets his message across. Sometimes he speaks in stilted cliches and sometimes he becomes so impatient with the inadequacies of words that he becomes temporarily incoherent.

He needs love, which is only a shorthand way of saying that he needs the reassurance of acceptance. His thrust is to shift his relationships onto emotional and social grounds and this is probably why you can depend upon him to keep his word or a promise to you. He is most comfortable when he has produced the situation where it is you and he against them. He wants and needs allies.

Some of the psychiatrists and psychologists who have examined him say, in effect, that his morals are totally compartmented. This is true. He is attracted by the sight of and the participation in strong familial and friendship ties, but this tender attitude is nowhere in evidence when he destroys the life of an Anthony Smith. Smith was a turkey. He was one of "them."

The psychiatrists also say that his huge bulk is due to an overpowering need of oral gratification. This seems only partially so. Other children leave environments where constant eating is equated with security and although they struggle with obesity for the rest of their lives, they do not become behemoths who strain to rise from chairs or who cannot walk without the aid of canes. He is monstrously fat only because of some genetic or glandular flaw. Sit beside him now for weeks at a time and you see him eat only a sandwich or some fruit during the day and a steak at night although he used to eat on the Diamond Jim Brady scale. But his weight never diminishes. The prison of flesh in which this wary operator resides never becomes less.

The words are his only form of release and as they cascade from him in zest and excitement and humor, the bulk gives way to his really extraordinary style. There is no trace of pettiness or petulance in him. There is no room in all that vast body for a personal concern with those who have tried to hurt or punish him. He takes their best shots and keeps on going, and whether you have nothing but contempt for his thieving activities or view him as an individualist who can beat the systems that manipulate the rest of us, you end with the admission that whatever he is, he is a major leaguer, too.

Although he will keep his word to his friends, he lies continually to himself, as well as to his targets. But his fantasies are those of a politician or a salesman. If he has first convinced himself, then a thick evangelical atmosphere comes into being as he tries to convince you.

You see the thin cold man inside of him when he protests too strongly about his love for his fellowman and his hatred of violence. You realize he loves his fellowman because acceptance is mobility for him and with violence comes the reminder that he is perpetually imprisoned. "Anybody wants me, they can come after me and get me with a pen knife," he says, and you understand that he feels a quick, frightened empathy for the object of anyone's violence.

Is he a total manipulator? Probably. But it is hard to say that there is nothing else in him. Too many people have held him in affection for too long a time to believe that he only calculates. He also gives. Spend any amount of unguarded time with him and you inevitably walk away with the feeling that he

143

can become a warm source of strength for you. It is hard to believe that can be counterfeit.

The naturalists ask: *Does a bird fly because it has wings or does it have wings because it flies?* and, unfortunately, some of that dilemma clouds every attempted description of Sylvan Scolnick. Was it his weight that caused him to become a resourceful and original criminal or did he become a criminal because of the excuse of his weight?

The answer must be subjective. The question about the birds can be resolved by an intensive study of living creatures adapting to their environment, but when you deal with the mind of a man like this, the variables that might have set him off onto one path or another are almost infinite.

So, you look at him pragmatically and you report: These are things he has done and said, these are the opinions of his associates and this is how he seems to me. Anything beyond that describes only the reporter's frame of reference.

His principal attorney during the days when he was swinging his hardest was a quiet, very sure-footed attorney named Irwin Paul. In commenting on Scolnick's intelligence, he said, "If you listen to Scolnick long enough, he will certainly charm and mesmerize you, but my profession is such that I must look a bit deeper and further into people. So, I'm not dazzled by Sylvan.

"I think he is intelligent. You never have to repeat the same statement twice to him because he understands exactly what you are saying the first time. He's very probing, so he analyzes every word. I think his IQ must be very high, but to me the mark of a man is the end result and not the beginning. I think Sylvan has had a lot of good beginnings and bad endings.

"He's fascinated by get-rich-quick schemes. He has a defi-

144

nite lack of patience and I think that is an off-setting factor to his tremendous mental capacity. He's good enough to sell a dead man an alarm clock, but his problem is that the guy won't buy a second clock from him.

"In other words, when people tell me that Sylvan is a genius but that he got mixed up with the wrong kind of people, I have to disagree with them. The way he ended up just doesn't spell genius to me."

Stanford Shmukler, the second attorney who played a large part in Scolnick's life, waged the long and eventually successful fight to get him out of prison. Shmukler says, "He's not easy to evaluate because he is a very complex individual. He has not learned from books, although he is very well-read. He considers himself a patron of the arts, but I don't think he is a cultured gentleman, even though he likes to think of himself in that way.

"Although he is tremendously acute, I don't believe he's the genius that the newspapers described. He has a passion for details and is a first-class organizer. For example, the PSFS [$100,000 bank robbery] was a masterpiece of detailed organization and it came damn close to becoming a perfect crime. Because he reads other people's minds and anticipates their actions even before they are aware of what they are going to do, he was able to foresee that there would be a time when the bank clerk would leave the safe deposit keys within reach. But this was the work of a good planner, not a brilliant mastermind."

These two opinions can be projected into what is probably a fair index to his mental capacities. The combination also fits the description of many classic con men, as well as quite a few respected and successful business leaders.

The common denominators that are always present in this kind of person are: mental agility, nerve and a talent for manipulating others, although this last factor is a quality that

145

is often denied. No one likes to be known as a manipulator. By admitting it, you somehow seem to lessen your accomplishments.

Logically, it would seem as if Scolnick would take pride in his ability to "move" people. He doesn't. He was once in a business deal with a syndicate of legitimate businessmen who had begun to suspect that he wasn't quite the reputable consultant that he had held himself out to be. When he became aware of their intent to push him off into a corner and run the business themselves, he approached one of the key men and, among the other things in their conversation, he said, "You know, I been watching you. You really pull an awful lot of stupid mistakes. If you was working for me, I wouldn't pay you thirty cents."

The man—who had made a sizable fortune representing the railroads—was indignant at the idea that this coarse-talking, grossly fat man would speak to him like that. He called a meeting with his associates and told them that Scolnick was a liability they could carry no further. The meeting ended with a joint agreement they would buy him out, which is exactly· what Scolnick had in mind when he disparaged the other man's abilities. He had banked on the other man's pride in his own accomplishments and knew that if he insulted him properly, vanity would blind him to good business judgment.

But later he flatly refused to accept that this episode represented his pleasure in manipulation. "Stone wrong," he said. "There's just more than one way to skin a cat, that's all. It's got nothing to do with manipulating people. I hate that more than anything else. You know, that's like telling me I like always to be on guard. If somebody would just stay by my side for a month and see the comers as they walk in, and everybody trying to rap you and cut you and this and that, and you fence and dance around and look to protect yourself and make the best deal, then you could see how I hate being on guard and always having to move people.

146

"Saying I enjoy it is like saying that I would just love to wear a suit of armor every night to bed, or that I'd like to walk around all day with a bulletproof vest on. I'd love to walk around with just a T-shirt, as long as I knew my back was covered and nobody is going to stab me with a knife.

"The only thing is, I understand people. I can read 'em so well. I can tell when a guy is leveling with me, and I can tell when he's full of shit. I can tell when a guy really wants to be with me and be my friend. I can feel it. I get what you call vibrations from it.

"As long as you don't forcibly take anything from another man, or as long as he's got the same opportunity to win as you, then it's a game. It's like chess, where they got a play called the Queen's Gambit, where you sacrifice the queen. The guy takes your queen and you move a knight in and you checkmate. You see, he's so anxious to grab hold of that queen that he don't see anything else. It's the most powerful piece on the board. He thinks he's getting something for nothing. So, what you've done is use his own greed against him. I don't call that manipulating. That's just letting a guy get so greedy that he gets stupid."

He was asked, "You keep saying that people are always taking a shot at you . . . ?"

"Right."

"But don't you find that even subconsciously you are always on guard against this?"

"No. Because if you guard against it, if you always have your defenses up, then people feel it right away. You can't always keep your defenses up. It's best just to be a counterpuncher."

"How many of your decisions in dealing with people are based on hunches or vibrations?"

He shook his head emphatically. "None. I don't go anything on hunch."

"You don't?"

"No."

"You make it your business to. . . ."

"Right. I make it my business to know. And only a sick person doesn't trust nobody."

"The trouble with Sylvan," said Big Murray Farber, "is that he trusts too many people. He's always too good-hearted to the kind of a guy that ends up taking him over. He fluffs off the people he should give to, but he gives and gives and gives to the jerks until they stick it into him. One time a cousin of his comes crying to him. It happened that he didn't have any money in his pocket, so he says to me, 'How much you carrying?' and I told him I had about a grand in my wallet. 'Give him seven and a half,' he says. 'He only needs it for a week or so.' I peeled it off for him and that was the last time I ever saw that seven-five-oh.

"He's supposed to be a smart guy, but they make a sucker out of him. He's plain and simple good-hearted. A guy screws up and then he comes to him with a sob story and, no matter how much Sylvan hollers at him, it don't mean shit. Five minutes later, it's all over and he's telling the guy, 'All right, pal. We'll take another chance with you.'

"He's done it time in and time out, and he'll continue doing it. Because that's his way. He's not going to change. A guy gives him a bunch of checks that come to four grand. All of them bounce. The guy gives him a hard-luck routine and he takes the pile of bad checks and tears them all up and says, 'You don't owe me nothing. Get the hell out.' "

His lawyer, Shmukler, in commenting on Big Murray's observations, said, "Murray is right. He always surrounds himself with people who will kowtow to him . . . and these are generally people who have sizable defects in their own characters. This kind of person will listen to him, obey him and, quite sincerely, make a a cult out of him.

"Big Murray, Billy Somerville . . . all those kinds of people find difficulty in making decisions for themselves. So they surrender their identities to him and they all live better, as a result. There is no way that a man like Big Murray could have enjoyed the life-style he had when Sylvan was moving in a big way. He got it by being a gopher for Sylvan, and this made him quite content.

"Most people think Sylvan is the complete realist. He's not. Actually, he is a fantasizer. He convinces himself that the people around him can do more than what they actually produce. And when they fail to carry out his plans properly, then he fails.

"If he had utilized people who were more efficient in carrying out his instructions, there is just no telling what he might have gotten away with. I don't know, though, maybe he subconsciously wanted to get caught, because that was the way to let everyone know about his exploits. Or maybe it is just because a con man always turns out to be the easiest mark of all. And, there's no question about it, Sylvan is a big mark.

"I can recognize it because I'm not a con man myself. So he can't con me. I've known him for six years, and I might be wrong in my opinion of his motivations and his life-style, but I'm sure I'm not wrong about the basic personal decisions I've made about him.

"I think he is an extremely humane person who has a deep concern for the welfare of others. Many times when I'd visit him in prison, he'd turn away the conversation from himself in order to try and get me to help a fellow prisoner for whom he felt sorry. I know that his wife and mother were having tough financial times during that period, but to my knowledge, on more than one occasion he got them to send money to someone he had heard was in bad shape.

"I'm not trying to be a psychiatrist, but I think he has a

great desire to be loved and that this is expressed by his generosity and in his conduct, where he always tries to throw the biggest party, to take down the biggest score, or to outthink everyone else. He equates admiration and respect with love. Maybe that's also one of the reasons he can always be depended upon to keep his word."

"And, you've got to keep your word to him," added Irwin Paul, "because when you don't, that's when Sylvan really gets upset. Suppose you say you are going to lend him a thousand dollars. He'll make a commitment based on that money and if you don't come up with it you're going to excite the hell out of him. You've got to remember that when he says, 'I'm going to do this because the other guy is going to do that,' what he is actually doing is fitting another jigsaw part into the broad picture he's got in his mind. He's always seeing things as part of a master plan. Sylvan is not interested, for example, in selling that lock on that cabinet over there in the corner of my office. He's interested in selling four million locks to the United States, and to the world after he gets through with the United States. He's already figured out how he's going to do it, so you'd better be damned sure to deliver that first lock to him.

"Sometimes his fantasies get him in trouble at the very beginning. He thinks, 'If I do this and this and this, then the whole thing just has to come about. It's just got to!' And it seems logical, while he's explaining it to you. But sometimes, after you analyze it, the follow-through on the other end just can't be depended upon. And then he's in trouble."

Quite a few of his associates and adversaries have said that Sylvan Scolnick finds it hard to draw the line between fact and fantasy, but this might be because so many of his actions can't be comfortably fitted into normal pigeonholes. His first impulse always seems to be to explore the situations that strike him as interesting, colorful, or just funny.

150

For example, once after being questioned by the district attorney's office, he completely blew the cool of the two detectives who were taking him back to prison. Hanna Zbik, a secretary in the DA's office, recalls, "He was walking down the corridors in City Hall between these two cops, when all of a sudden he began to sing 'The Prisoner's Lament' at the top of his lungs. You know, the song that starts, *Oh, if I had the wings of an angel.* Well, that's what he was singing, and at the same time he began to twirl his cane and strut like Charlie Chaplin. The detectives said it hit them so funny, they couldn't stand up."

On another occasion, he had just come out of the courtroom where he and a former associate named Al Carlucci had testified against each other on a bankruptcy fraud matter. Through poor planning, both defendants found themselves in the same City Hall elevator. The United States marshals escorting each of them were warily waiting for the hostility to break out between the two men, but Scolnick said very thoughtfully, "Hey, Al, when we get out of here, I got a hell of an idea where we can open another bankruptcy," and the tension turned into explosive laughter.

The accusation that he considered having his father-in-law killed to keep him from testifying in the M. Stein bankruptcy trial is probably pertinent here since it figured so prominently in the newspaper and magazine stories written about him. Most people repeated it as support for their own conviction that he has been an utterly unregenerate criminal.

One reporter who had heard the story tried to discuss it during a series of visits to Scolnick's home but the time and circumstances never seemed to be right for the logical introduction of the subject. Then, one morning while Scolnick and the reporter were having coffee, Mr. Stein who was in the kitchen, called out, "Sylvan, did you say you wanted some toast?"

151

Scolnick's face took on a thoroughly ominous expression. "I already told you twice, no toast. Do you want me to let a contract out on you?"

This domestic byplay convinced the reporter that there was no truth in the story and he came away thinking that sometimes the Fat Man's sense of drama and humor made it difficult for others to sift out the fact from the fantasy where he was concerned.

In discussing the difficulty of finding the proper yardsticks to judge him, his probation officer Eugene Kelly said, "He might have done very nicely in one of the islands of the South Pacific, where obesity is considered beautiful and his fatness would lead to his being considered as a very distinguished member of the community. In some of those places, he wouldn't be considered an anomaly; people would listen to him and respect him. He's out of his culture, here."

"If you ever found a Jekyll and Hyde, you've got one here," said Irwin Paul. "Sometimes he'd give you the shirt off his back, and other times you look at him and see nothing but cunning and conniving."

"He may be all of the things that people say about him," concluded one of the district attorneys who prosecuted him, "but no one can ever say he's a hypocrite. Harry Karafin was found guilty on forty or more criminal counts, but he went to jail still screaming he had been framed. Not Scolnick. He says, 'I did crooked things and I was punished.' I never saw him hide or lie to himself. During all the times we grilled and prosecuted him, there wasn't one occasion where he tried to win sympathy by justifying his actions."

"Why should I cop a plea?" Scolnick said. "I just know that you can't live your life based on somebody else's desires or requirements. You got to live your own life based on what you feel you got to have. You got to be able to bend when it's

152

necessary. If a tree can't bend with the wind, it gets torn out by the roots as soon as a hurricane comes along. But most people can't bend, so they keep getting moved by everybody. They just stand straight, not being able to bend in the wind and then end up like a guy in the middle of a hurricane and hollering for help. And who the hell is going to hear him?

"I'm not afraid to tell you who I am or what I am. I'm ashamed of some of the things I've done, and I can't say they're wrong when they say that Big Cherry was a thief. But I'll tell you something, Sylvan Scolnick wasn't always a thief. Sylvan Scolnick's been a hard worker all his life. I never thought anything of working eighteen, twenty hours a day.

"I don't figure I got to hide. I'm legitimate now, and when I talk to someone about getting involved in some kind of business with me, first off I tell 'em I did three years and eight months in a federal penitentiary. I tell 'em in front that I used to be a professional thief and I went to prison for it.

"But I also say, 'And I'll tell you one thing more. I was a successful thief. I never missed being a winner. I never had a loser in my life and that's what you're coming into. You know who you're doing business with now, and if you'll get off your ass and put in the hard work, we're gonna have a lot of good luck together.' I say it plain and simple. I don't look to hide who I am. Then if they want to go with me, it's with their eyes open.

"I learned a lot about life just from watching fleas. Sounds funny, but it's true. You know, if you take a flea and put it in a bottle and screw a cap on it, that flea will jump up and try to fly out of that bottle. Then, after a while of bouncing up and hitting his head on that lid, the flea from then on jumps just high enough so he don't hit his head.

"After a couple of hours, you take the lid off the bottle, but still the flea don't jump any higher than where he learned that he was going to hit his head, and he never realizes that there

153

isn't anything left to stop him from jumping out. That's pretty much what most people are up against. They've trained themselves to think they can only jump so far and no more.

"But I won't buy that for myself. I believe I can do anything I set myself out to do, I got that kind of confidence in myself. I don't limit myself to anything. I'm not going to be a flea in a jar.

"So what if I bounced my head a couple of times? Does that have to mean I can't ever go out farther? Like hell! Then I become a part of the pack like everybody else."

Sylvan Scolnick is a good and loyal friend, a cold and conniving thief, an explosive raconteur, and a quiet source of strength. He is forever radiating and asking back for love, but there are so many who say that he is violent, ruthless and contemptible. He is cynical and sentimental, bright, shrewd and sometimes surprisingly naive.

He is a good son and a loyal husband who has been a source of pain to his mother and an enigma to two wives. Monstrously fat, yet many men and women have found him attractive.

They used to say that Al Jolson hated his audiences because he was afraid of them, and when he went out on stage his assault on them was so total that their eventual cheering verdict was the result of a rape. There are also many who leave Sylvan Scolnick's company uneasily feeling that they, too, have succumbed.

# Chapter 9
# VARIOUS ROBBERIES

Q.  *To what extent was there planning for the actual execution of this robbery?*

A.  *How do you mean, to what extent?*

Q.  *How many hours did you spend and who participated in the planning?*

A.  *A great number of hours. For instance, the night before the actual attempt took place, we spent from eight o'clock P.M. to one o'clock A.M.; four to five hours.*

Q.  *Who set the master plan of the robbery, the ultimate plan?*

A.  *The ultimate plan, the finality and finishing touches, I would say, was set by Sylvan Scolnick.*

—From the testimony of
"Tommy Mitchell" at his
preliminary hearing,
October 3, 1966.

The popular but mistaken notion that a cashier's check or a certified check is as good as cash was the basis for the Fat Man's wildest project; he and his gang set out to loot a $28-million chain of department stores.

155

He had been sitting in an attorney's office one day when the subject of an apartment house sale came up. "The check they gave in payment," said the lawyer, "was a cashier's check for seventeen million dollars—biggest check I ever saw."

The Fat Man was impressed. "All that money in just one check? Do you really mean they put that kind of scratch in just one check?" Until that moment, he had always assumed that a purchase involving a sum that large was generally made by letter of credit or its equivalent.

"No," said the lawyer. "It's just the same as if you were buying a house. You sit down at the table and you sign the papers and you pass over a check. It's just like any other settlement."

The Fat Man recalls, "That really laid with me. I went home and I started to think, and I said to myself, 'Geez, it's true. Whenever you go to buy a business, if it's a bar or a construction company or anything, it's always the same; you give them the check and they give you the title and the keys to the place and the combination to the safe and everything else. And that's it!' And, also, I remembered that the settlements that I had seen always took place on a Thursday or Friday, I guess because that's when they closed the books for the week.

"My mind started wondering about making settlement on a big department store like Gimbels. I remembered reading one time about a guy who worked for one of those department stores had robbed it of a hundred thousand dollars in jewelry, but that he had missed the four or five hundred thousand in cash they also had on hand when it took place. It was money from the weekend's business.

"So everything started to mesh together in my mind and, after a week or so of planning, I got ahold of Tommy Mitchell, the guy that teamed with the other nut, Harry Cohen; only at that time I still didn't know how dumb Mitchell really was.

156

"I told him my plan and we set out to work. First, I told him he had to grow a beard because I didn't want any accidental recognizing of him while this thing was going on. Then I rented him a big apartment in some nice place over in Jersey and opened a bank account under a phony name I gave him to use. I also bought him a good, rich-looking wardrobe, including a black Homburg hat. I really dressed him up right. I even rented a limousine and a chauffeur for him.

"But I told him, 'Make no phone calls, at any time, from this apartment. You want to call me, you go out and use a pay phone. And don't touch nothing in the apartment with your bare hands. Always use gloves, even if you want a glass of water.'

"Then I pick the name of a very reputable lawyer out of the phone book and, when Tommy's beard has grown out, I send him over to this lawyer with the story that he represents a buying cartel which wants to buy some department stores, doing at least a couple of million dollars a year in jewelry, because they're looking to enlarge their operations.

"Tommy does it. He gives the lawyer a check for a thousand dollars as a retainer, which was good, and tells him he'll pay the balance of the fee as soon as it's all straightened out about how much work is involved. He also tells him he can't disclose the name of the people in his combine because if the word got out, the purchase price would shoot way up.

"This satisfies the lawyer. He calls Tommy a couple of times with details and this and that; and because he's already got his money in front, he's got no question that everything is legitimate.

"Finally, one of the business brokers that the lawyer has out looking for the right deal calls Tommy and says they located a chain of department stores up in Boston that's for sale. Tommy asks him if they have a big jewelry department and the lawyer says, 'Absolutely. They got one of the best in the country at their main store.' So, Tommy tells him he wants to make sure of bringing a strong, clean deal to his principals and that the lawyer should use the most accurate accountants he can find in order to go over their books. Tommy tells him it has to be a very tough audit because he wants the guys in the cartel to be totally satisfied.

"Now, all of this, between the time it takes Tommy to grow the beard and for the business brokers to bring us the right deal, is about two months; plus which I now got about seventy-five hundred invested. A lot of it was in furnishing the apartment because I didn't want Tommy to have an office; he had to look like he was from out of town somewhere. He had to say that for the moment he was looking in this area, but that he was willing to go anyplace for the right deal.

"You see, it had to be simple. Simplicity is what makes these things work. You have to operate within the framework of the law to break the law. If you work outside the framework, then you can't get away with it. If you do business their way, then you can bend the framework from inside. But it's gotta be simple and uncomplicated.

"Anyway, the deal is set. The guys who own the department store are so busy getting their books in order that they don't bother to check us any further than the respectable lawyer we got in front. Besides, all they want is a cashier's check at the settlement.

"So my next step is to go and print up some blank, legitimate looking cashier's checks on a big bank up in New York. I had about twenty or thirty of them made. I felt that the cashier's check would look stronger because, what the hell, to make a certified check all you got to do is to get a rubber stamp made up for ninety cents and that, when it comes to twenty-eight million dollars, which was the firm price they wanted for the department stores, wouldn't be as impressive.

158

"Everything was going along great. Tommy's lawyer and accountants was calling and writing their lawyers and accountants and they were calling and writing back, working out all the details and this and that. Most of the time, we kept them on the defense pretty good. Not that they had any real reason to check him. It was a cash deal, no credit involved. The most they would have done is check out the lawyer—and he didn't know who Tommy was, either.

"Now, the reason I hadn't wanted him to make phone calls from his apartment was because, after we took down the score and blew, I didn't want the phone company to be able to trace the people at the numbers he had called. Once they found that out, they'd be able to follow the lead right back to him and then to me. I think it's six months that the Bell Telephone maintains the records of the calls you have made.

"Then, one day, Big Murray comes in and tells me the deal's in trouble. I had sent him up to the apartment to just generally check out how things were going and he finds the phone banging away and the place is full of broads that Tommy is interviewing to hire as a private secretary. He's really carried away with the whole thing! He's using the apartment to bring up all his old girl friends, and he's making calls out to all over the place. I found out he had called his mother and his wife, he even had made two calls to me, which up 'til then, I thought had come from a pay phone.

"He wasn't supposed to have touched anything in the place, but Big Murray tells me they're all drinking and having a party and everything else. Him and every broad he ever knew had their fingerprints all over the place.

"So, right there, even though we were just about ready to make go with everything, I nixed the deal. Closed it down stone cold.

"So I lost the seventy-five hundred, but I figured that it was cheaper to wash that out than to pay twenty-five thousand to

159

his family while he was in jail, plus with the lawyers and everything else. Who the hell needs it? Plus the fact that I got a
dummy as a monkey on my back for the rest of my life.

"The deal would have been that we would make settlement
on a Friday. We turn over the check and they give us the keys,
the combination to the safes, whatever money was in their bank
accounts, and in the cash cages in the store. This is normal
business. They turn over their money to us, but we add that
amount to the check we pay over at settlement.

"Then, Friday night and that weekend, we would go in and
strip the place. Clean out all the diamonds, all the jewelry, and
all the cash. Then, Monday morning, we would clean out the
bank account. We would have had plenty of time, because it
took three banking days for that cashier's check to clear.

"It didn't even matter that the stores would be open Saturday. Everything that came in that day would go into our pockets. It don't make no difference to the clerks who work in the
place who the guy is who's sitting in the president's office, even
a dummy like Tommy Mitchell. Who's gonna question the guy
who owns the store how much he takes out of the cashier's
cages?

"Anyway, I blew the deal. When Tommy saw how serious
I took it, he made all kinds of excuses, telling me he didn't
realize and this and that and it wouldn't happen a second time.
I told him, 'Don't worry, there ain't gonna be a second time.'
And I never let him show up at the lawyer's again.

"So, to make expenses, we passed some of the cashier's
checks around; you know, cashed a couple of the pieces, and
we made some dough. I came out with a profit, but that was
only buttons when we were looking to clear at least a million
out of the job. So, Tommy didn't do me no favor by letting me
grab a few thousand. But more important was the time we
wasted. That cost me more than the few grand I took down. It

was at least a month in front and a month in back while we were setting the thing up. What with growing the beard and running down to him how to effect settlement; what to say and give him his cover story, it took a lot of time. We spent one week working late every night just training him how to act and what to look for at the settlement.

"People don't realize it, but to steal—it's a lot harder than being legitimate. A legitimate businessman, if he makes a mistake, so it costs him thirty bucks and he made a mistake. If he doesn't like somebody, he throws them the hell out of his place. And then he don't have to hear from him no more. But, when you're stealing and you make a mistake, you're talking about going away for ten or twenty years!

"That's a different kind of pressure. That's a pressure that's on you every hour and every single day until the deal is pulled off. That's why you feel like you had an orgasm whenever a deal is consummated. It's because the pressure, all the weight, is lifted off you for the moment. You're free-wheeling again.

"But people don't understand that. They think it's easy to steal; but it's ten times harder than being legitimate. Of course, I'm just talking about somebody who steals scientifically, rather than just somebody who goes in with a gun. That's no pressure at all; any dummy can go in and take a pistol in his hand and threaten somebody's life. But you just try and trick somebody out of their money . . . that's where there's pressure, because if you get caught you're going to do a lot of time because you're not talking about stealing five hundred dollars, you're talking about stealing large figures; and don't you think that a judge doesn't give you your time based on the amount that you steal.

"Anybody that says that it doesn't matter if a man steals a quart of milk or he steals twenty grand—he's still stealing and he gets the same punishment—stone don't know what he's

161

saying. A guy who steals milk they're sorry for because he's hungry. They don't want to know that the guy who stole the twenty done it because he was hungry, too. He was just a little hungrier. He just don't want to go back and steal milk three times. He only wants to go once.

"What made this thing so tough, was that we already had the buyers for the jewelry and other things we were going to strip out. There's never a problem for that, because we had already checked out the goods and talked it over with three buyers. I'd had them goods sold so fast it would have been like a sump pump sucking up water in a wet basement.

"Those guys don't have to actually see the stuff. You just tell them what type of action it is and they say, 'Okay, I'll buy.' In fact, sometimes, when you go into a deal where there's a lot of goods involved, and you tell them the type of score it is in order to get the right price with the guy, he'll give you a guarantee before you take the sting. In other words, if he locates for you . . . tells you that you can take a good score down at John Doake's place; so you say to him, 'How do you know?' and he says, 'Well, I seen it,' and you tell him, 'Well, you know, to set up a score like that, it takes time and an investment, and this and that; what will you do? Will you guarantee me?' So the guy says, 'Unquestionably. You got a hundred thousand for your end, no matter what it takes.'

"So you set up the deal, and if you come in with a lot more, you arrange a new price and he buys. But, if you only come up with—like seventy-five grand worth of goods, you still got a hundred for your end. That's the way you make those deals. If it hadn't of been for that jerk, Mitchell. . . ."

The arrest record for Tommy Mitchell began in 1959 when he was picked up for carrying a gun without a license. At that time, he was twenty-six and, over the next seven years, the record shows a continuing series of prosecutions for burglary,

162

larceny, aggravated assault and battery and other breaches of the peace. The long jail sentence he drew in 1966 probably reflected a comment on his career as well as punishment for an armed robbery during which he had viciously pistol-whipped the victim that he and Harry Cohen had selected as the night's target.

He looked respectable. Tall, slender, well dressed and well-spoken, he was operating a drugstore when he came to Scolnick in 1964, looking for $25,000 to finance a proposition that he was considering. He had almost convinced the Fat Man to back him, until he mentioned his attorney's name. During that period, Scolnick happened to be in another deal with the same lawyer and had come to the conclusion that the man was an out-and-out thief. "Right away," said Scolnick, "this guy is being too cute about playing dumb with me. A guy with a lawyer like that is looking to clip me for the twenty-five.

Mitchell didn't get the money, but he did get a job in the Fat Man's organization, where his respectable personal appearance could be used as an effcient front; and, by the time Scolnick found out that Mitchell's efficiency was totally illusory, he had decided that he liked the ex-druggist too much to get rid of him. He kept him around for laughs and, occasionally let him participate in a sting. He never knew about the man's capacity for criminal violence until long after the $100,000 PSFS bank robbery.

Mitchell and his sidekick Harry Cohen became the handymen for the gang. If a phony insurance company was being operated, the two sat in the office and talked to the occasional customers who wandered in. Mitchell fronted for quite a few deals where the advance man had nothing to do but look legitimate, and the two occasionally helped out as holdup artists when some of the boys temporarily left Scolnick to go out on their own.

Everyone agreed that there was a sizable bonus involved

163

in the employment of Mitchell and Cohen. They did funny things—sometimes by design, but most of the time because of their earnest stupidity.

Billy Somerville recalls the time that Cohen helped him buy a mink coat. "I was sitting in the office one night around seven, eight o'clock and there was a real blizzard going on outside. Little Harry was hanging around, keeping me company, and all of a sudden I said, 'Harry, what the hell. Let's go buy a mink coat.'

"Well, you know he was agreeable to whatever I wanted, so I looked through the phone book and picked out a furrier. Then I take a complete set of fake ID's out of the files and make them up for him to show he's a doctor. I also took some rubber pieces, fraudulent blank checks that Sylvan has laying around, and off we go.

"We hit the guy's store around nine o'clock. Remember, this is going in to buy a mink coat at closing time in the middle of a blizzard, which just goes to show that when you want to move people, what time it is makes no difference at all.

"The guy starts making general conversation with Harry. 'What do you do for a living?' and Harry, who can't remember what kind of a doctor he was supposed to be said he was a veterinarian. Well, the guy gets all enthused about talking animals with Harry, and Harry tells him he has just worked out a new idea; he's gonna create a Blue Cross and Blue Shield plan for animals, and that if it works out, he's also gonna throw in accidental life insurance in case your pet gets run over. Things like that. The crazier Harry talks, the more the other guy is impressed. Maybe, in his own way, he was as crazy as Harry.

"Finally, they get down to business. Harry picks out a coat, and, after I tip him the nod, he asks the guy what he wants for it. The guy says thirty-eight hundred. Harry starts to argue with him, saying that that was way out of line and he wouldn't go a cent over twenty-five hundred dollars.

164

"These two guys get to discussing it—back and forth—and I'm starting to feel edgy. Here it is, after closing time, the whole avenue is dark and in case there's any trouble, the snow is going to make it a hard getaway . . . and Harry keeps fighting with the guy. He finally gets him down to three thousand and then he says, 'The hell with it. You're trying to take me. I'm leaving'; and he says to me, 'Come on, let's go. This man doesn't want our business.' I was ready to choke him, right then and there.

"But the turkey don't let him go. 'Wait a minute,' he says. 'My father had that coat made up for my mother. Let me call him and see what he says. He's only down in Florida.'

"And that's what he did. Dials. Gets the old man on the phone, tells him he's got a live one. They talk a little bit and he hangs up. He turns to Harry and says, 'Okay, you win. My father says you can have it for twenty-five hundred dollars.'

Harry says, 'While you was on the phone, I been thinking. The best I got in my checking account is twenty-four hundred. You wanna make a cash deal at that price and I'll write out the check right now?'

"The guy agrees and Harry writes him out one of the pieces of rubber. He makes a little more talk, shows him his fake driver's license and the rest of the ID's, and the guy boxes up the coat for him.

"When we get outside and back in the car with the coat, I said to Harry, 'Harry, you son of a bitch, we could have had the deal made and closed an hour ago. Why didn't you buy it when it was three thousand?' and he answers, I swear to God, he answers real seriously, 'Well, he turned out to be such a nice guy, I didn't want to beat him for that much money!'"

If there ever was a born thief, it was Harry Cohen, whose record shows that he has been arrested for everything from armed robbery to impersonating an Internal Revenue agent. Another member of the gang once reported, "He used to get real kicks out of beating a dinner check. One time, we had just

165

come off a big score and we all had at least four or five grand in our pockets. So, to celebrate, we go to a restaurant and order a big dinner. When the tab comes, Harry says, 'I'll take care of it, you guys go on ahead.'

"As we're leaving, we hear him say, as he stops at the cashbox, 'Just a little bit too much . . . tell the chef just a little bit too much garlic,' and he walks out, stiffing the tab and joins us."

On one occasion when Cohen visited Scolnick's home in Cherry Hill, he noticed a Mexican sombrero and two silver-colored plastic six-shooters hanging on the wall behind the bar. He thought for a moment and then asked Scolnick, "Can I borrow these for a minute? I wanna try something and I'll be right back."

Scolnick, who was busy in conversation with another guest, agreed. Cohen strapped the guns around his waist, put on the sombrero and went out and got into his car.

He drove to a nearby Seven-Eleven grocery store. As he walked in, he said to the clerk, "All right, I want all the money in the register." The clerk stared at the weird looking little man and said, "Oh, get the hell out of here."

"In that case," said Cohen, "give me a pack of Marlboros." When he mentioned it to Billy Somerville later in the evening, he explained, "I just thought I'd take a shot at him. If the guy gives me his money, I made a robbery. If he doesn't, I needed cigarettes, anyway."

"He was funny," said Billy, "but never lose sight of the fact that he was also a very bad kind of a crazy. One time some guy told him about a move he was gonna make on a liquor store and Harry figured it sounded like a soft touch, so he went ahead and knocked over the place himself before the guy could get around to it. The guy was really steamed when he read about it in the papers because he knew from the description it had to be Harry.

"So he goes over to the motel where Harry lives and started banging on the door and hollering what he was going to do to him. Harry was in bed with his girl friend when all this noise started but, instead of getting up, he just reached under his pillow and got his gun and blew four shots through the door and then went back to his broad. Lucky the guy didn't wait after the first shot, he just made fast tracks the hell out of there and he never mentioned the subject to Harry again."

It was evident, from the relish with which Billy told these stories, that he considered Harry Cohen to be a far-out character. But it never seemed to occur to him that he, Billy, in his own way was just as colorful.

He grinned in tight spots and was at his best in situations where other crooks caved in. Scolnick's most bizarre plans were the ones that gave him his greatest enjoyment. For example, he laughed for almost a half hour after he learned about the Newark job and was told that he would run it.

"It was one of the most ambitious things Syl ever dreamed up," he says. "First, we rented this big empty store, and then we started running ads in the papers saying that it was gonna be the most fantastic jewelry store that ever hit Newark, New Jersey. Next, we picked up a local guy, who was well-known in the local retail business, to be our manager. He wasn't in on the play.

"The deal was this: After we had run the ads for about a month, we were going to have our manager contact all the big diamond wholesalers in New York and Newark and set them up appointments—spaced about a half hour apart—to come in and show us their line. We were going to do this in the little office that was just off the main store.

"As each guy would come in, we'd shove a toy gun in his face, tie him up, and take his bag. We planned to keep the tied-up guys in the warehouse until we had 'interviewed' everybody that was scheduled to come in. Naturally, the first guy we were gonna tie up and put back there was our manager. We could have scored a half million, easy, on this.

"But then I find out that somehow Sydney Brooks had got wind of what we were doing and he wanted in. I called Sylvan and told him and all he said was, 'Close up. It's over. Sydney's under indictment for something else right now and he'll give us up in a minute to make a better deal for himself.'

"Anyway, so we wouldn't lose the front money we had invested in the deal, Sylvan worked out another job for me to do so long as I was up there. He gave me a set of fake ID's and opened up some phony bank accounts in the name of 'Bill Simpson.'

"The scam was this: I'd go to the private jewelry stores all over the city; you know, the kind of guys who sell from some office on the second or third floor of some building. In each case, I say to the guy, 'My mother, Mrs. Simpson, suggested that I come here. I want to buy an engagement ring, but I can't go over fifteen hundred for it.'

"Well, of course, they'd always talk me up to twenty-five hundred or so, and then show me the piece. I'd say, 'That looks good. I'm sure Mother won't mind if I take it,' and I'd give him a small, legitimate check on one of the accounts and tell him I'd be back tomorrow with a cashier's check for the balance and I'd pick up the ring then. Naturally, the guy agrees to this, so I was able to set up about fourteen stores that day.

"That night I call Sylvan and tell him about it and he said, 'Now, let's not get hit from the blind side. Early tomorrow morning, you cut some of them merchants in on what we're doing. Tell them they're gonna get first crack at what we take out, and they're gonna get the pieces at very, very attractive prices. Then, if the police get wind of this, they'll warn you and you won't have no surprises waiting for you at any of the stops.

168

Because, sure as hell, if there's a stakeout waiting for you anyplace, there's a good chance you're gonna get shot full of holes. Just leave this number with the guys you cut in and tell them to call me at it if the deal suddenly gets hot.'

"Naturally, I do as Sylvan says; so, after I get three of the merchants to throw in with us, I set out to do the other places. Sylvan had also told me that I was to call him after every pickup.

"The first four went okay, but after the fifth, Sylvan says, 'Blow. There's a stakeout waiting for you at the next stop.' So, instead of going there, I headed for the train station. We pulled out of the deal with four or five nice pieces; but, naturally, it wasn't anything like what it would have been if Sydney Brooks hadn't got himself involved."

Brooks only occasionally became associated with Scolnick in the years between 1962 and 1966. Most of the time, he originated his own projects which he executed himself or, occasionally, with Herman Kutsher, another burglar. He worked alone as often as possible; not to insure secrecy, but because he hated to split with any part of the loot. There was no way he could outthink the Fat Man when division time came around, so he worked with Kutsher, who, over the years, made less out of his deals with Sydney than if he had put the same effort into legitimate occupations. Brooks paid a high price for this economical approach late in 1966, when Kutsher filled the police in on all the burglaries and the three dozen arsons the two had committed.

Among other things, Kutsher told the police that he had tried to persuade Brooks to undergo plastic surgery to remove the scar left after the fight with the shylock, so that Brooks would not be so easily recognizable. But according to Kutsher, Brooks was "too much of a creep" to spend the money.

169

The pair developed an MO for arson which, in time, became quite familiar to the police and the insurance companies, but they were so skillful at their trade that they were never nailed for a job until the day Kutsher made his confession. They used a flammable mixture of magnesium oxide powder and naphtha, which they would spread generously throughout the floors of the target building, ignite a time fuse, and drive away. Invariably, after they had put just a few blocks between them and the building, the sky would suddenly become bright with flames. No fire company ever reached the burning building in time to hold down any part of the insurance losses.

On occasion, Brooks tried to bring Scolnick into certain burglaries that required intensive planning, but Scolnick insists that he never participated in any of the jobs where violence was the basic key for success.

"Later, the DA nailed me on a couple of them," he says, "but I had no more to do with them than that Sydney and Herman—and once in a while Tommy and Harry—would discuss them in my house. I didn't even listen to them. They'd sit in my living room and talk 'em over, but I'd make it my business to be somewhere else in the house, doing something else, while it was all going down. I didn't want no part of that asshole stuff.

"One time, they sucked me into it in spite of myself and, later, when it all comes out, the papers keep talking about the 'Big Fairmount Park Robbery' like it was the stone knockover of the year. But there really wasn't anything to it.

"Sydney came to me with the proposition that I help out this jeweler that wanted to go bankrupt; but, after I talked to the guy, I told Sydney that it was no good, that this was a thing that was gonna take time—maybe a few months—to set him up as paying his bills and ordering merchandise and so on and so forth. And, besides, the guy don't want to go bankrupt my way

170

because he says it'll hurt his reputation. So I told Sydney the deal wasn't for me.

"Then Sydney says, 'Well, the hell, we'll go in and stick him up. The guy can get forty or fifty grand worth of diamonds in his store on a memo, so what we'll do is tell him to get set, in advance, and we'll go in with guns and he'll deliver them to us.'

"I said, 'Sydney, I'm not going to have anything to do with that kind of crap. This store is in the middle of Jeweler's Row. The police are always patrolling it. Sydney, you're going to wind up killing somebody. If a cop comes by and sees you down there with a gun, and he comes running through like a hero to stop you, somebody will shoot somebody and you wind up with a couple of dead people.'

"But there was nothing I could say to him to change his mind. All he could see was the score. Finally, I figured I'd better get into it to save everybody concerned a lot of grief.

"I told him, 'Don't do nothing for a while. Wait until a customer comes into this guy and asks to see some good stones. Instead of showing them in the store, let the guy tell his customer that he'll get a good assortment of stones on memo and bring them out to his house where he can look them over at his own speed. When he goes out to show the pieces, the guy should be sure to have with him, as company, somebody whose word people will believe, but who isn't in on the play. He shouldn't have any idea what's going on. Then you and the boys follow the jeweler in your car, stop him, stage the holdup and blow. The straight guy will testify it was legitimate and everybody will be out clean.'

"So that's the way it went down. The customer lives out in one of the western suburbs, so to get there the jeweler drives through Fairmount Park after first tipping off Sydney what his route's gonna be.

171

"They set out. The jeweler slows down at one of the cross-roads in the park and, at that point, Sydney pulls up and bumps into him. When everybody gets out to see what the damage is, Sydney pulls a toy pistol, says it's a stickup, and they take the things out of the car and blow. And that was the great Fairmount Park robbery that the papers made such a big deal out of. It was just a simple fake knockover, where we got the diamonds, and the guy gets the insurance."

Another crime of record in which Scolnick admits participation with Brooks, was the hijacking in 1966 of a trailer load of 210 air-conditioners worth $26,000 at wholesale prices. The felony was supposed to have taken place somewhere between Philadelphia and New York.

One morning while the police of both cities searched for the missing truck, the Fat Man received a call from the thieves, whom he vaguely describes as "a couple of guys I knew. Guys who worked in the truck depot. Now they can't unload the pieces, right? So the guy says to do him a favor and unload for him. I say sure and, after I make a couple of phone calls, I send Big Murray up to where the trailer is stashed."

Big Murray took over the story from there. "Before I left," he said, "Sylvan tells me that I should take along a padlock and put it on the truck before I get it out on the road so, in case I should get stopped, I wouldn't have a key and nobody can get in. He says to do it just in case because you never can tell about these things.

"Anyway, I'm on the road with the truck and, when I get to the Seven-Eleven store in Cherry Hill, I stop as I'm supposed to and meet the man that's going to take me to the warehouse. Sylvan doesn't tell me where the warehouse is in advance just so I wouldn't know to say anything—just in case something happened.

"So I'm sitting outside the Seven-Eleven store, drinking a soda, and there is a couple of kids walking alongside the truck.

172

I tell them to get away but instead of leaving, one of the little bastards goes to the public telephone and calls the police and tells them he heard voices inside the truck. This is a little eight-year-old kid that does this!

"While I'm thinking whether I should blow and run the risk of them chasing me all over South Jersey, a car comes racing down the highway and pulls in front of my truck. It's the Cherry Hill police.

"The cop gets out and says, 'You own this truck?' and I say, 'No, I'm just a driver.' Then he walks all around the truck, listening into it. I said, 'What the hell are you listening for, are you nuts?' and he says, 'Let me see your driver's license.'

"I showed him the phony that Sylvan had fixed me up with, and then he says, 'Okay. Open up the truck.' I got indignant, 'You want me to get fired? I can't open up that truck.' He says, 'You open it,' and I say, 'I can't,' and it goes back and forth until he says he's gonna have to take me to the station house and I'm telling him he can take me any place he wants, but I don't have a key and I'm not about to break a lock; that if he wants to break it, he can, but it's his own responsibility. Those goddamned kids!

"Finally he says, 'I guess I'm going to take you in,' and I tell him, 'Listen, suppose I call my boss and get the okay to break the lock?' I was looking and acting calm, but inside I was sweating bullets because this was the day after the heist and the radio and television was all full of stories about the missing trailer load of Fedders air-conditioners.

"So he said okay and I call Sylvan at a place where I know he is waiting for me. When he gets on the phone, I say, 'This is Murray, the truck driver. I'm hung up here without a key and this cop wants me to open the door and I can't open no door without a key. Can I break open the lock?' Meanwhile, the cop is just outside the booth listening to the conversation.

"Sylvan says to me, 'Are you in trouble?' and I say, 'Yeah,

yeah,' and he asks where I'm at and I tell him Cherry Hill. Then Sylvan says, 'All right. Let him take you wherever he is taking you. Meanwhile, you refuse to open up the truck and, if worse comes to worse, you tell him you want a search-and-seizure warrant for probable cause. Don't worry, Murray, I'll have it squared five minutes after you hit the station. But don't let 'em know you're scared or in bad shape. If you open the door, you're dead. You got to stand up there and just tell 'em *No.*'

"Well, I did what he said because Sylvan generally knows what he's doing, although I was really worried. I had just been pinched for something else and was waiting for the sentence and if they nailed me on this one, too, I'da been in a deep trouble. But I let him take me in and, just like Sylvan said, I was back out just a little while after I got there."

Scolnick was asked how he had managed to spring Big Murray so quickly. "Well," he said, "I made a few phone calls —this and that. By the time he got there, a friend of mine had called the cop in charge of the station house and told him that Murray had this load of automobile parts on the truck and he didn't have the key because we were worried that he might, himself, steal a big part of the load. You know, it's hard to count pieces of automotive supply. You got brake shoes in there, drums, points and plugs, stuff like that, which is easy to move out.

"My friend also tells the cop in charge, 'You open that truck and not only Murray, but anybody else hanging around your place is gonna steal me blind and, by the time I get there, it's gonna be too late.' So the cop says okay, he'll take care of it, and my friend says, 'And I'll take care of you, too, for the favor.' "

"It went down just like Sylvan said," added Big Murray. "I come in there; the cop on the desk wants to know what I got and I tell him the story again. I'm already breathing easier

174

because I can see he's been reached. And he tells the cop that pinched me, 'What the hell, we got more important things to worry about. Go ahead and let him go.'

"That's another time I learned something from Sylvan. You can't ever show you're scared. Once you do, you better forget about it. You got to be a better actor than they are a cop, that's all."

Scolnick was asked how he disposed of the load. "Well," he said, "I made about nine thousand on the deal. I gave the guys who pulled it in the first place three and a half grand for the twenty-six grand worth of air-conditioners. I split them up into two or three lots and made a couple of calls and got rid of them for thirteen thousand inside of the next two days. It was the kind of touch you make when you got a reputation.

"Not that I wanted any more deals like that. I only done it as a favor because these guys were stuck, so I moved off the load for them. But I didn't like it. Why should I go with things that are stolen, when I can get all the legitimate merchandise I want with just a phone call? I don't need to go with guys who maybe hit somebody over the head with a crowbar to get their merchandise.

"I never got into any of them deals with Sydney and the rest for any other reason except they were in trouble and I had to show them the way out."

# Chapter 10
# CREDIT CARDS, COUNTERFEITING, INSURANCE, AND OTHER SWINDLES

*Scolnick, having spent years preying on business, expects to emerge from prison as the businessman's benefactor, proprietor of a consulting service called something like Security Measures Against Fraud, Inc.*

—The Philadelphia *Bulletin*,
January 7, 1969.

When an honest man goes over his head in debt, life becomes a nightmare. Until then, the charge cards and the easy pays and the liberal credit plans were sunny horizon wideners, but once those convenient monthly payments begin to suck up the bare living expenses that his family needs, they become something else. They turn into a menacing barrage of collection letters and dunning phone calls, all threatening to destroy the good credit status that advertising had educated him to believe he needed.

That is, of course, if he is an honest man. To the crook, the credit systems are a flock of nice, fat turkeys.

176

There are dozens of ways in which credit cards and credit plans can be secured, used, and abused at a considerable profit and no personal liability. An operator can drive away from New York broke—but with a pocketful of hot credit cards—and arrive in Los Angeles with $10,000 in his pocket after having gone first class every mile of the way. All it takes is a knowledge of the way the system works.

No one knew this better than Scolnick and his gang. He, Big Murray Farber and Little Murray Packer met one morning in 1971 to explain it for the benefit of a reporter. Each of the three had completed their prison sentences and were now straight. Each had a wallet packed with credit cards issued in their right names and all were paid up to date, although Little Murray wistfully noted, "Man, could I bang them with these if I was still in action. I keep wanting to get 'em, baby."

Scolnick's opening description of a credit card company was rough, but essentially accurate:

"The reason there's so many holes in their operation is because they go on the basis that most people are honest. They build a cushion into their charges that takes care of maybe the one or one and a half percent of the people that beats 'em. They make so much money, they never miss it.

"Take, for example, American Express. Say they got two million members. Every year, they charge every one of these members fourteen dollars apiece to belong, and that gives them a cash flow of twenty-eight million dollars and they still ain't done nothing but send out a credit card that costs maybe two cents.

"Now they start buying the credit paper—a member's charges at an individual store. That twenty-eight million bankrolls their operation—even if they're doing three hundred million—because they're turning the money over every thirty days.

"Now, look what they do. A merchant pays them two

177

hundred forty dollars for the right to put their decal in his window and run charge accounts for his customers. In comes Joe Doakes and he buys maybe one hundred dollars' worth of goods. After fourteen to twenty-eight days, the merchant sends in the slip to the credit card company who then bills Mr. Doakes. Within ten days, Doakes pays forty, fifty percent of what his bill is. Within the next ten or fifteen days, the company has gotten about seventy percent of their charges. But, they still haven't paid out three cents of their own money!

"The merchant has laid out his money for the goods he sold Joe Doakes. Joe Doakes has paid for the goods he bought and, meanwhile, the company has picked up the fourteen dollars for the card, two-hundred-forty dollars from the merchant, plus the amount that's been paid on their bills. They got a good part of all that money earning them interest in the banks. In addition to which, they charged the merchant seven-and-one-half percent for collecting each bill. That's a cash float that allows them to operate with plenty of margin.

"All that goes on every year. Every twelve months, credit card outfits open up with millions of everybody else's money in the bank earning interest just for them. Is it any wonder the credit card companies want to get their cards in as many hands as possible, and what the hell does it matter if one percent goes bad?"

"Sure," added Little Murray, "I did time in jail for fraudulent bankruptcy, and still I got all the credit cards I want." He opened his wallet and fanned through a sheaf of them. "See these? They're all in my name. I just walked around one day and picked up all the applications."

It turned out that none of the issuing companies had taken the trouble to check back far enough on Little Murray. He had remarried and moved in 1967 and, as far as the companies he had burned before were concerned, he had a new identity.

178

"You can get all the cards you want if you know what you're doing. I put down on the application I make fifteen thousand dollars a year and I been on my job for five years. Actually, I make ten and only been there two years, but I asked my boss about it and he said sure, go ahead.

"To be truthful, I got over forty thousand dollars' worth of judgments against me. I never went bankrupt personally because I didn't have to and maybe I'll need it someday. But I think the judgments are only good for four or five years before they have to reprocess them or something, and what are they going to do; beat a dead horse? So I don't even know if they're still there.

"If they are, they're laying in some courthouse. That's where they'd have to be, because I rent my apartment—I don't own a house. Now listen to this; a couple of months ago I needed some tires, so I went over to some place in Jersey that offers instant credit. I fill out the credit form and the guy asks me if I got any credit references. I tell him I got charges at the stores and the Diner's and the American Express, and he says, fine, and he gives me the two tires—right there on the spot! No problem.

"The payments come to eighteen-ninety a month and, after I make two payments, I get a letter from the bank that holds the paper. They say that my credit is so good that if I want, they'll lend me thirty-five hundred—all I got to do is stop by their office and sign the papers. Now, I'll bet you anything I can go in there tomorrow and sign them papers and get the check. And I make a clear profit of thirty-five hundred just by moving."

He was asked, "Suppose you didn't want to leave your job and move somewhere else. Suppose you just didn't pay?"

"What are they going to do, shoot me in the head?" answered Little Murray. "The New Jersey outfit can't levy against me because I live in Pennsylvania. And that state don't allow anybody to garnishee your wages. The best they're gonna do is set a judgment against me and they can stack that one up alongside the other ones that are already on the books."

Big Murray chipped in. "Anybody with a common name who wants to get a new credit card after he's moved, all he's gotta do is drop his middle initial. There's nothing illegal about that. All you do is put your name and address down and that you lived in a place for five years, or better. They don't like grasshoppers. You're really in clover if you changed your wife, like Little Murray, because then when they check their files and pull the package on you, you come up clean. They got no bad history on you at all.

"And they can't go to the other credit companies for information. That's against the law. One bank can't even tell another bank how good a pay you are. These credit bureaus are ridiculous. They just don't check hard enough. They're happy if they know what you were doing last year. If it was me, I'd want to know what you were doing five years ago if it was my thirty-five hundred you were getting.

"And once you got one card, it's a cinch to get the rest. You put down on the application that you got an American Express card and then Diner's or Carte Blanche is tickled pink to be doing business with you. You'll get them cards so fast, your head will spin."

He was asked about the ordinary, honest man in a financial jam who is past due on his credit card or credit installment payments. Scolnick broke in with the answer, "He's in a world of trouble because they're going to scare him half to death. They will send him letters saying they are going to sue him, they are going to sell him out and shoot it to a lawyer, and everything else. If he's a legitimate guy, they are going to put a judgment against his house. They're going to call him at night, send him

180

collect telegrams and do whatever else they can to fill his life with hell.

"In other words, the whole credit system goes against the guy who is legitimate. He has no recourse. But the guy with the slightest bit of larceny in his heart is okay.

"So what happens? Well, if the pressure gets too tough, some guys sell off their credit cards to an operator. He gets twenty-five or thirty dollars apiece for them and waits a week or so and then reports the cards are stolen. That way, the legitimate debts get mixed up in the 'larceny.'

"Then the operator starts to move. It doesn't matter if he's using hot cards or cards he got through some fraud, he's ready to go because he knows that as long as he keeps his purchases under forty or fifty dollars, depending on the card, the merchant isn't under any obligation to precheck the transaction with the credit company. Some department stores put a limit of twenty-five dollars on a purchase before the clerk has to call in and see if it's okay, but the credit card checks all start around forty dollars. Go over that, and the merchant has a toll-free number that he has to use to call a computer who gives him a yes or a no on the deal. But, below that, you can buy all day long.

Big Murray, now that he is an honest citizen, showed elaborate disgust with the merchants who knowingly accept purchases on an invalid card. He said, "Most of them work something out with you. I go to a restaurant and I see a tab come in for seventy dollars. So what does the guy do who's running the joint? He knows the card is bad, so he makes up two checks for thirty-five dollars each, one for food, and the other—the bar bill. He don't give a damn, he's already scored. That's true of any merchant who's selling you a two-dollar item for twice that. He's just so thrilled to move his merchandise, he don't care about anything.

181

"If you go to buy something for a couple of hundred bucks, just give him a story. Tell him you're buying it on a company card and he'll be very happy to break the price into as many slips as he needs to, in order that he don't have to call the computer.

"And then there's the guys you don't even have to buy anything from. You find these guys by just talking to a store-keeper for a while, and he'll let you know if he's down to earth. If he is, then you tell him to 'sell' you something for forty dollars and he gives you the slip to sign, plus a twenty for yourself. He ain't out no merchandise, just a slip."

Little Murray volunteered, "I used to have a guy with a hundred-dollar slip. He'd give me eighty dollars for my end. Then he started cutting down the price on me. First it was seventy dollars, then sixty, and fifty. But I didn't care. I was still picking up dough every week on a phony card. It was like my father giving me an allowance."

Scolnick shook his head. "It's so easy to get credit cards, it's criminal. You can buy hot ones in any city in the country where they send them out by mail. The postman, everybody, knows there's a credit card in that envelope. The mailbox thief has a party. He lifts your card when you don't even know it's coming, and he's got thirty days to play with it before you get a bill. One outfit, Unicard, finally wised up. They mail you the card. Two weeks later, they send you a letter asking if you got it. But they shouldn't wait two weeks. They shouldn't wait more than two days. And, I understand, some of the other companies are finally getting around to printing a guy's picture on his card.

"But the credit card companies don't have to put themselves out, as long as their losses don't upset their profit. And that takes a lot of upsetting, because they're rocking and sock-ing everybody with all them ridiculous charges. Some of them

182

attach late charges of five bucks or so, or they charge you one-and-a-half percent a month on an unpaid balance. That makes it eighteen percent a year, and do you have any idea how much that comes to when you have as many customers as they do? My God, eighteen percent a year! They really don't need no guns! They just keep charging you interest on the interest they already charged you."

"I guess," said Little Murray, "that's part of the reason the storekeepers don't give a damn about the credit card companies. They don't care if it's a bad card, because they know the companies are obligated to pay them—as long as the card isn't on the 'hot list' [a printed list of stolen and revoked credit cards that is periodically sent to retail establishments by each credit card company]. Oh, maybe one out of a thousand might call in to check a card, but even that's generally because they're looking for the twenty-five- or fifty-dollar bonus they get for pulling a bad card for somebody.

"But the only time they really got an obligation to the company is when the card is on the list and that's because then it's their own money at stake. They don't worry about nothing but their own money."

"You can generally get as much credit as you need on one of them cards," said Scolnick. "I know one guy that took down forty-two hundred dollars on a gas credit card. I, myself, once banged out a credit card company for twelve grand on just one card.

"In fact, when I was in the business, I used to slaughter 'em. I had guys working twenty-four hours a day, getting cards with phony applications and then out on the street working them.

"It's so easy. The companies take some kid out of school and make him a credit man. They tell him that he's dealing with primarily honest people. Well, it's not that the people are hon-

183

est, it's just that they're novices. A lot more would be filling out phony apps if they just knew how.

"Now, when that kind of a kid goes to check a credit application, they first call all the numbers [credit references] that the man puts on his slip. But they don't call information or check the yellow pages in the phone book to see if that number is really what the application says it is. So, when somebody answers the phone, the kid says, 'Is this Johnston's Furniture Store?' 'Yeah.' 'Do you have an account under the name of Murray Farber?' 'Yeah.' 'What kind of pay is he?' 'Great!' And, all the time, the kid is talking to me or one of my guys.

"If I was doing the checking, I'd first call Information and find out from them the number of Johnston's. You see my point? All you have to do is something sensible like that. Most of the credit that goes bad is because the applications are phony in front. The landlord is a phony; the guy gives his brother's or his cousin's number, and when the kid calls up to check, he's told that the guy lives there and he always pays his rent on time.

"There's one bank in Philadelphia who won't give out information at all about their savings accounts. So, every con man in the area puts down that he's got ten grand saved up with them. How is anybody going to check? But if it was me, I'd want to see the guy's passbook, and he knows that if he phonies that up, he's in deep trouble because then he's got a federal rap tied into the deal.

"Another thing they all put down on their apps is the insurance information. No insurance company will ever answer a phone request for information because right away they figure it's another insurance agent calling up after one of their customers. Banks could find out if they wanted to process the loan properly, but they just don't want to go to the trouble. It's just too easy to build their losses into what they charge the legitimate guys."

184

He was asked about counterfeiting credit cards. Surprisingly he answered, "Too much trouble. No need to go into it when it's so easy to get hot cards or a card with a phony application. Besides, it takes a lot of talent to make a credit card. Credit cards aren't just printing. They have a center core with a printed piece on the front of it and the back of it. Three separate pieces of paper. Then it's laminated and then it's embossed. It takes too much talent and nobody needs to go to all that trouble."

He was reminded that one of the criminal indictments against him had dealt with his counterfeiting of American Express checks. "Well," he said, "that's something else. Now we're off credit cards and into what can be done with an offset printing press. You know what offset printing is? Well, the best way to explain it is that you take a photograph of whatever you're printing. Then that photograph becomes the plate you print from. If you're printing in black and white, you only need one plate. If you're printing in color, you have a different plate for every primary color.

"So, anyway, I set up a printing plant. I bought a second-hand press for around three thousand dollars, and I go out and recruit a printer. Now I'm all set to go. The first thing we do is start running American Express Cheques. I'm not bragging or anything, but later when the thing blows, the cops and the American Express people themselves say they are the best queers they ever seen made.

"It's easy to move these kind of checks, especially overseas. I'd send guys over to Europe with a complete line of bad credit cards, ID's, and maybe twenty, thirty thousand dollars' worth of Cheques. They moved off all the hundred-dollar pieces they wanted to. It's easy, because those Cheques take twenty-five days before they bounce back.

"This is where both American Express and Diner's Club

185

have a problem. They got the man in the store holding his slips for two and four weeks before he sends them in. You see, they pay twice a month. That always gives you a couple of weeks to move around before they bounce back.

"They don't want to change the system because of the interest they're earning on the other guy's money that they're holding. If it was me running one of them companies, I'd have an electronic scanner in every store wired into a central system. Put in a bad card, and it would kick back out, right there—on the spot. It might cost maybe six hundred dollars a store, for installation, but I'm willing to bet that they lose at least a thousand dollars a year on bad cards in every store they got."

He was asked, "Suppose I want to buy a set of hot credit cards. What would they cost?"

"You can get a set for five hundred dollars. But that's retail. Buy in bulk, and you can get 'em for fifty dollars a set."

"How many is a set?"

"Seven or eight."

"And, if I'm going across country. . . ."

"You can beat them to death. It's easy to take down twenty grand without even breathing hard. Half in cash and half in goods and living expenses. I once took a liquor store for twelve grand but, of course, I'm not the average guy. I go in with the right story, every time."

"What story did you give the liquor store?"

"I told 'em I was in the insurance business and we were going to have office parties in every one of our branches. The guy was very thrilled to do business with me. If you come up with the right story with your cards, you can get anything you want.

"But you can't go in on just conversation. You've got to make an investment. When you are stealing, it's a business. The men who get caught are men who don't treat it like a business.

186

They treat it just like what they are: nickel-and-dime thugs. But if you operate as a serious businessman, there's no way they can combat you because you're traveling within the lines of their operation.

"The normal thing is what you do. They want to see a driver's license, then you got it. They want to check your references, you got somebody standing by at the numbers you give them to call. You leave them no way to pierce the veil and say that you are crooked.

"We boffed out Las Vegas the same way. Vegas is easy because they operate the same as the banks. They go on the principle that most people are honest. Here's how you do it:

"First, you put ten thousand dollars in the bank under a phony name and give the bank the authorization that if a credit call comes in, they can say that you have a five-figure balance. Then you call Vegas and make a reservation at whatever hotel you pick out and you also tell 'em to set you up a line of credit.

"Then you go out to Vegas on—say a Thursday—and leave your markers, but you don't take them all down at one time. First you take five hundred, a thousand dollars in chips and make it look good by some plays at the tables. You only spend maybe one hundred dollars at the table.

"Next night, after the banks back east are closed, you start making your heavy plays. You go to the different tables and give markers for a couple of grand wherever you go. You see, it's too late for the casino's bookkeeping to call in to your bank.

"You always work with another guy. You keep looking like you're plunging but, in the meantime, you're going under with your partner in the men's room, or wherever, and giving him the chips and he's cashing them in. You keep looking like you're losing and giving out more markers until you've taken down eight, ten grand.

"Then you leave. You're out by Sunday. Meanwhile, just

187

before your bank back east has closed on Friday night, you had somebody go in there and clean the account out. They maybe cash a check for $9600 so the account is open, but it's bare when the markers you gave hit the bank next Thursday or Friday.

"It's foolproof. You can even go back a couple of times to various hotels because you ain't Charlton Heston or Burt Lancaster, somebody they're gonna know a second time.

"The main thing is to do it like a businessman. You make an investment in the bank account and you got a complete set of ID's and your front has got to be perfect."

Scolnick was then asked if he had ever printed counterfeit money. He indignantly rejected the thought. "I done a lot of things, but I always had a funny feeling about printing this country's money. I'd do driver's licenses and passports and even, once, the Great Seal of the United States, but I just think there's something stone wrong about getting into that kind of a proposition. It's against your country.

"Besides, most of the guys in it are nuts. Some years ago, when I first got involved with the printing plant, a guy comes to me with a package of queer, you know, funny money. At that time, they were buying it for fifteen dollars a hundred. I asked him how he passes it, and he says it's no problem, they just go out and buy things. That wasn't for me. No way.

"But this guy insists. 'Come on, I'll show you,' he says. So we drive out to a roadside stand and he buys some chickens and gives the lady a queer twenty-dollar bill. When we get back, he looks at his wallet and says, 'I'm a son of a bitch. That lady shortchanged me three dollars!' And, do you know, he went there and made her give him his three dollars back! I guess to be in that line, you gotta be stone crazy.

"But, I really got interested in that printing plant. I studied all kinds of books on printing and learned how to do silk screens and everything. The whole thing paid off on just the Du Pont paint deal, and that was only one out of hundreds.

188

"The big thing there was to print accurate labels; so what we did was to buy some different cans of Du Pont paints and take the labels off. Then, I cut a thin sliver off of each color and I took them over to an ink company which had a spectograph, which is a machine that tells you what kind of inks are used to produce each color. I bought a lot of pounds of every one of the colors they indicated and I had plates made and started to run off genuine Du Pont labels.

"I bought a couple of trailer loads of some cheap paint at fifty-five cents a can and I had them all wrapped with my Du Pont labels. These we sold off to all the painting contractors for two, two-fifty a can. One guy wanted to know how good it was and Big Murray tells him, 'Are you crazy? It's Du Pont. It's as rich as sour cream!'

"The guy takes a load and uses it. First time it rains, it washes off in streaks and he come back screaming, 'You son of a bitch, that *was* sour cream!' "

Before long, the printing plant's output of passports, driver's licenses, Social Security cards and bank checks had become efficient enough to put the gang into the business of selling their products to other crooks. Their forgeries were so craftsmanlike that robbers and con men came from all over the country to buy these items for their own schemes. Twenty sets of driver's licenses, owner's and Social Security cards, brought $1000 and the customers were figuratively standing in line to get them.

From here it was only a short move into the insurance business. The rationale for the move was that an insurance company only gives one tangible in return for premium money —a printed policy. And they had a printing plant.

They printed and sold fire and casualty, life and accident, and almost any other kind of policy that anyone would want. True to his own principle of always proceeding in a businesslike manner, Scolnick began advertising his product in the newspa-

189

pers and over the television stations in the area, and the sales volume reached flood proportions after he discovered the ghetto merchant.

In recent years, these businessmen have had little or no chance to insure their operations. Riots and the proliferation of armed robberies have reduced their stores to very poor or untakable risks, as far as the insurance companies are concerned.

"They welcomed us with open arms," says Scolnick. "They can't get no insurance from anybody and here I got salesmen going in and offering them a deal. They was willing to pay almost any kind of a premium in order to get our coverage.

"Handled right, a deal like this is good for a couple of years. All you have to do is to pay some small claims and, on the big ones, you go piecemeal. In other words, you write letters back and forth and so on, and before they know it, six or nine months has gone by while they're waiting to get paid.

"And, all the time, you're annualizing the premiums. You tell a merchant that all he has to do is pay twenty-five percent of the annual premium down and we can finance the rest through his bank. He's got to grab the deal and so does his bank when he goes to them with the Insurance Company of North America policy we give him. The bank don't check with the insurance company; they'd need three hundred people to check out every policy that's brought in. Do you realize how many policies are financed? To check them out right, you'd need a hundred extra phones in the bank and even that wouldn't be enough.

"Finally, I ended up buying a legitimate company that wasn't doing too much business and I used that as a front. I didn't pay off any claims out of that, either. But we really started to move big, then. We used to advertise on television with a guy dressed up like a doctor with one of those mirrors

190

on a band around his head and a white coat and all. Real borax. 'Protect Your Family for Pennies a Day.' That kind of thing.

"We were moving so good, that I brought in a legitimate guy as a partner. He knew the insurance business from back to front and his wife was so happy about this big break he was getting that she decorated all our offices with paintings she brought in from home.

"Well, after a while, this guy and his wife see my guys hanging around, and Sydney Brooks and his friends coming in and, every once in a while, Harry Karafin with his big mouth, and they can't understand it. They keep saying to me, 'What kind of a place are we running with all these thugs?' and this and that. Pretty soon, I get the idea that my partnership with the legitimate guy is dissolved. He didn't show up at the office any more, and she come in and took down all her paintings.

"Worst of all, was that reporter from the *Inquirer,* Harry Karafin. When I first met him, he was taking shirts and ties and radios from guys so he wouldn't write one of his investigation stories about them. He was leaning on me for this and that and I really got tired of it. So, I said to him, 'Harry, why don't you wise up? Instead of taking nickels and dimes, why don't you hold yourself out as a public relations man? All these guys would put you on their payroll just to keep you quiet. Stop looking to do everybody so much frigging harm and do them some good for a change.'

"Well, he took the idea. He and I sort of went into partners. I'd talk to guys for him and they'd say okay, and first thing you know, we're taking down a couple of thousand dollars apiece. But most of the time, I just let him do his business as long as he let me do mine. I'd step in and help him whenever he needed it, and I guess, all in all, I ended up with maybe ten grand out of him.

"It was my suggestion that he start this Home Remodeling

191

Association of America that the DA finally banged him on. I explained to him that instead of just shaking down all the home remodeling guys individually, he should get them into one association which could pay him a nice annual fee for his public relations services, which was mostly that he don't write stories about the way they did their business.

"That went down fine. As a matter of fact, it worked out so good that I got into the home-mod business too and, through that, we went into the debt consolidation field. That was a beauty."

When he paused to consider the legitimate pleasures of operating a debt consolidation company, the reporter shuffled through his notes and then said, "Sylvan, I have ads here from all over the country pushing for this kind of business. Start from the beginning. How does it work?"

This is the kind of question that Scolnick likes. Almost every interview with him ends as a tutorial discourse. But, because he is a good storyteller, he is always entertaining, as well as instructive. Both Murrays, who had been sitting by as he described the gang's counterfeiting and credit card operations, were interested even though they had, themselves, participated in every one of the projects he was describing.

"It all began," he said, "with a young fellow named Joe Cox who got a dream while he was working in the collection department of a bank. He dreamed up the idea of a man being able to put all his debts in one pile and pay them off over a longer period of time, with a lot smaller payments going out than when the man was trying to pay something individually on every debt.

"He took his idea to another man, named Matty, who was in the finance and home improvement business, and sold him on it. A month later, Joe left the bank and went to work for Matty at a hundred twenty-five a week. Within a month, every

192

morning when Joe and Matty came down to their office, they had people waiting twenty deep to consolidate their debts.

"What they did was this; they made the people sign a home-remodeling-loan paper. Then they went out and tapped a pipe in the guy's place and charged him twelve hundred dollars, which covered everything he owed. They used the twelve hundred to pay off the guy's debts and he paid them back the money over a five-year period. And that's the way they started. It went over so big that within a couple of years Matty was a millionaire. Joe Cox didn't get the ride with him, though. After a little while, Matty dropped him and now Joe is back brokering paper somewhere. Everybody made money out of the deal but Joe. Debt consolidation companies started all over the country and, everywhere they opened, they done big.

"It's really a good idea. Nothing bad about it at all, except human nature. A guy gets clear of his debts and maybe he stays that way for six or eight months, but pretty soon he gives in to the pressure that everybody puts on to sell him something and, the first thing you know, he's back to Household Finance or one of them other companies. Naturally, they're glad to see him. He already made one loan good with them. Then it starts with the other companies; the department stores send him literature, he believes all the advertising that he needs a new car instead of the one he's got. Before you know it, he's in hock again. Only this second time around, he blows his house. They all close in on him and he's got nothing to go back with for another debt consolidation.

"Worst thing about it is that the guy don't have to go to the debt consolidators or to the finance companies in the first place. But he's a novice. He don't know how to borrow from a bank, which is the place he should go instead of buying so many things on credit. He thinks the people that give him credit

are his friends. They ain't. No way. They're the toughest enemies he's got!"

Big Murray said, "Now tell him about Partridge Development."

"I ain't finished. I was going to describe how I ran my
company."

"That's okay," said the reporter. "I get the idea. The rest
isn't hard to figure out. What about Partridge Development?
Was that another one of your companies?"

He smiled and shook his head. "It just was fantastic! Unbelievable how smart businessmen sometimes operate! There
was this guy, Richard Partridge. He was a promoter and he had
a television show which had on it all new inventions. His deal
with the inventors was that they come on his show and, if he
liked their item, he would put together companies to make and
merchandise it. He got half the royalties for his end.

"Well, he runs the show for a couple of years and he's up
to his ass in inventions, only he hasn't got anything off the
ground yet. Meanwhile, he's holding half of all these patents.
So he gets a group of ten or twelve respectable businessmen, all
rich, together and they put up over a million dollars into the
company and they go public. They're selling stock in their
company.

"And still they don't do nothing. They burn up all but
about a hundred grand in promotion and planning and big
offices and a fancy staff, but they got nothing to show for it.

"Right then, one of the deals that come to me was a guy,
Joe Costanza, who says he's looking to promote a deal he's got
in Puerto Rico to manufacture marble terrazzo tiles. He says
it's gonna be the construction material of the future. What it
is, is a precast block of concrete, about an inch thick and a foot
square, with some marble dust sprinkled on it which they grind
down and call it precast marble terrazzo. They can pour it in

194

big sheets if they want, so it's got all kinds of romance going for it.

"Costanza asks do I want to do something with it, and I ask him if he's got a plant or a contractor down there to make it. He says he can get one; all he has to do is go down and get one signed up. Well, to make a long story short, he goes back and forth to Puerto Rico a couple of times and Sam Koff, who came in as my partner, and me are bankrolling him now for about thirty-five hundred dollars, and what we got to show for it is a contractor who says he can make it and a bunch of pictures Joe gives me of the contractor's plant and which I print underneath, 'The Biggest Terrazzo Manufacturing Plant in Puerto Rico.'

"So now I go to Partridge Development, who I hear is now out looking for someone to generate sales. I talk to the board of directors and I wind up selling them the American rights to 'Portacor,' which is what I called the tile, for ten thousand cash and forty-five thousand shares of their stock—which, at that time, was trading for four and an eighth on the board.

"Well, the first couple of weeks that I'm there, I don't say too much. I just look and listen. I see their fancy staff sitting around, betting baseball pools and all that kind of crap, and I say to myself, 'What the hell am I in?' I know that our next move is to dump their stock. By giving them a little pressure here and there, I get the board of directors to buy half of our stock from us at two dollars a share. That makes fifty-five grand, so far, we took 'em for. And still they ain't seen one block of Portacor. Just my pictures.

"I wait a while and then move them into buying the rest of our stock. Now we're in a hundred ten grand from all these businessmen who are so smart and successful in their own fields, and we tell 'em goodbye.

"Six months later, Partridge Development is still flounder-

195

ing and down to three, four thousand dollars in the bank. They're in big trouble. I run into one of the directors one day in the street and he tells me the story. 'Look,' I said, 'that company is basically sound. It can be a big winner—if the right sales effort is ever put together.' Well, with one thing and another, next thing I know, I am invited back to address their next board meeting. I lay out a plan, showing what we can do with a publicly held company—you know, going into financing and things like that, and I really set the place on fire. When I finished, the treasurer of the company wrote out his own check for five thousand dollars and gives it to me to use to put the company back on its feet. He's afraid that his reputation is gonna get hurt if it goes bankrupt. I tell them I'm willing to do it, but not for nothing. I need some more stock for my end and this they agree to.

"Well, I maneuver around a little bit and, meanwhile, Sam and me strips the place of most of the assets they got left. Then I call for another board meeting. But before we go in, I say to Sam, 'I want you to positively keep your mouth shut in this meeting. No matter what I say, just listen and don't make no comments about anything.'

"Now the meeting starts. I get up and start pitching them how great the company could be and what can be done and this and that. I really sold my heart out. I outlined all kinds of plans that had their eyes popping, but then I end by saying very sorrowfully, 'But, Gentlemen, I must tell you I'm not the man to do it because of this and that.' I talked for about an hour and a half, always making it sound good and then explaining why I can't go forward with the company and they can have all my plans if they're willing to buy back the stock they give us the second time around.

"Finally, Sam can't stand it no longer. He gets up and says,

196

'Gentlemen, will you please excuse my partner and me for a moment. I'd like to have a word with him in private.'

"They say sure, and me and Sam walk out into the hall. When we get there, and this is the stone truth, he says to me, 'Sylvan, if it's so good, why don't we keep it for ourselves?' "

# Chapter 11
# THE LAVISH LIFE

*He states that he has had no homosexual experiences and that he has no problem achieving sexual satisfaction with women.*

—An extract from the
presentence report ordered
by the sentencing judge.

Many of the country's thieves and con men heard about the Fat Man. They came from all over to Cherry Hill for his help, or recommended his services to their friends because of his reputation.

A larcenous stockbroker in Ohio offered him $10,000 to counterfeit some of the bonds in his customers' portfolios. He wanted to sell off the real securities to cover his personal losses in the market and was brought to Scolnick by a fly-by-night insurance operator who had made a profit out of the gang's accurate replicas of legitimate policies.

He accepted some deals and turned others down because he saw a personal risk or that the scheme was bad, but he spoke

198

to no one until he had received a few thousand dollars in advance. He began to regard himself as a crime doctor who could and did prescribe the ways to add vigorous safety to a faulty scam.

They came to him for financing, too. As a loan broker, he helped set up phony unions, bankrolled insurance companies and bankruptcies for other operators and, occasionally, bought into projects that promised fat, fast bucks.

The MO was always the same; he got his—first—in front. If a crook needed $15,000, he took him to a friendly bank or shylock and, after repayment schedules were arranged, $3,000 was sliced off the top for his end.

The money came pouring in, and he lived like a maharaja. Life seemed to be one big candy store—to which he had the key. To this day, he is unable to approximate how much came in, what he spent on himself, and how much he shunted off to friends and acquaintances as "business expenses." Within the space of one particular week, he bought three new Cadillacs and three Chryslers and gave them away as gifts.

Another time, he happened to be window shopping along a street in the northeast Philadelphia business district. He was taking a few days vacation away from his office and was wearing an old shirt, ripped and baggy trousers and a pair of scuffed space shoes. A furrier's window caught his eye and he went in.

"The lady inside saw me," he recalls, "and maybe she thought it was going to be a stickup or something because I looked so much like a bum. She says, 'What can I do for you?' and when I answer, 'I'm thinking about a mink coat,' she got even more worried looking and says, 'Wait a minute,' and runs in the back to get the boss.

"He comes in, a real smart guy and, after sizing me up, he says, 'Do you have any idea what a mink coat costs?'

"Well, that really burns me. So I figured I'll straighten this

199

guy out. You know how I straightened him out? I made him keep bringing me mink coats until I found one that I liked. Then I said, 'That's it. Give me two of them .' 'Two?' he says. 'Yeah. One for my mother and one for my wife.' He looks at me long and doubtful and finally says, 'That's over eight thousand dollars!' I looked back at him as scornful as I could make it and answered, 'So what?'

"Then I reached into my back pocket and I bring out the ten or twelve thousand dollars I have with me and start counting out fifty- and hundred-dollar bills. I get up to five thousand dollars and I tossed it over to him, saying, 'Here's a deposit. You bring them over to my house tonight and, if they like 'em, you got a deal.'

"That's how I straightened that guy out; by acting like a big-time jerk. But it was worth it. That night, when he came with the coats, I took one of them out of the box and tried it on Ruth. Mom was sitting there in the living room, watching her and telling her how beautiful it was, and then I said, 'Now it's your turn, Mom,' and I reached back into the box and brought the other one out and put it around her shoulders and she just burst into tears. She looked so gorgeous in that coat!"

He was asked the logical question, "Why did your mother continue to work when you were making so much money?"

"Well, she wanted to be self-sustaining. Mom never wanted to be obligated to nobody. After I was indicted and she found out where all my money was coming from, she cried for days. She said to me, and I'll never forget the way she looked when she said it, 'Your daddy never had to do that. He never took anything in his life that didn't belong to him. Why did you have to?' Boy, that was strong. Of all the problems I was facing then, that bit the deepest. I knew she had lost an awful lot of respect for me, but what could she do? She bought the deck of cards and she could only play the hand she was dealt.

200

"I had kept all of my business dealings away from Ruth, too. It was seldom I ever let anybody who came to the house discuss their deals, unless she was out to a movie or visiting, or something like that. She never handled the house money, I just gave her what she wanted for her pocket and paid the rest of the bills myself. She never really knew anything until one time a reporter came to the house, after the *Philadelphia Magazine* story, and started asking her questions. That's when she found me out and, my God, she was unbearable to live with for the next few weeks. See, she only knew about my legitimate deals, and that's where she thought the money was coming from."

Actually, the large chunks of cash that he was accumulating had become an embarrassment to him. He was still in his early thirties and although he knew how how to manipulate bankers and other moneymen, he lacked the financial sophistication to channel his income into a form that could be reflected in an annual tax return.

He decided to retire, and this lasted a year and a half, until the inaction almost drove him crazy. He went to every motion picture and play that seemed even remotely interesting and he rebuilt his house into a place crammed wih unnecessary conveniences, such as downstairs showers, billiard rooms, and a swimming pool that would have been too ornate for an estate.

For a while, he spent three and four solitary hours a day in the billiard room, trying to regain and then surpass the youthful proficiency that had earned him a minor reputation as a pool hustler.

"None of it was no good," he says, "and I was going batty. I had a ton of cash and I didn't dare invest it in anything. Do you realize how hard it is to get rid of cash? To even hide it?

"I didn't trust nobody with it, and I sure as hell didn't want to try sending it to Switzerland because when it's my money, I want to be near enough to watch it. One time, me and

201

Pop [his wife's father] spent the night ripping out all the paneling in the den. We was drilling and sawing and chiseling and then, when we got all the panels off, we took the packages of money and stuck them to the bare wall with masking tape all around them. Then we put the paneling back up and, to make it look absolutely right, we even hammered in beading all around the edges.

"We finished about nine in the morning and were sitting back, admiring our job and having a cup of coffee, when in walks one of my older brothers who's there to see how Mom is. He takes a look around the room and says, 'Man, all that paneling would sure be a great place to hide money behind! So, as soon at that son of a gun left, me and Pop got out the hammers and chisels and pulled all that goddamned paneling down again.

"Another time, I figure to hide some in somebody else's house. I pick an aunt who lives in one of the old houses that have things like fifteen-foot ceilings. I had the key to her place and, one day when she was away, I go over with a package of diamonds and, even with my bulk, I'm up on a ladder, pulling away the trim from over a door. I'm in the middle of it and my cousin walks in. He says, 'What are you doing, Sylvan, hiding money?'

"So I figured—the hell with all this bullshit, and started spending like a drunken sailor. It got so I was even sorry I had the frigging money. It used to work on my nerves. I mean, I never used to worship money for itself—I just liked the things it got me and what it represented in the way of my abilities.

"If money really was my goal, I'd a used what I had to try and build some kind of an empire. But, I figure, why take a chance? If somebody grabs me, I'm through and, 'Next case.' I finally come to realize that I knew I didn't need no more money, but I sure did need something that was going to occupy

202

my mind besides pool and the picture shows. Of course, now that I'm older, I would know what to do with it. I'd know how to get it into the hands of investment groups in a way that would make it all legitimate.

"I guess what I missed most of all was the feeling you get when you take down a score. There's nothing in the world like it. The excitement is something you just can't match anywhere else. It's like a junky shooting dope. It's a real high.

"Your hands get wet. Your feet start sweating and your stomach is fluttering. Then, afterwards, there's such a relaxed state of mind; I just can't explain it. You feel great. Maybe it's like a woman feels after she has a baby. It ain't the money, it's the victory.

"That was true of every scam I was ever in. Especially the bankruptcies; man, that's like having an orgasm every two hours! It's because you're dealing with five hundred turkeys. Every time one comes in, it's another win. In the beginning, you're so careful with the financial statements, setting the store up right and placing the orders and buying the proper merchandise. Pretty soon, you owe fifty—a hundred—two hundred— four hundred thousand dollars, and you're still parlaying, you're still paying the bills with their own money and you say to yourself, 'Holy Mackerel, I'm a year in action already and I still don't have any money. And everybody's straining at the bit because they want to stop paying the bills and pocket. But the more bills you pay, the more goods you get at the end.

"So you hold off until ten or twelve weeks before the Christmas season, and you place orders with everybody in the country, and there's a line of trailers a city block long waiting to unload, and there's guys coming in with suitcases full of diamonds and you're sitting back, wheeling and dealing with everybody.

"You're sitting back and selling off all that stuff and taking

203

the cash and not paying nobody. Every night, you sit down with twenties and fifties and hundreds and you divide it out with your guys. Everybody you got is walking around with their pockets just bulging with cash.

"Then, when it's over, you really need a rest for a couple of weeks, because you're all spinned out. Maybe it's like an actor with an opening night on Broadway, and he don't know whether the show is going to be successful or not. You've had all this hard work and all this pent-up emotion and then, all of a sudden, you got it.

"So you sit back afterwards and relax and you think of all the things that went through and the things that you could have done better. But it don't matter. It's not a dream anymore. It's reality. You scored!"

This kind of a reaction can probably be extended into an explanation of why a majority of the con men and thieves are almost always broke. No matter how big or how recent the score, they all seem to suffer from a chronic case of "the shorts."

Billy Somerville thought that this condition was because "you just don't consider it your money. In your heart, you know you haven't earned it, so it has no value for you. It's like markers in a game. Taking down a good score, in the right way, is one of the most important things involved because then you're showing how much smarter you are than the turkey."

There must be some truth in Somerville's analysis. Otherwise, there is no way to explain the foolish risks that some con men add to the game in order to lengthen the odds against them. They don't do this as a deliberate thing, they explain that some erratic action was undertaken because "it was funny. It really tickled me."

When Scolnick was printing insurance policies, one of the members of his gang, although he was using a phony name, had

204

his picture printed on the stationery. Scolnick, himself, swears that he was the essence of prudence in every caper, but he still, occasionally, signed flagrantly bogus names to checks he counterfeited. "Harold Fink," as a banking officer, was one of his favorites; and he made the aged clown, "Maestro Joseph Fisher," an officer of many of his corporations.

"It was arrogance," Scolnick says. "All the guys was getting away with so much, for so long a time, it just became a game to see how far you could go."

Somerville was asked, "Billy, you're a young man. Over the years, you've made as high as fifty thousand dollars in one shot. Why are you always broke?"

"I'm not, now," he answered. "Now I got money in the bank. But when I was on the con it was a different story. You take a businessman who gets a five-G sting. He runs to put it in an investment and gets maybe eight percent on his money. That's four hundred dollars. But what use was four hundred dollars to me? I wasn't a businessman, I was a moneymaker and, if I needed four hundred dollars, I'd just go out tomorrow and get it in a dozen different ways. I always knew there was a lot more where that came from. Now I know I got to work to put money in the bank. But I didn't then. I just played games for it. Maybe the reason I feel different now has got something to do with the fact that I'm older. Now I got a wife and a baby, and it isn't a game anymore."

There was no question that the gang considered their activities as a game. Almost every one of them admits that he had a buried realization in those days that there would be an eventual reckoning; but, as Little Murray said, "Sure, I knew deep in my heart that someday I had to take a fall. But I figured what the hell. I'm having a ball, the money is rolling in and, if I have to do a year or so in prison for all this, it'll have been worth it."

"We had parties all the time," Scolnick says. "It got so I couldn't wait to get down to the place in the morning to see what craziness they was dreaming up for the day. We always had a couple of warehouses where we kept the swag and we had some blasts there you just wouldn't believe. They'd get drunk and there'd be naked broads running all over the place. I'll never forget walking in one night and seeing big Murray balling on a fork lift.

"When we really wanted to have some fun, we would go down to Atlantic City. A friend of mine owned a big hotel there and he used to close off some of the floors during the wintertime. I'd make him open up for me, and I'd rent the whole floor just for eight or ten of us.

"One time, Big Murray—naked as a jaybird—gets himself a spear and a shield and he's chasing this broad all over the hotel, going through crowds of people in the lobby and everything. So the guy that owns the joint gets me on the house phone and says, 'Please, Sylvan, give me a break. I'm going to have every cop in Atlantic City here in the next ten minutes.'

"So I tells him okay, and I tell the guys and the broads that I decided we're all going for a boat ride. I call up a place that rents these big yachts—you know, the kind that carries a hundred forty people—and I make them take one out of dry dock —or whatever the hell they call it—and we go out and continue the party on the boat. I was wearing a costume they had gotten me someplace. It was like the eunuchs used to wear; the turban and the scimitar and the baggy trousers, and I went out and waited in the lead car while they got some more broads. You ought to of seen the faces on them broads when I got out on the pier!"

On another occasion, the gang decided to spend a weekend in Las Vegas. Scolnick flew out first with Little Murray who lost no time in turning the flight into four hours of mortification for his boss. He began by driving his car onto the apron where the plane was waiting. A policeman, seeing this, began racing toward them, blowing loud, piercing blasts on his whistle. Naturally, the other embarking passengers and the onlookers in the gallery above watched the scene with great interest.

When the policeman reached their car, Little Murray explained that his boss was so fat, he couldn't walk, and that he was so frightened of flying that he couldn't catch his breath. Both statements were lies, but since they succeeded in turning the policeman into an escort for them the rest of the way, this only whetted Little Murray's appetite for a scene.

Once aboard the plane, he made his way to the pilot's cabin and explained to the air crew that his boss was no ordinary man and needed at least three safety belts—which was another exaggeration.

"In no time at all," Scolnick recalls, "they had radioed the tower and gotten permission to reopen the plane so some extra guys could come aboard and strap me in. I had three or four guys working on me, and there I sat, feeling like a real jerk. But, I didn't want to start nothing with Murray. All I wanted to do was rap him in the mouth.

"Then, after I'm strapped in, he stands in the aisle and looks at me. He hollers out, 'Hey, I never seen nobody that fat!' and then he sits down alongside of me, still hollering, 'What are you, a gangster? Some kind of big racketeer?'

"Now all the people in the plane are stretching forward and backward to look at me, and I see 'em doing double takes and asking each other did they ever see anybody so fat.

"As soon as we get up in the air, he tells the stewardesses that he's my medical advisor and I need at least a dozen steaks for lunch. So they go around telling the other people that whoever don't want their lunch, they'd like to have it for the fat man sitting over there by the wing because he might go into collapse from hunger if he don't get enough to eat.

"They bring me a whole tray full of steaks and I'm so mad,

I won't even eat one. I'm fit to be tied, but I can't say anything because I know, if I start arguing with Little Murray, he'll go at it even more.

"Now, the payoff is, I don't know what he says to the stewardess, but when we land, the pilot says over the cabin radio that everybody should keep their seats. Then the door opens and two guys comes in and gets me and they take me out, and I see this thing; it's like a little tricycle with a pad in the back, and a beautiful girl driver sitting up front. There's no way I can say no; so I go down and sit on the back pad of it and when I do, the whole front end lifts up in the air.

"Now Little Murray really starts hollering. Everybody in the airport was looking. He's yelling, 'He's medically unfit! You're giving him a heart attack. Oh, my poor boss is gonna die from a heart attack!'

"The beautiful girl who was driving was stone scared. She looked like she was going to cry any minute. So what did he do? He goes to the girl and makes her position herself a little bit different. Then, he makes me lay down in the back, so my weight is more forward on the tricycle. He perches himself up on the front and says, 'Let 'er go!' And that's the way we drove to where there was a car waiting for me. I was never so embarrassed in my life.

"What a wild weekend we had! It ended up costing me about seventy-five grand, but it was worth every cent of it. First thing I done, I hired one of the chorus lines. I got six girls and paid 'em two hundred dollars an hour from Saturday afternoon to Sunday afternoon.

"We had a really magnificent suite at the Flamingo Hotel. When we go in, the first thing I notice in the bathroom was a bidet. I'll be honest with you, I didn't know what it was, myself, but I don't say anything because I don't want to appear stupid. But not Little Murray. He comes out of the bathroom wiping his mouth, saying, 'It's really convenient having a water fountain in there, only it's set too low.'

"Most of the time, while they was partying, I was playing blackjack down in the casino. At one time, I was twenty-five or thirty thousand dollars ahead. I had busted out all of the twenty-five dollar chips and they put a rope around the table to keep other players out; and I was sitting there, playing five hands by myself.

"They raised the limit up to one thousand dollars and I'm betting five hundred dollars a hand and pressing everything under eleven, which left me betting three, four thousand dollars a hand. Then, out of the crowd around the table comes a beautiful broad who must have been no more than twenty-five, twenty-six years old. She goes under the ropes and sits down next to me and leans up against me and says, 'My, you smell good.'

"Meanwhile, I'm all excited. I say to the dealer, 'Artie get this whore out of here, will ya? I didn't come here for this kind of crap, I came here to gamble!' Man, it was just like a movie scene. I sounded just like Humphrey Bogart!

"And I sure gambled. I think they sent some mechanics in next, when the broad didn't work, because I ended up stone broke. I got so carried away, I didn't pay any attention to what I knew about the game, which was stupid because blackjack is your best shot when you go to Las Vegas.

"You see, you shouldn't ever fight the dealer. He's only a machine, not a human being. He's got to hit sixteen and stand at seventeen. So, you're not tricking him. All you got to do is never hit anything over eleven, unless you got an ace and a three, or something that makes it worthwhile going for five cards. Otherwise, you got a little edge. You can stick at twelve and he's got to hit fifteen.

"Anyway, we had a good time. We had a lot of good times,

209

though. For two years, there, I was cheating on Ruth pretty good."

His move into infidelity began with an apartment he rented in order to have a meeting place somewhere away from home. When the others would talk about their girls, it was always tacitly understood that Sylvan wanted privacy and whatever he did in the apartment was his own business.

"But you know what I was doing there?" he said. "I was watching television. I'd go over to this place and everybody figured I was moving on my own, but all the time, I was doing nothing but sitting around waiting for it to be time to go home. My secretary, who was going to night school, used to watch the place for me. She'd do her homework there because she was studying to be a bookkeeper and it was a good place not to be disturbed.

"Understand, now. At that time, I was thirty-three years old. I had been married to Ruth over ten years and, during that time, I never even looked at another woman. I was never tempted, never had the desire to mess around. Then for two years, up until the end of 1964, I went crazy and since then, I've never looked at another broad again.

"Sam Koff got me started. I used to go to a nice place for dinner with him, which was some bar out on Roosevelt Boulevard. But that was all. I never went out with him afterward because I was ashamed—you know—my weight. I figured I didn't want no broads laughing at me. But one night Sam says, 'Listen, you go with me and there ain't no worry. Just take your time and do whatever you want to do.' So he keeps bugging me and bugging me and, finally, I go with him. He gets me this girl who was really lovely and, I got to admit, I was so excited, I was through even before we begin. That was the first time, and I felt terrible afterward. I came back home and took four show-

210

ers and I still didn't feel clean. I just didn't know how I was going to get in bed with my wife. I felt like I had done something that was so wrong. . . .

"But I got over it. From then on, every time I got the urge, I got a broad. They was all hookers, but I thought—what the hell, I'm spending all this money on the guys, why not spend some of it on myself.

"I never had to pay those broads after the first or second time. Like Carol. She was stone gorgeous. After we got to know each other, she wouldn't take any money from me, so I used to buy her presents—things for herself. Sometimes she'd call me at the office, just to take her to a drive-in, or something. She'd feel like going out, but didn't feel like going out on the turf. It got so, I was seeing her once a week. But one time, I was down in Atlantic City with her and Big Murray and another girl, and Big Murray was swearing something awful, so I told him to cut it out in front of her.

"He looks at me and says, 'What the hell are you, in love? Do you think you're at the junior prom?' And, with that, he grabs Carol by the arm and says, 'Come here, whore,' and he orders her to do some things, which she did, and it made me sick to my stomach because I had liked her so much. I never wanted her around after that.

"That was the closest I come, in all those two years, for having any personal feeling about the broads. You know, when you see them in the morning, man, I mean, they was broads. In fact, most of the time, after I was done, I used to think, 'Boy, am I sorry I ain't home. Ruth could make me a sandwich, a cup of coffee, or something, and we could watch TV.' But I used to have to sit there and listen to their dumb shit in my ear all the time.

"It all ended one day when I took a good look around and saw what I was running with and the money I was throwing

211

away, and I realized it was totally ridiculous. So I just stopped stone cold.

"Years later, after I got out of prison, one of the guys, who was trying to get me for something, came to the house while I was out and told Ruth she was a damned fool for worrying about me and having it so hard while I was in jail. And then he told her about them two years.

"When I got home that night, after looking upset for a couple of hours, she finally told me about what the guy had said. I answered, 'Ruth, I'm not going to deny anything and I'm not going to admit anything. You believe what you want to believe. You been married to me, going on eighteen years, and you know me well enough to know whether I did anything wrong or not. If I did do something wrong,' I said, 'I was the victim of circumstances. I was with other guys and there was naked women running around. But you know how difficult it is for me to get laid—I got to be in a special position and this and that. Now, you just use your own judgment as to what I did.' "

Before Scolnick would reminisce in this area of his activities, he made his wife leave the living room where he and the reporter were sitting. Although he did not say that he was about to discuss sexual activities, she understood immediately. As she left the room, she noted, "I'll read about it in the book and then it will be fiction, right?"

There are reasons beyond the story for recounting these episodes. There are those who say that Sylvan Scolnick's capacity for evil approaches insanity, but if he were truly psychotic, it would seem that one form of kinkiness or another should stick out of these anecdotes like a sore thumb. Instead, he describes only a fat man who was unsure of himself. He stayed with the whores, although several nonprofessional women have

212

indicated that they were attracted to him by his personality and humor. He was obviously capable of achieving sexual gratification in quite conventional patterns.

Of course, it doesn't necessarily follow that insanity and sexual difficulties go hand in hand, nor does a prosaic marital approach always indicate "normality." This aspect of his personality is introduced here only for the sake of the record.

The term "evil" often occurs in the descriptions of Sylvan Scolnick by his adversaries and victims. But no one ever advanced a specific example of an abnormal approach to life or to others. Several stories were told that he had planned to have one man or another killed, but none of them stood up under a close investigation. There is no question that violence was an element in some of his crimes, but it was never the hinge on which the scheme would swing.

One attorney who had the opportunity to observe him closely over a long period said, "He says he hated violence, but I think that's only because he's so imaginative. He's not a violent man, but he has admired violent people. He's fantasized about them like a kid admiring an athlete. However, this is something that he's unquestionably outgrown.

"He's not even amoral, no matter how often they've said that about him. The only difference between him and the businessman who screws you twenty ways to Sunday is that he never respected the rules of the game that other men drew up. The legitimate businessman or banker gets around those rules in legitimate ways, but he used to feel: The hell with the rules, it's your mind against his. I think that's why he's never been ashamed of the description of 'thief.' As far as he is concerned, that term also describes the businessman and banker who technically stay inside the law, but end up being just as rapacious as Big Cherry ever was."

His personal physician, Dr. William Block, was asked

213

whether Scolnick could benefit from psychoanalysis. He answered, "I doubt it. He's who he is because of what he was; a fat kid, clawing his way up and out of mediocrity. He had a drive that wasn't too dissimilar from many of the successful businessmen that I've treated. But there's nothing about him that needs correction except this drive, and I think he's already begun that by himself. He's really been in a state of flux ever since he left prison. While he was there, I think he came to the realization that he must live within the same rules as the rest of us, and now he's trying to find the ways to channel that drive into more acceptable areas.

"But I never would agree that he needs psychiatric help. He'd pay too big a price; the chances are that he would lose the balance that he has had a hard time achieving. He's a gentle and considerate man and I accept his word when he tells me something. His problem, I guess, has always been that his quick mind and driving need for success has, in the past, made him too impatient to attain his goals through legal means."

Scolnick says, "How the hell do I know what I am? For a while I used the fat to excuse my being a thief. I said, 'Nobody ever give me a shot at doing things the right way.' But now I think that maybe I learned one thing too early; I learned how easy it is to make money by playing off people's dreams.

"I'll put it this way: Suppose tomorrow in a federal prison, it comes over the loudspeaker: 'All inmates who wish to go home must leave the prison by two in the afternoon.' Now, this is Friday. The loudspeaker then goes on to say, 'If you like, you can wait until Monday and the same program will be in effect.'

"I will bet you that seventy percent of those prisoners would stay over to Monday! They would use excuses like, 'I need time to get my clothes and things together,' and, 'I got to see a couple of the guys in the bricklaying class to say goodbye,' and things like that.

214

"You know why they react like that? It's because they're comfortable where they are. They won't ever admit it, but they know who they are when they're in prison. Some men even commit stupid crimes, which they don't realize they done it because they really want to go back to prison. That's where they're somebody. They know their way around, know how to get clean, pressed clothes, feel easy in the routine, and things like that. Outside, they don't know how to get two dollars they don't steal. They have to bum a quarter for a cup of coffee. They don't know it, but their dream is to be safe in prison where everything is taken care of for them.

"Well, if you really understand that principle, then it gets to be easy to move people around. All you have to do is find out what their dream is. It took me a long time to understand what all this means to me, but I finally saw it. My dream was moving people around. Not only for the money, but also for the power that comes with it. So, moving people got to be my own weakness. I was in deep trouble until I got to where I could see that about myself. But they had to put me in prison, where I could think, before I got away from that big-time racketeer crap."

The primary key word to all of the foregoing is probably "arrogance." This term covers the attitude of Scolnick and his gang toward the rest of the world; and one more anecdote describes it all:

Billy Somerville had gone to Florida for a gambling vacation. But the Hialeah Park ponies quickly cleaned him out to the point where he didn't have money left for the plane fare home.

Of course, he wasn't worried. He simply went to the airport and presented a rubber check in return for his ticket. To his surprise, the girl behind the counter refused it, saying that her company was going through a period where they would honor only company checks, since so many of the personal ones bounced.

He began an argument with the girl that was overheard by someone standing in the passenger line whom he had met during his stay at the hotel. This man obligingly lent Somerville some money.

When the man got aboard the plane to walk toward his seat in the tourist section, he passed by Somerville seated comfortably in first class.

# Chapter 12

# THEY FINALLY
# TAKE THEIR FALL

*Your honor, in the last couple of weeks, I think we can't
ignore the fact that there has been quite a bit of publicity about
Mr. Scolnick being arrested on several charges, and I think it just
has to be faced. It can't be ignored. I would like to point out that
taking the allegations that are involved in these charges that we
have read about in the newspapers at face value, it should be
pointed out that the alleged dates of occurrence of these events
were before Mr. Scolnick pleaded guilty to this bankruptcy charge
and it should also be pointed out that these charges are being
vigorously disputed. They are being made by alleged coconspira-
tors who have confessed—to men who have confessed carrying
loaded weapons and robbing people, and it is evident at this point
that they are just going to involve everybody and anybody in an
attempt to save themselves whether it is true or not.*

> —Closing statement of Sylvan
> Scolnick's attorney before Judge
> Higginbotham in the United States
> District Court, October 7, 1966.

217

The gang had operated too flamboyantly and accumulated too many victims.

Their activities had come to the attention of the FBI and various state and local law enforcement agencies as early as 1962.

In 1964 their string of fraudulent bankruptcies was the subject of a *Philadelphia Magazine* story entitled, "Bankruptcy for Fun and Profit." It was written by two investigative reporters named Gaeton Fonzi and Greg Walters, whose references to the Fat Man included:

> There's no doubt that Scolnick has some associations among the very top men in the Philadelphia underworld, but he seems to realize he's in a tough business. He takes care of himself. Often seen in his company is a hood named William ("Slats") Sladko, a former holdup-man and convicted murderer. Scolnick, of course, carries a gun himself, but he still takes precautions, which is why he usually gives the parking lot attendant, at the nightclubs he frequents regularly, big tips to park his car under a bright light.

However, in spite of this story and intensive police surveillance of most of the gang's operations, no prosecution followed until several more years had gone by. And then everything caved in.

It began in late 1965 with a federal indictment of Scolnick for concealment of assets in the M. Stein bankruptcy case and the pressure it brought with it caused the gang to almost tumble over each other in the rush to make a good personal deal by squealing on everyone else. The next two years were a storm of arrests, trials, and convictions for what appeared to be every offense the gang had ever committed, and keeping score turned out to be one of the toughest jobs the prosecutors had.

It serves no point to place these events in chronological

218

order now. It is much more interesting to trace who did what to who.

It was Meyer Mauer, the patient, plodding attorney known as the Bald Eagle, who located and began pulling on the first string in the raveled mess. "Several of our clients," he said, "had suffered heavy losses in some of these bankruptcies and it didn't take too much digging before I discovered that someone, described as the Fat Man, was the common denominator in most of them. Then, coincidentally, the *Inquirer* reporter, Harry Karafin, came walking into my office one day.

"Now, I trusted Karafin about as far as I could throw my left eye. My past experiences with him indicated that no one could completely believe the things he said. But, he was there to propose a deal, so I listened. He said he was authorized by the district attorney to give me a detective to work with me in my investigations—if I would keep them informed of my own discoveries.

"I agreed, but said that I would only give twenty-four hours advance notice of anything I found that he could use in his newspaper stories. He said all right and then he began to boast about what an influential guy he was, that all the big companies had put him on their payroll as a public relations man because they were afraid of him. And, as he rambled on, talking about all his investigative work in the bankruptcies, he mentioned the name of Sylvan Scolnick, which was the first time I had heard that name in connection with the cases I was digging into. Up until that point, I had only heard rumors about a Fat Man.

"The detective the DA assigned me turned out to be an absolutely first-class investigator. There were some charges about him later on, but I never believed them. To me, he was a totally reliable source of information."

219

This detective, Tom Smith, brought Mauer the information that Scolnick carried a gun and that the character witness for the gun permit was Harry Karafin. Mauer, who was sharing his information with the FBI, also learned that Twin City Distributors, one of Scolnick's headquarters and a place often frequented by leading racketeers, had listed the name of its president with Dun & Bradstreet as Harry Karafin.

Mauer says that all of the information given him by Tom Smith was of the greatest help in cracking the bankruptcy ring. "Smith laid it on the line," said Mauer. "He was able to warn me about other pending bankruptcies and I was able to get the creditors out in enough time so that they didn't suffer losses, and he also told me that Scolnick had been pressing him to get out of the case. At one time, Scolnick met Smith and began to abuse him. Smith said that while this was going on, he kept his hand on his gun, hoping that Scolnick would make some kind of a move that would justify blowing his head off."

Scolnick's version of the confrontation with Smith is quite different. "This guy Smith, was really cutting into my business. He was obviously out after my butt, because he was contacting everybody I dealt with. So I figured I'd go to him direct and answer any questions he asked me, but not really give him any information. I had already been told that I had to see Smith alone because he was a bastard and if he was gonna take, it wouldn't be in front of anybody.

"Anyway, through a guy I knew, I set up a meeting with Smith at a road behind the Northeast Airport. I remember it was raining hard, and when I drove up, I got right behind the car he was parked in. He got out and came over and sat down in my car and the first thing he did was put on the radio because the jerk thought the car might be bugged.

"Right off, I asked him, 'What the hell are you looking for? You're causing me a lot of grief and you are working on your own time, as well as the DA's, in order to do it. Now, there is something wrong when a guy works overtime and doesn't get paid for it. What will it take to get you off my back?'

"He says, 'Nothing,' and then he goes into a lot of this and that, which made me realize he was figuring out a price. So I said, 'I want to know what you've got. I understand you are working with the guy from the FBI, and there's going to be a hearing where Mauer and everybody is going to come up with surprises. I don't like surprises. What have you got and what do you want for it?'

"He says, 'Twenty-five grand.' Everybody always has the same figure—twenty-five grand. So, I told him, 'I'd sooner leave you under the wheel of the car, because it just ain't worth that figure. You already done most of your damage.'

"So we talked for a while and he came down to five thousand dollars and agreed that for it he wouldn't turn in nothing too strong, and he would let me know everything they had— in advance of the hearing. I kept my word to him and he kept his to me. I paid him the money in two installments because I didn't want him to think that money could be gotten that easy and, at the hearings, they didn't ask no questions that I didn't know about in advance."

Word of this alleged deal reached the district attorney who promptly fired and then indicted Smith for accepting bribes. However, since Smith was not convicted by the jury, much of Scolnick's account of the transaction is questionable. It was clear that he had advance notice of the facts the creditors were going to present to the referee, but this information must have reached him through other sources. The inference is strong that he hurt Smith with the district attorney because the man had crowded him too hard.

At any rate, the FBI, Mauer and the district attorney's office methodically tightened the noose around Scolnick and his

221

associates. A referee's hearing was held on the M. Stein bankruptcy, and despite Scolnick's advance knowledge, the facts were enough to cause the referee to turn the matter over to the United States attorney for a criminal prosecution. This first indictment was based on "fraudulent concealment of assets" in the amount of approximately $600,000. The looting of the M. Stein company had been Scolnick's first crime and it turned out to be a long-burning fuse.

On June 8, 1966, Scolnick and his associates pled guilty to the charge of concealment of assets, but this was only the beginning. A few weeks after his sentencing, he and Sydney Brooks were indicted for the $100,000 robbery from the safe deposit box at the Philadelphia Savings Fund Society, as a result of information given to the police after a deal made by Tommy Mitchell and Harry Cohen.

The robbery might never have been solved if Cohen and Mitchell hadn't been arrested in connection with a $10,000 holdup. In order to try and get a better deal for themselves on the sentence they suddenly admitted the bank robbery and implicated Brooks and Scolnick the Fat Man.

The four men were tried for the larceny of a tin box. If Cohen had simply switched the boxes the way he had been told by the Fat Man, the robbery, according to the police, might not have been discovered for months and, in the bargain, there might have been no valid charge of robbery at all. As Brooks's lawyer said at the trial, "My defendant is only guilty of removing without violence, his own money from the bank in an unusual manner."

The tin box was worth about two dollars but, in the end, that proved enough for the prosecution to win a conviction against the four. There was even great doubt that any crime had been committed by the violation of the Internal Revenue Service lien because, in the opinion of most of the lawyers follow-

222

ing the case the lien had been improperly obtained in the first place.

The conviction kept Brooks from following through on the final part of Scolnick's plan which involved bringing suit against the bank for its negligent loss of the money that Brooks had entrusted to their safekeeping. Incidentally, Brooks was so pleased with the gall of this last part of the plan that he had already agreed to split the proceeds from the suit on a fifty-fifty basis with the Fat Man.

The idea of a "deal" between the police or a district attorney's office and a criminal isn't necessarily an unsavory one. Many crimes are solved and quite a few crooks, who would otherwise be walking the streets, go to jail because some law enforcement officer was astute enough to trade the promise of a recommendation for a lighter sentence in return for information on other offenses. Two rules generally cover these trades; the information must be of usable value, and the crook must understand that the best the lawman can do is to tell the judge about the cooperative help that was involved. Hopefully, the judge bears this in mind when awarding the sentence and, as a matter of practice, most of them do because they are aware of the law's need for a flow of this kind of information.

So, Mitchell and Cohen, the "Batman and Robin" who had been kept around as comedy relief, made a deal on the bank robbery after they were picked up during an armed robbery spree in suburban Philadelphia and New York. In one Long Island home, they placed a gun at the temple of a child who was a cerebral palsy victim, telling his father that the boy's head would be blown off if all of the family's money and jewels weren't immediately forthcoming. They pistol-whipped a jeweler so severely that the man required extensive hospitalization after they had finished with him, and, on another occasion, stuck up the hotel in which they were staying because they needed pocket money.

These activities were unknown to Scolnick and Sydney Brooks. Until the day that Mitchell and Cohen were caught, the gang told each other funny stories about the pair.

Tommy Mitchell had the distinction of being the first man prosecuted for a bomb scare. He boarded a plane the day the law against this offense was passed and told a stewardess that the transistor radio he was carrying was actually a bomb. He received five years probation from a judge who didn't think he was funny.

Harry Cohen once visited Scolnick's house dressed as a priest and riding a motorcycle. He had a bible under his arm and pistols in the saddlebags. Scolnick wasn't home, but his wife Ruth thought the little man was making a joke when he told her that he was going out on a job dressed like this because no one would suspect a priest and he'd be able to make a clean getaway.

Another time, the two bought, through mail order, a gun that fired tranquilizers into animals that required sedation. They conceived the idea that using this kind of a weapon would eliminate the possibility of accidental murder on their jobs. But, first, they wanted to test it.

They went to a busy street intersection where they saw a man, about sixty-five, waiting for a bus. Walking up to him, Mitchell asked, "How do you feel, Pop?" When the man said he felt well, Mitchell took out the gun and shot him—point blank—in the stomach. As the man fell over, a bus pulled up and the two boarded it and went on their way. Cohen later told Scolnick, "We never did find out if he was sedated. He was bleeding too bad."

Scolnick treated these incidents as only further examples of the pair's desire to become big-time racketeers, but one day

224

Sydney Brooks came to him and demanded that they be stopped or sent away. "They're security risks," he told him.

"Well," said the Fat Man, "I found that kind of hard to believe. At that point, I didn't know they were out sticking up houses and I most certainly didn't know that Sydney had gone partners with them in a couple of the jobs.

"Then he mentions that he had helped them a little here and there and, after talking all around it, he admits that he had set up a couple of things for them and, afterwards, helped move off the swag.

"I asked him where they were and he says, 'They're over at the motel now. They're going out on a job tonight.' So I made him drive me over to the place.

"I waited downstairs while he went up after them. When he comes down, he says, 'Tommy will be right here, but you'd better make it strong. Their room is full of blackjacks and walkie-talkies and shotguns and pistols.'

"So, when Tommy come in I grab him and I say, 'If I find out that you or Harry have anything to do with these busts or stickups or anything like that, I will personally see to it that they cut your head off. I don't want nobody involved with me to be into armed robbery or any of that bullshit.'

"He answers, 'Syl, I swear, I just found out that this is what Harry has been up to. I been up there arguing him out of doing these kind of things.' I knew he was a stone liar, but I told him to go back up and bring me Harry.

"When they return, I said to them both, 'Are you crazy? Don't you realize you are going to jeopardize me and Sydney and everybody that's been around if you get busted with this bullshit you're doing? What do you think this is, a grocery store where you can go take what you want and if they catch you, the lady who owns it will just slap your fingers and throw you out but you can come back in buying again tomorrow? It ain't

225

that way at all! They catch you, they're going to bust your ass all over the place. And, if they don't, I will!'

"Well, they promised me that they weren't going to do that kind of business again, but they didn't keep their word. They just went back out and stole everything in sight, including a bunch of art treasures they lifted in Dallas and tried to peddle in New York."

When they were finally caught, they admitted to enough crimes that they could have drawn prison terms of fifty-five to a hundred ten years. However, the judge sentenced them to three to twenty years in prison, which was an admitted slap on the wrist, but was given in return for the information the two provided on a variety of unsolved crimes, including the $100,000 bank robbery.

The squeals of another caught crook resulted in Scolnick's indictment for subornation of perjury, during this period. Only hints of the seriousness of this crime are evident in his version of the episode.

Brooks and Herman Kutsher had burglarized an expensive center-city apartment. When Kutsher was picked up on suspicion of having committed this caper, he promptly claimed that he had only forced the lock and that sole responsibility for the burglary and the assault and battery that went with it belonged to Sydney Brooks.

"What happened was," says Scolnick, "that while Brooks and Kutsher was robbing the apartment, a silent burglar alarm went off. The building's maintenance man got the signal and went upstairs and caught them at it, but Brooks whacked him around so good with the billy he was carrying that he fractured the guy's shoulder blade. Then he knocked him out.

"Kutsher runs down the steps, but Sydney leaves by way of the main elevator. When he gets to the lobby, he bumps into a guy he knows and later, when they grabbed him and this guy identifies him, he claims he was just visiting somebody he knows in the place. This guy died between the time the job was pulled and the time that Sydney went to trial, so nobody could shake his alibi on that count. As a matter of fact, Sydney got a hung jury the first time they tried him because somebody got up on the stand and swears that he overheard Kutsher say that he had done the job himself, but was pinning it on Sydney because he didn't like him anymore.

"Now, Sydney is out after the first trial, and he's waiting for the second trial to come up. So he comes to me to see what I could do. I thought for a while and I said to him, 'Do you know what would make it a positive win? All we have to do is come up with a guy who would say it was him that was with Kutsher. Such a guy wouldn't get in trouble because, as far as he is concerned, the statute of limitations has already run on the charge of breaking and entering.

"Sydney gets all enthused and asks me if I know such a guy and, as it happens, I do. It's a crazy artist that's been bugging me because he wants to get into the rackets. His name is Chickie Kevan and he's about six foot three and weighs about three hundred pounds. He always wears dark glasses. And he's a little bit mixed up.

"So I get him on the phone and I tell him I finally got something for him to do. He wants to come right over, but I tell him I'll meet him on the corner of Castor Avenue where there's a pizza joint we know, La Strada. He says, 'Great! Shall I bring a piece?' and I said that it wouldn't be necessary right away.

"Me and Sydney drive over and there he is, on the corner, waiting for us. I forgot to mention—he's also got a long, white beard. He gets in the car and I introduce him to Sydney and I say, 'Now, Chickie, I'm going to tell you something. Syd's a friend of mine and he's in trouble.' I run down the whole story for him and then I say, 'So what I want you to do is to take the witness stand and say it was you who was with Kutsher when the robbery took place at Park City West.'

"He says, 'You mean you want me to admit, on the witness stand, I was in a robbery?' 'No, Chickie, I don't want you to say that you went for a robbery. I want you to say that Kutsher came to you and he told you the guy in the Park City West owed him some money but he threatened that if Kutsher came to collect it, the guy would beat him up. You went along to protect Kutsher. So the only crime is breaking and entering and there's a two-year statute of limitations on that, which has already passed. So you ain't in no trouble and, meanwhile, you get Sydney off the hook.'

"Then Sydney says, 'There's five thousand dollars in the package for you, Chickie. We'll arrange a drop at Las Vegas, where a friend of mine will pass you the chips, and you go cash them.'

"Well, Chickie goes for the deal. Next morning, Saturday, we meet to brief him on the layout of the apartment house and what he is supposed to say on the stand and so on and so forth. We hold this in a lawyer's office and we was all standing around and helping brief Chickie. Honest, it was right out of Perry Mason! Everybody was having a party, taking turns at cross-examining Chickie so he'd have the story perfect.

"It was foolproof. The best Billy Wolfe [assistant district attorney] is going to get is a hung jury. No way for anything to happen. At least one member of the jury has got to believe that only a straight guy takes the witness stand to say it was him, but that he was afraid to say anything until now, but he hates to see an innocent man go to prison. He was going to say, 'I only went there to protect Kutsher and after it took Kutsher three seconds to get inside, I come walking in and, before I

228

knew it, there was guys in there fighting and swinging; so I punched a couple, whacked a couple, and the next thing I knew, we ran out of the place.' Everybody was cheering as soon as Chickie got the story right and they were all having a ball.

"Monday morning, Chickie goes on the stand. He was dressed to kill. Sport coat, dark glasses, everything, just like he was going in to get married. He tells his story, how it went, and the courtroom just busts up. Ryan and Schneider from the crimes division are sitting, looking like they wanted to take out a pistol and shoot him right off the witness stand. Billy Wolfe is hollering, everybody is hollering, and nobody knows what to do.

"Only, there was one mistake. Sydney Brooks. Before the trial, I tell Sydney to be sure and take care of Chickie's wife, to give her a few hundred to get her out of town until after the trial. Before we go in, I asked him if he took care of that. 'Oh, sure. I took care of it.' But, because it costs a couple of hundred, Sydney took care of nothing. He's so tight, his ass squeaks when he walks. He's the only guy I know that went to a hospital to get operated on and used somebody else's Blue Cross. The toughest candidate with a dollar I ever saw.

"Anyway, the DA, Billy Wolfe, gets nowhere with Chickie on the stand. When he finishes, he tells the judge he wants the man held on the B and E charge, and the judge says he can't because it's past the statute. So they let him go.

"But the DA ain't finished. That night they grab Chickie's wife. Sure enough, Brooks hasn't given her any money and, anyway, the wife hates Chickie more than Brooks hates Kutsher, so she tells the cops she's positive there's a fix.

"Next day, they put Chickie's wife on the stand and she says she knows that Chickie was home with her that night because it was Valentine's Day and he hit her in the face with a box of candy. Chickie gets so steamed up that he hollers,

229

'That's a lie! It wasn't candy. I hit her in the face with a cake!'

"And that blew the whole story. Later, he told the way the whole thing went down, so me and Sydney also got indicted for subornation of perjury."

Other charges against Sydney Brooks began mounting right after he was picked up on the Park City West job. Kutsher admitted to eighteen robberies and arsons, and named Brooks as having participated in a majority of them. The district attorney said that Mitchell and Cohen, as well as two other witnesses against Brooks, had received death threats. At times, it seemed as if every crook under indictment in the city wanted to come forward to discuss his relationship with Sydney Brooks.

The judge set his bail at $300,000 and this worried Billy Wolfe. He asked the court to reduce this amount to $100,000, saying, "If you put together all the charges against him, it's almost inviting him to flee the jurisdiction."

When the judge refused to take this advice, Brooks lost no time in accepting the "invitation to flee." As soon as a bondsman posted his bail, he left town and disappeared. This was in October 1966.

Some actual newspaper headlines during the following three months encapsulate the next part of his story:

BROOKS SIDESTEPS DRAGNET
SPREAD BY FBI IN CHICAGO

---

FBI LAUNCHES WIDE HUNT
FOR ELUSIVE BROOKS

---

IT'S COSA NOSTRA vs. FBI
IN EXTENDED HUNT FOR BROOKS

230

By the end of October he had surfaced. The next headline read:

BROOKS FLEES TO AFRICA;
U. S. PONDERS NEXT STEP

Evidently the United States didn't ponder overlong. On November 22 a Philadelphia *Bulletin* story was slugged:

BROOKS FRETS IN RHODESIAN CELL;
CHARGES HE WAS 'SHANGHAIED' THERE

The follow-up story was:

BROOKS HAD JOB SELLING INSURANCE
IN RHODESIA, PLANNED TO SETTLE THERE

Three days later the Rhodesian authorities had made up their minds. Since they had no extradition agreements with the United States, the migrant burglar was sent to a place which did:

SYDNEY BROOKS DEPORTED
BY PLANE TO S. AFRICA

BROOKS FLOWN TO SOUTH
AFRICA; SAYS "I'M DEAD"

BROOKS DROPS FIGHT
AGAINST EXTRADITION

On December 3, 1966:

BROOKS FLIES HOME
TO A WAITING CELL

231

·

The story was obviously an exciting one. So much so, that the *Philadelphia Inquirer* sent its ace investigative reporter, Harry Karafin, to write a series of "color" stories on Sydney Brooks's trip back. The story he filed on December 3 began, "I spent a half hour on Friday with an old acquaintance—Sydney Brooks . . . a man I met sixteen years ago when he was tending bar in Philadelphia." The story went on to describe the reaction that Brooks had to the Rhodesian way of life. Evidently, he liked it just fine, but "I could have beat this for years and years. But I called my wife every day, and believe me, Harry, I cried."

Next headline, December 6:

JUDGE ORDERS RECORD $1 MILLION BAIL
FOR BROOKS; TRIAL WILL START ON JAN. 9
*Carroll Scoffs as Burglar*
*Hints He's Short of Funds*

Now, jump forward almost a year. The concluding headline in the series makes the episode complete. On September 10, 1967, a sports-page item of the *Bulletin* was headlined:

DA'S ALL-STARS FACE
BROOKS' ARSON KINGS

and the story began: "The District Attorneys, divisional champs in the Municipal Employees Softball League, have accepted a new challenge from an old face. They're going to play Sydney Brooks' all-star prison team of the State Correctional Institution here."

Everything came tumbling down. Because of the information supplied by Kutsher, Brooks, Sam Koff, Mitchell and Cohen, and almost every other one of his former associates, the mountainous figure of Sylvan Scolnick was now totally visible amid the rubble.

232

His printing plant was raided and all of the employes united in describing him as a master counterfeiter. He was indicted for the $643,000 arson that he had commissioned Brooks to accomplish. He and Brooks were implicated in the highjacking of the trailer load of air-conditioners and, for good measure, the burglary of a wig factory was also placed against their door. Cohen and Mitchell identified him as the mastermind of a "theft ring" and, at their pretrial hearings, said that he had worked out the operational plan for a long list of burglaries. Even the half-million-dollar cashier's check he had given Gazzara to pass came to the attention of the law. The only reason there was no prosecution on the hundreds of phony bank loans and fake deposits was because the statute of limitations had already run out on most of these offenses.

Finally, the Fat Man was going to jail. His planning of the thefts had been models of simple precision, but he had failed to allow for one element—the human one. When a reporter, covering his arraignment, asked him why a man as smart as he was reputed to be, had put so much trust in a covey of songbirds, he answered, "Do you know how hard it is to get good help nowadays?" and the reporter wasn't sure he was joking.

Scolnick says, "Sydney wanted me to go to Rhodesia with him. When I saw on the TV that Cohen and Mitchell had named us in the $100,000 robbery, and that there were warrants out to find 'the mystery mastermind'—actually, I was just sitting home in Cherry Hill—I figured I'd better get myself in order. I had somebody pick me up and I left the house for a few days while I made arrangements for bail and a lawyer.

"During this time, Sydney gets in touch with me. He wants me to go overseas with him. I said, 'You may be going overseas, baby, but I ain't going overseas. I ain't done nothing that bad.' You see, I really didn't expect all the shit to hit the fan at one time.

"But he says, 'Syl, they're going to railroad us and you

don't have a chance.' But I said, 'Look, Sydney, I already gave it some thought and my advice to you is not to breeze. I'm going to surrender myself as soon as I make arrangements with my lawyer, and you're going to get the same bail as me because it's the same charge.'

"So he said okay, and I told him to wait until he heard from me. Then I go to the bail bondsman who had put up for Sydney's burglary charge and I says, 'Lenny, Brooks is going to breeze, so you'd better get off the bail bond—otherwise, it's going to cost you thirty, forty grand.' Lenny asks me if I can get in touch with Sydney and I told him I would, as soon as my own bail was set.

"So Lenny sets my bail. It's fifty thousand with the city and ten thousand with the government. Then I go into a bar and call Sydney and tell him it's all set, but that Lenny wants off the bond. He agrees and arranges with some crooked bondsman to take it over; you know, post a phony bail bond.

"Anyway, they bring me into court to plead on the safe deposit box, and I hear the bailiff hollering, 'Sydney Brooks! Sydney Brooks!' in the courtroom, and I knew he wasn't going to show. And I take a look at Brooks's lawyer standing there, waiting, like a donkey. He trusted Brooks to pay his fee. What a chance he had! So Brooks don't show and I plead, 'Not Guilty,' and the marshals took me up to the Lewisburg Penitentiary.

"Next day, the war ain't on the front pages no more. Everybody's hollering, 'Sydney Brooks has escaped!' Well, you know the rest. He goes to Rhodesia and when they get him, they want him back so bad, they had the President of the United States come into his office on a Sunday to get his extradition papers signed. For a time there, he was the most wanted man the FBI had on their list. He was really hot. But, when I heard he was coming back, I knew he had made some kind of a deal that wasn't good for me."

The indictment of Scolnick became a local circus. The national, as well as the Philadelphia, press enthusiastically chronicled his ingenuity and his bulk, and it was a question which item played the most important part in their stories. When the United States marshal wheeled him into the courtroom on a mail dolly, the wire services sent pictures of the event all over the country.

Almost every headline contained some reference to his weight. One reporter, who had seen the film about a pool hustler named Minnesota Fats, described Scolnick as "Cherry Hill Fats," and this term became a favorite with the editors who wrote the banners, although it was never used by the people who knew him.

He was ideal grist for the newspaper mills; grotesquely heavy, colorful, articulate and reasonably suspected to be the mastermind behind a hundred major felonies. Within a short space of time, he was catapulted from anonymity into unwavering public attention.

At any rate, he was tried and found guilty of charges arising out of the M. Stein fraudulent bankruptcy that he had operated seven years before in 1959. His friend and lawyer, Irwin Paul, defended his father-in-law instead of him during these proceedings.

Paul says, "Sylvan took full blame at the trial. He said that whatever happened, it was as a result of his planning and that his father-in-law had nothing to do with it. What Sylvan wanted the other lawyer and myself to do was to try and get a fair shake for the old man, who was really only a dupe in the situation. He never had the mental capacity to attempt a thing like this.

"I don't know if Sylvan could have beaten the case if he had not pled guilty, because you never know what the prosecution witnesses are going to come up with. In this case, there were such a vast number of potential witnesses that we wouldn't have had the slightest idea of who they were going to put on

235

the stand. We didn't want to advise him which way to plead because, what the hell, we were shooting crap with someone else's life. He made the decision to plead guilty because it was what he wanted to do."

Scolnick said, "Well, it was the right thing. I told the prosecution that I'd cooperate with them if they took the heat off my father-in-law and off Big and Little Murray and the rest. And that's the way it went down. The boys only got one indictment apiece and I told the judge that he could take any consideration he wanted away from me and give it to Pop. That's what he did. Pop ended up only getting four months and some probation."

Little Murray received nine months, a sentence which he obviously regarded as a mild deterrent. He and Big Murray ran another bankruptcy during the time between their sentencing and the date fixed for them to go into jail. "Big Murray give me the bug," he said. "He came to me and says, 'You know, when we get out of jail, we won't have nothing left to come back to.' So him and me gave some guy a few bucks as an option for his business and we worked it up until the time the US marshals said, 'Let's go.' "

The same unrepentant spirit had been in evidence at their sentencing. When the two Murrays and another gang member named Hotsy came before him, the judge asked if they had any good reason to delay the beginning of their sentences.

Hotsy said, "Well, Judge, my son is getting married next month and I'd like to be there. Can I wait until then?" and the judge agreed to the delay.

Big Murray asked for a similar delay because he had a daughter who was due to graduate shortly from high school and he, too, was granted a stay.

Little Murray had no plausible reasons for a request, but, seeing that the judge was in a cooperative mood, he said,

236

"Well, your honor, I been invited to Hotsy's daughter's wedding. . . ." This stay was denied.

Scolnick did not take the matter as lightly. Because of his implication in a number of other crimes, he felt certain that, at the very least, he was going to serve out the full five years that he had been sentenced. And he was aware that jail could be a very special hell for a fat man.

## Chapter 13

# LEWISBURG
# PENITENTIARY

*After sentencing Judge Higginbotham turned down Scolnick's attorney's request that the Fat Man be allowed time to straighten out his personal affairs.*

*Scolnick was loaded immediately into his own automobile which has special reinforcements to support his weight, and taken to the city's Detention Center. Normally, a convicted man is kept there for some time until room is found for him in a Federal prison.*

*Local authorities, however, reputedly balked at feeding Scolnick any longer than necessary on the $6-a-day maintenance allowance paid for federal prisoners. The Federal Penitentiary at Lewisburg, Pa., was said to be readying a place for the Fat Man within a week.*

—From an October 7, 1966,
*Philadelphia Daily News* story,
headlined: "Fat Fraud Gets
Hefty Jail Term."

He remembers:
"When they wheeled me into court on that dolly, I felt

238

what a stupid ass I was. If it hadn't been for the weight, I wouldn't have had all this bad publicity, which was going over onto my family. So, what I did was to tell my wife to divorce me so she wouldn't have the notoriety. Wouldn't be involved in the way they were turning me into a circus. I told her to sell the house and she and Mom go away, but they wouldn't hear of it.

"It was a sideshow. I was Sylvan Scolnick, the freak, with their bullshit stories about how I could eat fifty-four hamburgers and gallons of milk for one meal. There was so much of it, I started to believe it myself when they pictured me as some kind of a monster.

"But, finally, I was able to shut 'em out of my mind. I faced the fact that I really was going to prison and that I was in big trouble. I was worried about my legs; they hurt so bad, and I wasn't able to walk, and I just didn't know how I was going to make out behind the walls. I was jittery. You know, you hear so many stories.

"When I got inside, the first thing they did was take away my identity as a man. They made me strip in front of the bullpen and bend over and spread my cheeks and then hold my arms out, so they can look in the armpits—you know, looking for drugs like some cons try to smuggle in—and everybody was laughing like it was a real freak show.

"But I didn't let 'em know. I didn't complain, and I kept a smile on my face, saying things like, 'Well, maybe I'll get some special treatment for all this.' You know, trying to ward it off by acting like it didn't bother me that much.

"Naturally, they didn't have the clothes to fit me. I couldn't wear their shirts and I couldn't get the pants over my hips, so I had to wear my civilian clothes while I was in the detention center, waiting to go to the federal pen.

"The first night, one of the wardens told the guards to lock me in solitary confinement because he couldn't have me around the jail in civilian clothes, so they put me in a cell that was about four foot by ten. The bed in there was twenty-four inches wide and was bolted into the wall. The mattress was about an inch and a half of rubber foam. I tried to lay down, but there wasn't room for me to get on it.

"So I sat up on it for a couple of hours, and then I started to bang on the door, telling 'em, 'Listen, I can't lay on this bed. There's not enough room for me.' After a while, this major of the guards came in and says, 'Well, sleep on the floor,' and he threw a half a dozen of these rubber mattresses on the ground. But I told him, 'That's no good. If I lay on the floor, I can't pull myself back up. I don't have the ability to lift myself from the ground without help.' He walked out, saying, 'That's the best you're gonna get.'

"It went on like that for a while. The days kept going by and there wasn't anything happening about sending me on to Lewisburg. Then I understood that the US marshals didn't want to use their cars because they had heard so many stories about my weight, they were afraid I'd break the springs in their cars. They had read, I guess, that I had special cars made for me, which wasn't true. The best I ever done was to have the seat moved back a couple of inches so I could get behind the wheel if I wanted to drive.

"I laid there some two weeks and, when they still didn't move me, I started to figure what I was gonna do to get 'em to ship me out. I understand there was a regular hospital at Lewisburg where if I could get some kind of care, I'd start a diet. I felt that whatever time I spent in prison, that I was not gonna let it all be to my disadvantage.

"So that night, I laid on the floor—to make it look like I had fell off the two beds that had been bolted together for me.

240

I laid there all night and, in the morning, the superintendant came up with eight or ten guards and rolled me over onto two of these thick sheets of plywood. It took all of them to stand me up because I said my back was hurt and couldn't help 'em none.

"That was on a Friday. On Saturday morning my attorney came up and he got me moved into the hospital where they had some facilities that was better. But not much better. I still couldn't get into the shower, which was a single stall. So the same major had a couple of inmates come in and wet me down with a hose for me to bathe, instead of letting me come downstairs where they had this big, open shower. They hosed me down like I was some kind of an animal.

"The food was just awful. They'd bring me plates with everything piled on top and mixed with each other and, all the time, the newspapers were running daily stories about what a sideshow I was up at the detention center. They must have figured their readers was anxious to know how a fat man got on in jail.

"The only thing good was the way the other prisoners tried to help me. Prisoners have some sort of a common bond; I don't know if it's against the prison system or the guards or just against people in general, but when another prisoner is sick or really in distress, most of them look to help. One guy used to make my bed and another guy used to bring over the best food he could find, saying, "Kid, why don't you eat something? Don't pay any attention to these fools.'

"But now that I think of it, most of the help came from the black population. The whites were the wise guys. They thought I was a big shot and tried to get in with me so I'd make a connection for them when they got out and things like that. But not the blacks. The colored people honestly cared about you as an individual. Oh, sure, some of the young ones who

241

were in for drugs, got fresh, but the older guys would straighten them out.

"Anyway, they finally let me call my brother, who came up with my car, and he and the marshals finally drove me to Lewisburg. When I got there, they opened a door in the back of the prison and that's where we drove in. Then the others got out of the car and I saw I was on one of those scales they use to weigh truck shipments. So first they weighed my car with me in it and then I got out and, when they just weighed the car, they found that I was six hundred forty-two pounds.

"I was wearing a gray, bulk-knit sweater that my aunt had knitted for me, and they took me into the receiving area and I stripped and they went all over me with a flashlight, and then they took me in an elevator up to the hospital where they had two beds bolted together. I really couldn't walk. I didn't realize it at the time, but I was overdigitalized. The doctors in the detention center had been pumping so much digitalis in me for my heart condition that I just couldn't catch my breath if I walked only a few steps.

"Right off, the prison doctor at Lewisburg asked me if I would go along with a theory he had about diets. He wanted to use me as a test case for a starvation program. I said sure, so they took all my measurements and everything, and started me right in. Within eight months, I had gone down to five hundred five pounds. But, that diet was the only special consideration I ever received all the time I was in the federal pen.

"The first thing I saw in prison was that all they want is not your rehabilitation, but that you shouldn't give them no trouble. You can do anything you want within their framework, but that's where you stay. You don't make waves.

"I learned not to value anything. I didn't let myself put a prize on material things because if I did, this was the way they could punish me or get at me. I've seen men who used to save magazines, maybe they'd have a hundred different newspapers and magazines stored up. And the minute they'd say anything or some guard would get sore at them for something, they'd come in and say, 'Well, you are only allowed to have five magazines in your cell and three newspapers . . .' something like that, and they would take away what you valued, and this was the way they'd punish you. So I found out that if I didn't value anything, there was nothing they could do to punish me. What could they do, take away my pillow? What I mean is, there was nothing for them to take so long as I kept myself stripped of contraband.

"As far as the rest of the prison population, I tried to keep to myself as much as possible. But they must of heard about me because a lot of them kept pushing themselves on me. I don't know what was in their mind. Maybe they were looking for me to tell them how to do it without a gun. In all the time I was there, I must have had hundreds of guys asking me to lay out schemes that guys could use when they got out. But I didn't give anybody anything but general conversation, and all the time I kept thinking to myself, 'Boy, what am I into!'

"I thought that when you go to prison, you do your time and that's that. But when you get inside there and you see who and what you are dealing with, you know that nothing is worth going to jail for. If I could have done it over again, I wouldn't have let me and Ruthie have clothes on our back rather than do something that gets you in prison. I was dead bang wrong, dead bang wrong. After I was there a month, there was no doubt about it in my mind. No amount of money is ever enough to go to prison for.

"That's not only because of what it's like, physically. It's also because of the people you're living with. It's full of people that have no understanding of what life's all about. They have no values, no understanding, no respect. A guy gets cut, his arm is hanging off, and some of them will laugh. There's degenerates, perverts and rape artists; and it's like they're my brothers, my pals. Everybody travels together, all brothers of the sword.

"And pretty soon, you find that their values don't seem so lopsided to you any more. The place is full of homosexuals and you start to think that homosexuality is normal. A guy would call himself 'Susie' and I start calling him 'her' or 'she' when I made reference to him to somebody else. A guard would say, 'Where's Parker?' and I'd say, 'She'll be down soon, she went up to the nurse to get medication.'

"It's unbelievable. I had one of them come into my cell to give me a rubdown. My back was bothering me. So she'd come in and make it feel better and one time, I swear, I got an erection; so I chased her the hell out of there.

"They all wanted to be around Big Cherry. 'How ya doin, Cherry?' and 'I want to be your friend' and things like that. I tried to treat them the same as I would anybody else and I talked to them on their level. So, soon, I got to believing in it myself. It's like when I play with a poor chess player, I play poor. When I play with a better chess player, I play better. See, you find yourself on the level that everybody else is if you stay in prison long enough. It's awful tough to fight.

"There's a lot of problems in prison, but homosexuality is one of the toughest. Most of the prisoners went that route. At night you could hear the mattresses being thrown on the floor so they could make love to each other without anybody hearing the springs working.

"I've seen new prisoners coming off the van and the old-timers standing there by the windows looking, and guys saying, 'He's mine,' and, 'I'll give a carton of cigarettes for that one.' They'd be buying and selling the new guys before they were even into the population.

"And the new guys would be scared to death. What happened, usually, is that an old guy would give a new guy some candy or cigarettes because they hadn't been allowed to go to the commissary yet, and the new guys would take it, not realizing that later there was going to be demands made on him for his manhood.

"The first time after that, when the old guy approaches the young guy, he generally gets fought off because he hasn't picked the right time and spot just yet. Then later that night or the next day, or whenever the time is right, five or six guys will grab him and gang-bang him. Rape him. After that, the kid is so scared that he'll pick one of the tougher or bigger men because he's made up his mind he'd rather have just one rather than five or six gang-bang him. And the kid becomes a homosexual. He starts referring to himself as 'Susie,' and I guess that stays with him for the rest of his life.

"The only time I was ever approached was once in the hospital. There was a white fellow, about thirty-eight, who played the piano just beautiful. He was a ward nurse. One night I was lying on my bed and, all of a sudden, I realize there's somebody else in the room. It's this guy, wearing a white, terry cloth robe and he's dancing quietly all around, letting his terry cloth robe flop open so I could see he wasn't wearing anything. When he got close enough, I grabbed him by the neck and said, 'Look, I don't want none of this shit, now or ever!' and I gave him a push that sent him spraddling over the floor. After that, none of them bothered me that way again.

"I've seen guys that were laying out, half dead, on a bed in the hospital ward, and some of these homos would pull him out and take him in the back and do everything they could think of to him. The guy would be so sick, he couldn't defend himself, or even know what they were doing.

"And the guards know what's going on. I've seen a lot of men complain to them that somebody is propositioning them, and the guard says, 'There's nothing I can do about it, unless he does something.'

"A lot of the guards are homosexuals themselves. They'll go into the cells to get themselves laid. You would hear them talking when they get together and they're laughing about this guy got knocked off, or they're gonna get this other guy, and it's a big joke.

"You see, when you're out on the block, the guard is supposed to keep all the cells locked so nobody can come back into their cell. But the guard leaves a few doors open in the back, so the guys can go in and take care of their business. Some of the cons prostitute themselves for the guards so they can get special favors.

"This is what I mean when I say that when you live in a lopsided society, pretty soon you start thinking lopsided yourself. You aren't surprised any more about men sleeping with men, or involving themselves in oral sex. Out on the street it's against society, but inside it's an everyday occurrence and there's nothing strange about it. Inside, men send love notes to other prisoners; 'I love you and I'd like to get hold of your body,' things like that. And you see men that gets three dollars a week from their wife or a mother or father, who are poor people, and they take that money and spend it on a fagot—just so they'll have a girl friend, somebody to get love letters from.

"One old guy, he must have been in his fifties, told me he'd rather have a young boy than a woman, any old time. He enjoyed it more and, he said, he could love a boy more than he ever loved any woman. At first I thought he was kidding around, but he wasn't. He meant it.

"In the beginning, I used to think this was funny because I didn't realize how deep-rooted and serious it really was. But then I saw it for what it was; a world full of people who were totally sick. They thought, for instance, that if they delivered

246

the penis instead of receiving it, that made them no homosexuals, but real virile men! They'd laugh at me and say, 'Ah, you just don't know what good is, Cherry,' and after just a little while, I stopped trying to reason with them. I minded my own business. Sure, I'd have wet dreams once in a while, but I had too many other things on my mind to get myself bogged down with their bullshit. That's all they had.

"There's other guys in prison. Take the repeaters. I guess that maybe seventy-five percent of all prisons is full of guys that have been there more than once. You know why? Because when a guy gets probation or parole and goes out on the street with maybe thirty cents in his pocket, all they say is, 'Good luck, and we don't want to see you again.'

"What's he gonna do? He's got no job. No place to go because, in a lot of cases, his wife has left him, so he goes to the least line of resistance. He goes out and sticks somebody up because he's tired of having no dough and holes in his clothes and just flops to sleep in. He don't have a trade or a job to keep him. He's just got to go back to dope or being a burglar or whatever.

"Prison looks good to them. Back there, they know what to do. They're jail-wise and they can wear pressed pants and pressed shirts with creases in them so sharp they'd cut cheese. They get swag, special food from the kitchen where their pal works, and they know how to act with the rest of the population because everybody is in the same boat. So in their hearts they're glad when they come back. In a sick kind of way, they're home again.

"What they should do is to have some real experts on the parole boards. Maybe social workers, or guards who have already worked in the prisons. They'd know when a guy should get out. I've found that when a man is in prison, he generally reaches what they call a peak in his rehabilitation. That's the

247

point where he's ready to be released, ready to do the most good for himself and for society. If he isn't released then, because of notoriety or because some parole board doesn't really understand penology, then he starts to decline. He'll go back to crime whenever they do get ready to spring him.

"There's got to be some change made. Otherwise, instead of having a grocery store on every corner, you're going to have a prison on every corner. The answer can't be with hiring thousands more policemen, with finer guns and finer weapons. They already got all of those that they need. There's got to be a better answer than that.

"How the hell can you decide what prison is or what it should be, if you've never seen the inside of one? People read about prisons and the rapes and the homosexuality and unbalanced diets and no medical facilities or sports or schools, and they say to the wife, 'Gee, isn't that horrible?' and then they close the papers and forget about it. The only way it bounces back at them, is when their kid or their sister or brother is arrested. And then it smacks them—right in the face.

"You got to do something about these men. They could be human beings if people just cared about them. But nobody cares. There's no instruction, no trades taught; except some half-assed thing in cooking and cleaning and mending clothes. I offered to teach some shorthand, and they didn't want to hear about it. I offered to teach real estate, Spanish, anything I could do, but the authorities didn't want to hear anything at all. They just don't want nobody to rock the boat. They figure they got it going along fine just as it is. That is, until an Attica or one of them kind of riots busts loose.

"Anyway, I seen what was going down, so I kept mostly to myself. Oh, I made a few friends. I played a lot of chess with a colored fellow named Knight. He was about the best chess player I ever seen in my life. I didn't know much about chess at the time, and I got started with this Knight by one time meeting him in the dental lab.

"We got to talking and I asked him, 'What do you do around here to pass the time, besides talk about jail and stealing?' and he said, 'Well, I play chess.'

"I said, 'I just started and I don't know whether or not I can play well enough to give you a game, but if you don't mind taking a shot at it with me. . . .' And he said that was okay with him. Then I got into it, and we played whenever we could. Sometimes we played eight, ten hours a day. And when we wasn't, I got all the books I could, to read about it and study up on it. That was better than listening to all that bullshit about who you robbed and who you figured to rob and who drove big Cadillacs. There was really no conversation you could have, except with some guys who were in there like Di Angelis, the big salad oil king, and Jimmy Hoffa. I learned a lot about life from chess. You learn to put yourself in the other guy's position. What would you do if you were him, and how you try to foreread what they're gonna do and the plays they'll make. How to counteract, you know, try to lead 'em into one area and then actually strike from another.

"I also learned from Jimmy Hoffa about how a major leaguer really carries himself. We played chess together a couple of times, but we never got close because he never wanted anybody to get too close to him. He didn't bother people and he didn't like people bothering him. When he talked to a guard, he said, 'Yes, sir' and 'No, sir' and that was all. No conversation, and he never asked for special favors. He was satisfied with being left alone; all he wanted to do was be nothing special, just another inmate.

"He never asked me anything personal, either. A lot of guys would question me about how much I weighed or how I figured out jobs, but not him. It's a funny thing about people

249

who have been to the top rung of the ladder. Their thinking is different. They never pry into your personal life. Intelligent people just don't ask personal questions. They figure if you want to say something, you'll say it.

"The only stranger I ever really got close to was this colored fellow, Knight. He was about twenty-six and he was in for using drugs. We used to play chess every single day, and at night we'd sit and write letters home. We would eat together and talk together, about everything other than prison. He was the first man I met in prison that I felt really had ability. He never had a chance on the outside, but he knew what it was all about. He'd talk business to me more intelligently than a lot of businessmen I had come up against on the outside. He would also tell me what it was like being black and on the loose in New York City. The pimps and the whores and how they operated and what drug dealing was all about. He'd explain to me the weights and measures they used and how he'd seen men take a shot at dealing for a couple of months and end up with thousands and thousands of bucks.

"I found that fascinating from the viewpoint that some kid in his twenties can make himself six figures in a month in a business that was totally set up to destroy people. I've seen some of the things that drugs does, and it's anything but pretty. I think more of somebody that beats somebody in the head or takes a shot at another man than I do of somebody who sells drugs to other people. Man, there's no humanity left when you get down on that level!

"Poor Knight. Nothing ever worked out for him. After I left Lewisburg, I heard he went to another prison and he got sick and they had to cut his leg off. I saw him only one more time after that. He was passing through Jersey, so he stopped in Cherry Hill to visit me. He wouldn't take any money from me, but he liked my sunglasses, so I gave them to him, and I never heard from him again.

250

"But he sure taught me a lot. I remember once I was playing a white guy named T.V. Charlie, who claimed he was some kind of a chess champion on the outside. Well, I was holding my own with him and then, somehow, he got in a game with Knight. He kept saying how he was going to slaughter Knight and, finally, they bet two cartons of cigarettes on the game. You know, in prison you never count money. Everything is paid for in cigarettes. It's the only currency there. Anyway, Knight knew how to pace himself. He never played any better than he had to because he didn't like to flash. He kept himself to himself, like Hoffa. Neither one of them ever went around the prison in them starched shirts or sharp creased trousers like the rest of the guys, trying to show themselves big shots. Both of them were satisfied just to be part of the population.

"Anyway, I said to T. V. Charlie, 'You want to play this kid, you're on your own. I won't take no part on your bet, because I think he's too good for you.'

"Then I watched. Charlie never stood a chance. The kid just slaughtered him. After it was over and he collected his bet, him and me were walking away and he said to me, 'Cherry, when I beat this Charlie, I had two things going for me. I not only play chess well, but I got the need to win.' I said, 'What do you mean?' and he answers, 'You're twenty times stronger when you *have* to win. I couldn't afford to lose because I didn't have any cigarettes to pay him if I got beat.'

"That taught me something important. From then on, I always carefully watched people who had to win. You got to be twice as careful when you're up against somebody who has to have something very bad, because you never know which way they'll go to get it. There's no way to chart them because they got a terrible need to win, which is pushing them on.

"Knight was a big influence on me in prison. He was soft-spoken and he never tried to get into my life and I never tried to get into his. We respected each other, and all that

251

counted was that he was extremely intelligent. I mean, that's all that counted in turning him into a good friend as far as I was concerned. He never tried to change himself into anything but what he was and that was all right because he, himself, respected what he was; never mind what anybody else thought. He didn't have to make himself into a big shot. And I respected that because I remembered how many times I had tried to create the illusion in other people's minds that I was a big shot, and how sour a taste it had left in my mouth. I learned from him to be satisfied with who you are and that is a very important lesson.

"And then, of course, there was Tommy Mitchell and Sydney Brooks. Yeah, they were in there, too. I played chess with Tommy a couple of times, but I never said anything about what I felt or what I thought. I didn't care any more what he had done. It was over and I was willing to sit down and play chess with him, as long as the conversation stayed general.

"As for Sydney, I still felt a friendship for him. When he did the singing about me, I guess I felt he did what he had to do. He was wrong, but we all make mistakes. A couple of times he wanted to talk about it, saying that it didn't go down the way the newspaper said, but I always discouraged discussing it with him. What the hell, we were both in trouble and it would be like two skunks pissing at each other. The more you piss, the more you stink. Talking about what had gone down wouldn't prove anything. It was all past, so it didn't matter at that point, anyway.

"Matter of fact, we even got to be better friends in prison than we had been on the outside. He used to keep an electric skillet in his cell and we'd fry pork chops and onions and french fries. Sometimes we had a lot of fun. He kept them things stashed away in a false compartment built into the cupboard where you're supposed to keep your clothes. One of the guards

252

was a pretty nice guy and he'd come in at night and we'd plug in and start cooking. The 'refrigerator' was the window.

"And while we were together there I came to understand that Sydney was a real man. He was the kind of guy that when he done something, he was willing to say it was him and there was no con about how he didn't mean to do it. I enjoyed talking with him because there wasn't any of this bullshit about what was going on in jail and who remembers when this lieutenant was a guard in that other prison and all that kind of crap that everybody else went in for.

"We used to play gin rummy together and I would boff him out something awful. He thought he was the greatest gin player going, and I used to clean him regular. At one time he owed me over a hundred cartons of cigarettes, but being Sydney, he never paid me. If he had, I'd a smoked myself to death so that was one time it was okay that he was so tight.

"That fault of his, about being so cheap, was probably Sydney's biggest, single weak spot. It always kept him in the minor leagues. He'd never invest in a legitimate business venture unless there was a back door for him. When he ran the bars, his back door was burning the place down for the insurance when it wasn't doing so good.

"He could also be totally obnoxious. I had a pretty good relationship with most of the guards because I didn't look to abuse anybody or ever try to make anybody feel too small. In my own mind, I always felt that a guard's job wasn't anything that I would want to do, but I can understand if a guy doesn't have the ability to do anything else. A guy has to eat and if you had to make your living being a guard, well, that's okay, because it's better than going around and getting it with a gun. But not Sydney. He was abusive. He was arrogant and he didn't care whose feelings he'd hurt. He'd tell them they were bums who couldn't get anywhere except in prison and make fun of

253

the way they'd talk. They'd take it from him, because most of them were afraid of Sydney, and he pressed it every inch of the way. He could make a guard feel like two cents, if that's the way his mind was working that day. I'd say, 'Sydney, why don't you cut that out?' and he'd say, 'Ah, screw him,' right in front of the guard. And most of them took it, too.

"There was this retarded fellow, Gierch. Sydney would even make fun of him, too . . . make him scrub the floor or walk around with his pants pulled down, things like that.

"Gierch had been off and on in prison since he was sixteen, when they got him for stealing a bicycle. Now, here it was, twenty years later, and he still couldn't read or write. So what I did, was to take some index cards and put an *A* on one and *B* on the next—right on down the alphabet. Then I pasted pictures I cut out of magazines on each card which had a subject starting with the letter on the card, and I used these to teach him the alphabet. Then I taught him to count up to twenty, so he would know how much cigarettes cost and be able to get himself a couple of little things, without having to get somebody to do it for him.

"And I made myself a pain in the ass for the social service department; you know, bugging them with, 'He don't belong in prison,' and this and that; and, after a while, they started taking him to a ball game now and then and then they finally released him to some kind of a home where he got care and, as I understand it, is getting along pretty good.

"I used to pay Gierch to make my bed for me, so he would understand about having a job. That got to be a little problem because when I was tired and wanted to take a nap in the middle of the day, he'd come in and make me get up, and say, 'No, Cherry. I got to clean the cell. This is my work and I got to do my job right.'

"Poor Gierch."

254

# Chapter 14
# HIS TURN TO SING

*Sylvan Scolnick, a 640-pound criminal mastermind, had made a fortune running a fraudulent bankruptcy ring in Philadelphia until the Government caught on to him a couple of years ago. In fact, the Government did not really move in on Scolnick and the ring until the* Philadelphia Magazine *exposed the ring in May 1964.*

*In any event, Scolnick was sentenced to five years and early this year began "cooperating" with the District Attorney's office in Philadelphia. Among many other things, Scolnick began to talk about his relationship with Harry Karafin. According to the* Inquirer, *Scolnick's singing, performed with "ill-disguised gusto" has put the reporter very much in the soup.*

—From a *New York Times*
story headed "The Press,"
April 23, 1967.

While Sylvan Scolnick was away in prison, the two women who loved him continued to live together in the house in Cherry Hill.

255

It wasn't easy. Although Ruth went to work as a secretary and his mother continued as a sewing machine operator, most of the money, plus the few thousand dollars he had kept out of the millions he had stolen, now went down the chute of his legal and other expenses. He needed $5000 to pay the fine the government had assessed as part of his sentence in the M. Stein case, but raising it was out of the question. The men he gave expensive cars or kept on the payroll had dropped completely out of sight.

He had been proud of his friendships with the gangland chiefs, but none came forward with an offer of help for his wife or mother. He had made a deal with some of his associates that if he shielded them from the rap, they would—in return—take care of his wife and family. Not one of them honored this pledge. His closest friend, Billy Somerville, went to Florida to work a new scam and, occasionally, called them to see how Sylvan was making out in prison. But he never volunteered help, nor would the two women ask for it. Later he said, "How was I to know that a couple of hundred bucks would have meant something to them?"

Each Sunday, the two drove from Cherry Hill to Lewisburg, Pennsylvania, to visit Scolnick. The distance for the round trip was five hundred miles and they took turns at the wheel because, by making the trip in a day, they saved the money that a motel room would have cost.

But he never knew of any of this. He'd meet them in the visitor's room and ask, "How are things going?" and the answer was always a smile and, "Great." They knew how dependent he had been on them for his bodily needs and did not want to increase the emotional pressure on him as a prisoner.

And then Ruth had a severe heart attack; a coronary.

His mother recalled, "One morning Ruth got up and she said, 'I don't feel well, Mom, I don't think I'll go to work today.' But I didn't like the way she looked so I called Dr. Block

256

right away and said she had terrible pains and to come right over. He was there by seven o'clock and he gave her a shot and said to call him again if she didn't feel better, but that he was going to reserve a bed in the hospital, just in case.

"Well, I watched her for an hour and she didn't sleep and her condition kept getting worse. Then she sat up and said that a terrible pain had just grabbed hold of her and that frightened me, so that I got her dressed and drove her to the hospital.

"I couldn't believe it. After they put her in bed and got her to sleep, I just stood there and, finally, I cried. I thought, 'How can I hold on any longer? If Ruth goes, what will happen? I got nobody else.'

"I just looked at her laying in that bed and the tears just wouldn't stop coming. I was crying about my whole life and what it had been. For forty-five years I had never known what it was not to work, and now I didn't know who to turn to. I couldn't go to my other sons, their families need them. Where could I get any more help for Ruth even if she came back to me, or Sylvan, if there was any chance for him?

"But we came through it. Ruth finally got well enough to come home. I couldn't leave my job to stay with her, so I hired a maid; and to this day, I don't know how I squeezed out the forty-five dollars a week to pay her salary.

"I couldn't even sell the house because people felt it was Sylvan Scolnick's, and all anybody would offer was less than the mortgage I had to put on it when Sylvan went away."

But her strength took them through. After a lengthy convalesence, Ruth recovered and went back to work. They told Sylvan it had been a minor attack and that although she was recovering rapidly, the doctors did not want her to drive the long, weekly trip until she had completely mended. This generated a strong desire in him to secure a transfer to a prison nearer to his home.

At this point, the two women met the young lawyer, Stanford Shmukler, who had already achieved prominence in Pennsylvania through his appearances for the defense in criminal cases.

Shmukler says, "I was first consulted by Sylvan's wife and mother in November 1966. I had read about him in the papers, of course, but since most crime news isn't very accurate, I didn't go into it too far. All I knew about him was that he was connected to the theft of enormous sums of money and had been wheeled into his trial on a mail hand truck.

"By asking around, I heard the rumors that Sydney Brooks had been sat down by the DA, given a pencil and paper, told to spill his heart out, and that he would get a deal if he cooperated. Everyone agreed that he was implicating Scolnick as had Harry Cohen and Tommy Mitchell.

"After examining the charges and evidence in the $100,000 bank robbery, I thought there might be a chance of winning the case. Everything in it was based on the testimony of this nut, Mitchell, who I thought I could tear apart in a courtroom. I understood that Cohen would not be a very effective witness and I didn't think that Brooks would be testifying. I was sure that when I said to a jury, 'Look at this grotesque seven hundred-pound man sitting there. Does he look like a mastermind?' They would go our way.

"So I went up to Lewisburg to see Scolnick. I said to him, 'Sylvan, if you want me to represent you, you've got to tell me the absolute truth. You can't hold back on me, because if we want to work out a deal, I need to be able to speak fully and openly to the DA's office. I will never enter a plea of guilty without making a full disclosure. There can't be any half-truths.'

"He agreed, and I went on. 'Now, I've never represented a man who turned state's evidence just to save his own neck.

258

I've never represented a fink and I don't want to start with you. But you are already the object of three people who have turned on you; Brooks, Cohen and Mitchell. They're trying to save their own necks, and there's nothing dishonorable in you trying to save yours. But you must remember, the judge doesn't have to give you leniency—no matter how much you tell the DA. Maybe the best you'll get is a lighter sentence because you've saved them the expense of lengthy trials.'

"Well, he agreed, and after a while began to talk openly. I think I was there with him for about four hours and during that period he gave me some material of a fairly substantial nature not only on the matters for which he was indicted, but also information involving other people who were fairly prominent in the city. This intrigued me and I saw the possibility of maybe getting him better than just a light sentence.

"When I came back to the city, I went out and checked his statements with some of my own sources. Although he gave me no false information, I did find out that some of this first information consisted of half-truths. So I went back to confront him with this and told him that I wouldn't represent him if he kept this up. After that, he was completely candid with me.

"Then I checked with the DA's office. I think it was Bill Wolfe who said that the only way they would make a commitment would be if Sylvan gave them something of 'star value.' That's the phrase he used.

"When I relayed this to Sylvan, he said, 'Fine, let's go' and began to talk. During this and a series of other meetings, he gave me many hours worth of hard facts, including some startling material about Harry Karafin which, I thought, certainly was of star value.

"I was fully convinced at that time that he was telling me the truth and that he never, thereafter, held back or lied to me. In the five years since then, I have found him to be completely

259

straightforward and honest in his descriptions of things he did during his career.

"There were many instances where he would tell me the same incident in almost exactly the same way; giving dates, details and facts that never varied. He couldn't be lying about those things. I think, many times, he glosses over areas that are embarrassing or sensitive and it takes some probing and prodding until the full picture comes out. But he's not a pathological liar because that, in my book, is someone who doesn't know how to tell the truth.

"At any rate, I was his only hope at this point. I started negotiations with Dick Sprague, the first assistant DA, who is an honorable guy. I had to start with Sprague and Arlen Specter, the district attorney, because I knew we were going to get into some very sensitive areas—actually involving some public officials—but after I had generally outlined what I was going to deliver, they gave me the approval to work with Bill Wolfe, who was the head of the city's organized crimes division.

"Thereafter, we got down to specifics. We worked under the agreement that everything Sylvan gave them would be off the record, and if the material turned out to be as valuable as we anticipated, they would then enter a recommendation [for leniency] which we would jointly agree upon. If it wasn't of value, then all the notes of these materials would be destroyed.

"Well, it didn't take long before they saw they had a gold mine in Sylvan. We entered into an agreement that Sylvan (who was under a five-year federal sentence, which meant that he'd be out in three and a half years if he served good time) would get a substantial break from them on any state or city offenses.

"Now, at the same time, the federal authorities got interested in having Sylvan cooperate. He had a lot of information that they wanted because they began to see that there was a pattern in fraudulent bankruptcies developing all over the

260

country. But, unfortunately, it is very difficult to negotiate with them because US attorneys do not control the sentencing or the parole boards in any way. All they can do is make a recommendation which you can't count on. Obviously, you are better off dealing with the state authorities.

"So, we were torn between the state and the federal prosecutors. Both of them had an interest in him. The best we were going to get from the federal would be an early parole, but there was no sense in getting a federal parole while he still had all these state charges hanging over him. He would just have gone from one jail to another. By dealing with the state, we had the chance of holding his whole time in prison down to three and a half years.

"Finally, Dick Sprague and I agreed that he would recommend a sentence for Sylvan of three to fifteen years, to run concurrently with the federal sentence . . . and this meant that he wouldn't be getting any time for all the offenses that the state had on him. The only question left was whether he would serve the time in a state or federal prison because there was no question that he would be in a dangerous position after giving so many people up. Since there is more control in a federal prison, that's what I asked for. After all, it isn't hard to get a lifer in a state prison to kill or hurt somebody who has a contract out on him for talking.

"Well, Sprague and I agreed in all details and we dictated a memo—of which there was only one copy made. Sylvan, Sprague and I signed this and we gave it to Sprague for safe-keeping because if anything happened to me, there would be no question of the kind of a deal we had made. As I say, Dick Sprague is a very honorable guy.

"Now that that was locked up, we then made our deal with the federal authorities. Sylvan agreed to testify against Brooks and the others in return for a recommendation by Sprague to the sentencing judge that no additional sentence [to the one he had already received for the fraudulent bankruptcy offense] be imposed. And, ultimately, that's what happened. Dick Sprague even appeared in court and personally made this recommendation to Judge Higginbotham.

"And, of course, Sylvan did end up by giving the federal authorities hundreds of hours of valuable information concerning bank frauds and other bankruptcies. He also was able to get some of his former associates to give them information.

"All of this was of such value to the state and federal authorities that, actually, over the next three years, he spent very little time in Lewisburg. Most of the time he was down here in Philadelphia, testifying, and because of the great problems in transporting him back and forth, they finally just kept him at the detention center. From there he'd be taken down to the Philadelphia City Hall, sometimes as many as five days a week, where he would work with the various district attorneys. As a matter of fact, he spent the last part of his sentence at the House of Correction, right here in Philadelphia."

Scolnick's version of this episode contains the dimensions that are missing from his attorney's description of the deal that earned him a lighter prison sentence.

"First of all, you got to know," he says, "that if I had sat down in the beginning to give them what they wanted, I could probably have got off with a suspended sentence, not spent one day in jail. But, I had made an agreement with my friends, guys like Koff and the rest, that if I took the weight, they would see that Ruthie and Mom had everything they needed. There was supposed to be a minimum of two hundred dollars a week come to the house for as long as I was away.

"Well, the first thing that went wrong was that the judge didn't let me have any time to settle my affairs. I went right to jail from the courtroom. They said it was because they thought

262

that Tommy Mitchell's and Harry Cohen's life would be in jeopardy if I was out on the streets. They were afraid I would kill them or have them killed.

"So here I am in jail and the first thing I know, in comes the guy who was US attorney at the time, and he wants to know about Brooks and the BR's and that other stuff. But I just chased him out. I told him I'd do my five years and that would be that.

"Then, Ruthie and Mom gets Shmukler up to see me. By this time, I have started to hear some things. A guy who was in another jail had a way to get to a public telephone. He used to call me through a connection I had developed at Lewisburg and he'd give me the news.

"He told me that Koff and a couple of other guys had backed down on their word to Ruthie. The first week they showed up, they give her one hundred dollars. The next week, it was sixty and, after that, nothing. I also heard that Karafin had made a statement in one of the bars that, 'I could help Sylvan, but screw him. Whatever he gets is too good for him'; and that was something else that added to the load. Everybody on the outside had froze. They all ran from the sinking ship.

"So when Shmukler talked to me about cooperating with the DA's office, I only mentioned Karafin, but I hinted at the rest. I really didn't have too good an opinion of Shmukler. It just didn't make good sense to me when he said he wanted to know all about everything I was involved in. Why, I mean, how do you tell a lawyer what you ain't been arrested for? Bad enough I got to tell him what I been arrested for. So I tell him some things—mostly what's past the statute of limitations— and he leaves to meet with the DA.

"Then he came back and said that I had lied to him and that he wouldn't defend me if there wasn't any trust between us. He told me some things that he found out, three of which

263

only Sydney Brooks knew. I know it meant that Sydney was cooperating with the DA. So I figured, what the hell, I didn't owe nobody any more than their word was worth, and they were proving how much that meant; one gang by singing and the other by the way they stiffed Mom and Ruthie. I realized that the only allegiance I owed was to my family. So I gave the whole story to Shmukler and he took it from there."

"We increased the pressure on Scolnick with a parade of warrants," says Richard A. Sprague, the first assistant district attorney of Philadelphia. Sprague is one of the most respected criminal prosecutors in the country. He is thought of so highly that other communities ask to be represented by him whenever a particularly important criminal case arises in their courts. The latest such request came from a mining center which asked the governor if Sprague could be made available to help them get a murder conviction against a group of men who had been accused of killing a prominent union executive. He is an implacable, thoroughly straight district attorney whose name is enough to frighten crooks and worry their attorneys.

He says, "When Scolnick was convicted of his basic sentence [in the M. Stein case], one of the steps undertaken by our office was to step up the pressure on him to the point where he had to cooperate in order to help himself. By having a parade of charges placed against him, we put him in the position where he saw that he had to do this. He had to see that if he didn't cooperate, we would have banged him so hard it would have been snowing in July before he got out of prison. This process began before the sentencing and was continued until he eventually gave in.

"Don't misunderstand when I say pressure. We had already learned of Scolnick's involvement with crime and his connection with other criminals. As a result, our pressure was to have him open up concerning his own involvement and contacts with others wherever that would lead to. This was put, not to Scolnick, but to his counsel. And, if his stories could be corroborated, we'd discuss an agreement as to his sentence. And this is what set us ahead. Thereafter, as far as I was concerned, he was completely truthful."

The parade of charges mentioned by Sprague fills three solid, single-spaced pages in his attorney's file. Had all of the possible sentences been imposed, Scolnick could have served a minimum of one hundred six years and, short of being let loose with a license to resume his career, there was no possible way he could ever have paid all of the fines that could have been assessed against him. It was obvious that Sprague's pressure left him only with the option of spending the rest of his life in jail.

A March 29, 1968, Philadelphia *Bulletin* story supplies the results which flowed from Scolnick's decision to cooperate with authorities:

## SCOLNICK GETS LENIENCY
## IN BANK THEFT

*Federal Judge Gives DA's Star*
*Informer Five Years Probation*

Sylvan Scolnick, down to 505 pounds, got off lucky in U.S. District Court here today after he was pictured as an informer for a number of law enforcement agencies.

As a reward for talking to the authorities about past crimes and informing on criminal associates, Scolnick escaped additional prison time himself.

Currently serving a five-year sentence at the federal penitentiary at Lewisburg for concealing assets in bankruptcy, Scolnick came up on another charge today, that of master-minding the theft of $100,000 from burglar Sydney Brooks' safe deposit box.

After hearing how cooperative Scolnick has been—and

265

contines to be—Judge A. Leon Higginbotham gave him a 3 1/2-year sentence to run concurrently with his present sentence, suspended a ten-year consecutive sentence, and placed him on probation for five years.

This came about after Scolnick, who in his prime weighed 741 pounds, was described as changed and "repentant" by his attorney, Stanford Shmukler.

To show how repentant Scolnick has been since he was caught, his attorney called on First Assistant District Attorney Richard A. Sprague.

Sprague testified that so far Scolnick has spent 1,200 hours talking in the DA's office here.

Shmukler interjected that he has spent more time talking in Philadelphia than he has behind bars in Lewisburg, which would postpone the date when he can become eligible for parole.

"The time in Philadelphia is costing him parole time," Shmukler said.

Sprague said that Scolnick has not only cooperated with the DA's office but also with:

The Federal Bureau of Investigation; the intelligence division of the Internal Revenue Service; the Securities and Exchange Commission; the Philadelphia Police Department; the Pennsylvania insurance commissioner; the prosecutor's office of Atlantic County, N. J.; the district attorney's offices of Queens and Nassau counties in New York, and in Allegheny, Montgomery and Bucks counties in Pennsylvania as well as nongovernmental agencies such as the Philadelphia Bank Detectives and a national credit card agency.

Sprague praised Scolnick for having brought about the arrest of 35 other persons.

Scolnick, said Sprague, was responsible for solving a $26,-000 hijacking, a $27,000 diamond theft, a $650,000 arson case and the recovery of over $200,000 in stolen goods.

"And he's still cooperating," Sprague said.

Shmukler told the court that Scolnick's arrest was the best thing that every happened to him.

266

"It has changed his whole life," the attorney added of the man who claims Cherry Hill, N. J., as his home.

Judge Higginbotham asked Scolnick what he had to say for himself.

"I guess I was on a merry-go-round," Scolnick responded, "with no chance to get off and no chance to look around.

"But since I have been in jail, I have looked around and seen what was happening to myself and my friends and my family. I have seen the great harm I have done to others. That's about all I can say."

Judge Higginbotham asked Scolnick if he knew what would happen if he violated the probation just given him.

"I'll go to jail for another ten years," said Scolnick.

Scolnick, 39, was sentenced in the bankruptcy case in October, 1966. Subsequently, he pleaded guilty to helping arrange the theft of a federally impounded safe deposit box of Brooks, allegedly containing $100,000 stolen from the Cottman Ave. branch of the Philadelphia Saving Fund Society.

His attorney was afraid that Scolnick was in physical danger from his former associates because of this cooperation, but the real threat was not from Brooks or his associates in the bankruptcy and bank swindles, but from organized crime. Everyone knew that Sylvan was singing, but the district attorney kept the theme of the song a top secret matter.

As a result, the rumors began to grow that he was telling the law what he knew about the Cosa Nostra and other syndicates. A few of the weeklies even printed "transcripts" from this supposed testimony. Little Murray, in another prison, said, "I figured somebody was sure to take a shot at him. Blow him up or something. People up there who knew I knew him said, 'You're never gonna see your friend again. They're gonna bury him.' "

This was a real fear. Both Scolnick and his attorney knew that he had said nothing about organized crime figures except

267

to describe the brief period that he had been in the loan-shark business with some of them. But they also knew that just a general suspicion that he had said more could prove fatal to the Fat Man. Fortunately, it soon became generally known that Harry Karafin (quickly fired by the *Inquirer*) had written the story that served as the source for the others. The headline of that story read: "Master Criminal Names Big Shots: Authorities Fail To Act."

The story of Scolnick's fingering of Harry Karafin was considered nationally important enough for such publications as: *Time, Newsweek,* the Washington *Post* and *Star* and the *Los Angeles Times* to assign reporters to work on it.

*Time* Magazine received the following telegram from Karafin:

HEDLEY DONOVAN
EDITOR IN CHIEF
TIME MAGAZINE

YOU ARE HEREBY ADVISED, AS I HAVE CAUTIONED YOUR REPORTER WHO TELEPHONED ME FOR INFORMATION, AND I REPEAT AGAIN THAT THE STATEMENTS CONTAINED IN THE PHILADELPHIA MAGAZINE CONCERNING MY ACTIVITIES ARE ENTIRELY FALSE AND MY ATTORNEY IS IN THE PROCESS OF BRINGING A LIBEL ACTION IF YOUR MAGAZINE PRINTS ANY INFORMATION SUCH AS THAT CONTAINED IN THE PHILADELPHIA MAGAZINE ARTICLE ON HARRY J. KARAFIN TITLED "THE REPORTER," YOU DO SO AT YOUR OWN RISK.

HARRY J. KARAFIN

However, nothing came of the threat and the magazine went ahead with a full-page story on the reporter who went sour.

Scolnick says that he supplied much of the material that Gaeton Fonzi and Greg Walter used in their story on Harry

Karafin, and which triggered his arrest when it appeared in the April 1967 issue of *Philadelphia Magazine*. But Assistant District Attorney William H. Wolfe says that his office had Karafin under surveillance long before the article appeared.

The point is important because it represents one of the yardsticks used by various law enforcement agencies to gauge the value of Scolnick's cooperation with them.

His attorney Stanford Shmukler was put on the witness stand at Harry Karafin's trial. He was asked by Richard Sprague, who was the prosecutor in the case, "What I am trying to find out, sir, is [whether] the information which led to the investigation, the entire subsequent prosecution, in terms of this defendant [Harry Karafin], ensued from you having talked to your client Scolnick? The district attorney's office did not approach you on it at all, did we?"

Shmukler answered, "That is perfectly correct. The information came from my client to me, to Mr. Wolfe. Mr. Wolfe had never mentioned Mr. Karafin's name prior to my raising the question."

Karafin, who had threatened to sue every newspaper or magazine that mentioned his troubles, subsequently dropped the suit he instituted against *Philadelphia Magazine*. His trial ended with a "guilty" verdict on forty separate counts, including blackmail and extortion. He was sentenced to a term of four to nine years in jail and was later indicted by the federal government for income tax evasion.

"Karafin's name was the last thing I mentioned to Shmukler after I finally agreed to tell him everything, and I was surprised at the reaction it got," says Scolnick. "I didn't know everybody would think he was so important. Later, when Billy Wolfe asked me if I'd mind confronting Karafin, I said I wouldn't, but when he came in, I felt bad for him. I had been in the same position as Harry just a few months before.

269

"I felt that way, but I got to admit that Harry was the most vicious man I've ever met in my whole life. He hurt people for personal pleasure. He hurt them in a way that he destroyed families. And the worst thing, after people paid him off, sometimes he still went ahead and wrote the story. He was like a ferret. If he got his teeth in ya, that was it. You'd never shake him loose."

During the next year, Scolnick spent almost 2000 hours describing the operation of past and potential swindles and crimes to the district attorney's office, scores of other law enforcement agencies, as well as a number of business and community organizations. The Canadian police asked to be filled in on the fraudulent bankruptcy operations because they believed that much of their own problems in that area might be conceivably traced to Scolnick and his gang.

At one time, it was estimated that over 200 people had been called in for interviews by various district attorneys in order to check or corroborate some of the allegations in his stories. One individual, accused of concealing assets in three separate bankruptcies unconnected with Scolnick, sent in a private offer to the Fat Man of $7500 if he would keep from giving any information that might somehow damage him. Scolnick reported this offer and the man was also indicted for attempted bribery.

The people and the offenses described by Scolnick began piling up to the point where, finally, Arlen Specter, the district attorney, called a temporary halt to the singing until the material could be evaluated. "There's a whole backlog of these cases," he explained, "and I want to see if we can get convictions in these, first."

"He made a tremendous contribution," says Shmukler of his client, "and it resulted in his becoming very well known in law enforcement circles across the country. After all, someone who was involved in somewhere between twenty and fifty million dollars' worth of thefts had to be listened to. You would just have to describe him as an expert."

When asked to assess the accuracy of Scolnick's testimony, Richard Sprague said, "As far as I am concerned, he was truthful. I think, having decided to talk, he took great pride in his ability to remember each and every detail, almost trying to show his own powers by recalling details of time and events. When he decided to adopt the imagery [of being a friend to the law], the only way he could come across good, was by being truthful.

"If he ended up lying, he is not going to remember the following day or the following week what he said before. Therefore, he would be diminishing or tarnishing what he was trying to present. The only way he could present the kind of figure he wanted to project, was by sticking to the truth and, as far as we are concerned, he did exactly that."

Mickey Rotman, who was the chief of the detectives assigned to the district attorney's office during that period, was asked how the Fat Man was regarded by the prosecutors and the law officers during his visits to ther offices. He answered, "First of all, you have to understand how law enforcement officers think and react to certain things. For instance, some policemen think nothing of accepting graft. But they take it as a personal affront when someone else commits a crime. They have two sets of standards; one for themselves and the other for everyone else. Now, if you take an officer or a DA who's been sitting down talking with Sylvan, they'll probably regard him as a nice guy. But when they walk away from him after the conversation, they still have in their mind that he's nothing but a criminal, a hood. In spite of all the friendship that went on during the talk, they only remember him within the frame, 'once a criminal, always a criminal.' As far as they're concerned, he'll never fit back into a normal life.

"This is twice as strong when you come to a guy like

Sylvan. He can overwhelm you with his personality. So the people he talks to, later react twice as hard against him. They mention it to other people and then the story starts to grow. It ends with him being a two-faced monster, as far as people who have never met him are concerned.

"A lot of the stories about Sylvan got started that way. Some law enforcement officer might have heard a little bit about the way he acted while he was in our office and then he repeats it to someone else. But he has to inject himself into it to make himself more important.

"And, of course, there was another factor that had to do with the way he was regarded in the office. How many criminals do law enforcement officials come in contact with who had Scolnick's capacity? Very few. A guy who's investigating crimes, generally comes across burglars who take some television sets or stick somebody up for a few bucks.

"So they really can't compare the routine criminal with the criminal acts of Sylvan Scolnick. It was too vast, too much contrast. How many people have busted out places to the tune of twenty million dollars? It isn't too difficult for Sylvan to outmatch the ordinary law enforcement officer, so there has to be some envy of him on their part. That's why some of them went out of their way to hurt him.

"Those people who actually had a lot to do with Sylvan, all had a high regard for his intelligence, his manner of speech, and the articulate way he had of providing an afternoon's entertainment. Everybody enjoyed his stories. But when they went away from him, he was still Sylvan Scolnick and very few of them would think about going out with him socially. They just wouldn't do it because, you know, he is still a hood. And those that didn't know him at all ended by causing him a lot of aggravation and grief by the stories they told about him."

"I sensed," says Scolnick, "that in every one of the discussions I had in the DA's office, there was never any personal regard for me whatsoever. The only reason they give me any courtesy at all was because they were using me for their own ends. I felt it and I knew it all the way along. But, as far as I was concerned, they were entitled to their own opinions. They only knew what they read or what they heard that I said. They didn't know what was inside my head.

"But even so, some funny things happened. You know, every once in a while they'd take me home to Cherry Hill so I could dig out some more of my records or canceled checks for them. Well, one night, a prison guard took me to the house so I could see my family, but I told him to park around the corner because some of my old, ex-friends like Sam Koff were keeping watch on the place to make sure I don't get no breaks.

"So when I'm leaving, I tell the guard to walk ahead of me because, for some strange reason, I think that if I walk behind him and don't carry the cane like I usually do, then nobody will see me. He says okay and we head for his car, him in front.

"All of a sudden, a red car pulls up alongside me, real slow, and I look over, saying very casually, 'Real cold out tonight, isn't it, officer?' and he says, 'It sure is.' Evidently, I don't look like no second-story man to him.

"When I get around the corner, I see the cops in the red car had gone ahead and stopped the prison guard as a suspicious character. They got him spread-eagled against his car and they're shaking him down, frisking him. The floodlights are on, the guns are out, the whole works!

"I said to myself, 'Oh, my God!' and my heart went down to my stomach. All this because the guy was doing me a favor to let me see my family. But I said nothing and kept on walking past him. Ten or fifteen minutes later, he caught up with me and told me he had to give them some kind of story that he was over here involved in a narcotic investigation.

273

"The police used to bring me here because I had all the books and records and, besides, sometimes they wanted a place to talk with me where there was no danger of being overheard. So what we did is maybe we came here about fifty times. Sometimes it would be during the day, and a lot of times after they were done questioning me at the DA's office, they'd bring me here at night. But I never spent a weekend here like some people said. I was always back in prison by midnight.

"One time, it came close to getting me in real trouble. The officer who came over with me as a guard passes out around ten thirty, and I can't get him up. I even drawed his pistol out of the holster and he still doesn't move.

"So I put his pistol back in the holster and I call Billy Somerville, who's at home. I tell him, 'I'm in big trouble, my guard has passed out and if I'm not back by twelve o'clock, they'll claim I broke prison.'

"He says, 'What can I do?' and I said, 'Well, it's mischief night, they're all dressing up for Halloween, so try and get a policeman's uniform and come and get me.'

"And that's what he did. He rented a cop's outfit from some masquerade place, and him and his wife took me back to the detention center. She waited in the car while he went in and surrendered me. He really got carried away, though. When he brings me in, he grabs me by the back of the belt and gave me a pull which like to broke my back. I wanted to smack him in the mouth.

"The guard at the entrance where you come in looked at Billy and says, 'You look familiar. What district are you from?' and Billy answers that he's from the Ninth. Of course he looked familiar, he had been locked up there a couple of times himself.

"So he signs me in and he went back to Cherry Hill and took the guard home where he could sleep it off."

Another view of the Fat Man's appearances at City Hall

274

is supplied by Hanna Zbik, a secretary in the office of the district attorney. She's young, attractive and, obviously, quite sentimental.

"The difference between Sylvan and the other people who came in here as witnesses," she says, "is that the others were always conning . . . trying to put something over on us. You could see it a mile off. They always tried to let everyone know they were big shots. But, right away, I could see he wasn't trying to put anything over on me. I've been working here for about six years and, at first, I was a little bit impressionable, but not now. And, since Sylvan came in almost every day for a long time, almost a year I think, I got to know him very well.

"My job was secretary to Bill Wolfe. The other girls sat outside, but my desk was in the same room with Bill, so I used to watch them.

"I had the strong impression that he hated prison life and that there was no way in the world that he wanted to stay there. He used to say, almost to himself, sometimes, 'If I could help myself . . . if I could just clear it all up. . . .'

"When the office first started buzzing with rumors that he was going to be brought in, we were all wondering what he would be like. From what we had read in the papers and heard some of the detectives say, we figured he was going to be a sharpie. He was supposed to be very hip with the language, and totally aware of everything. But I was shocked when I first set eyes on him; his size, mostly. I didn't know how to react to him.

"But after he was introduced to me, he sat for almost an hour before they called him and during that time something very nice happened. I realized he was interested in me—as a person. Not as a girl, even though he hadn't seen a girl for a long time. He came on straight. He wasn't nervous, he spoke freely, and was easy to talk to.

"He was always that way. If you asked him a question,

there'd never be just a one-sentence answer, it would go on into a fascinating story. And all the time he treated everyone, not only me, as if they were human beings, not someone he was trying to manipulate for his own advantage.

"I remember, about two months after he finished up in this office, an FBI man came to the door. I knew who he was because I had seen him in there before. He asked, 'Are you Hanna Zbik?' and when I said I was, he said, 'I have something for you,' and he dropped a cardboard cylinder on my desk and walked out.

"I wondered what the hell it was, and when I opened it, it turned out to be a scroll of art paper. It was a picture of me. Sylvan had taken a snapshot off my desk and carried it back to prison. From it he had drawn my portrait in chalk pastels, and put a little, personal, shorthand note at the bottom. I was very touched. I have it framed, hanging at home. You see, he didn't have to do that. He had no more contact with the office and I certainly couldn't do him any good.

"During the time he was here, I learned all about his childhood and background and he learned all about mine. He'd be sitting just a few feet away from my desk, and we'd talk while he was waiting to be called by one of the DA's. He'd talk by the hour about his mother and his wife.

"I used to call my mother at noon, every day. I had told him a lot about my parents, how they had been in a German concentration camp; so, once, when she was on the phone, he started to sing old Jewish folk songs in the background. You know, he has a beautiful voice and she wanted to know if I had the radio playing. When I told her it was Sylvan, she insisted on speaking to him, and they talked for almost a half an hour. That night she told me that by the time he hung up, she was in love with him!

"I never saw any evidence that he was such a glutton as

276

the newspapers said. Whenever lunch would be brought in, the most I'd ever see him eat would be one or two sandwiches. His appetite was nothing like they led people to believe.

"He was just totally different from what I had read about and what they said about him. They'd bring these other guys in—Brooks, Kutsher, people like that—and right away they'd be out to jam me up. Like they'd got hold of an envelope with the DA's seal on it and try to put something in there with my name as a return address on top so it would get mailed out without question. These were the con merchants and I knew from the start they'd try and take any advantage they could. To them, I never said much more than, 'How are you feeling?'

"But Sylvan became a friend. I used to feel so sorry for him around five o'clock when we had to take him to the sheriff's office for transportation back to prison. He just hated to go back. I got the impression that he'd rather die than ever have to go back to prison again after his sentence was served.

"A lot of the fellows in the office felt the same way that I did about him. Whenever things were slow, there'd always be five or six come in just to rap with him. General things. They enjoyed being with him.

"I have really come to believe that he is actually a very truthful person. He is one man I would trust in a pinch. I wouldn't say that about the other guys he had around him. Murray Farber, Billy Somerville . . . we've had them all in here. Sylvan used to care for them a great deal, almost like they were his brothers, but I always had the feeling that they would and did take advantage of him. He's so open, he thinks everybody else is, too. Which is a funny thing to say about a guy who has done the things he has. But—I still believe it.

"I remember, one time, when we knew Sylvan was going to be in the office until eight or nine that night, I went out to get sandwiches for everyone. Billy Somerville, who was just in for questioning, went along to help me carry the bags. We were talking and I tried to find out if he would ever go straight and try to help himself instead of having Sylvan get him out of every kind of a jam that he got himself into. I said to him, 'Billy, you've been in jail before and you know what it is like. How could you be so stupid as to go trip yourself up again?' and he answered me something to the effect that it would never happen again. But I didn't believe it, the way I would Sylvan. I knew that if there is ever a dollar laying around, Billy would go after it any way possible."

Considering his record and who he was, the first year in jail was not a total down trip for Sylvan Scolnick. He had dieted away almost 200 pounds and, judicially speaking, lost more than that in criminal culpability. Most important, he was about to learn conformity in the strictest society we have: prison.

# Chapter 15

# A PRISONER IN THE HOUSE OF DETENTION

*During my final visit with the Subject, I spoke briefly with Mr. J. A. Stieber of the Social Services Staff at the House of Correction where the Subject is incarcerated. Mr. Stieber sought me out to volunteer a reference for the Subject and Sydney Brooks. He states that the Subject has done an outstanding job in helping with some of the younger inmates and with some of the very old inmates at the institution. Mr. Stieber is unstinting in his praise of both the Subject and Sydney Brooks and says that he hopes that they will receive some consideration for the fine work they have done.*

—From a recommendation to
the sentencing judge,
May 16, 1969.

In July 1967 Sylvan Scolnick left the Federal Penitentiary at Lewisburg, Pennsylvania, for imprisonment at the Philadelphia detention center. He was kept there for approximately a year and then transferred to the House of Correction, a minimum security prison, where he remained until his release. Most of this latter stay was under the supervision of Warden Lewis Aytch.

"Rumors are a hell of a thing in jail," said Warden Aytch, "and when the staff and the prison population heard that Sylvan Scolnick was coming here as an inmate, the stories really moved into high gear. Everyone got worked up. Things like, 'This big-timer is coming in,' and 'Big money, watch out!' The staff's feeling was, 'We don't want to be tied up with him, why should he be here? Why didn't they keep him in the federals?' This is what the setting for him was like.

"I tried to get over to staff not to be frightened because fear itself is what really can destroy a situation. I knew that he had to be a disruptive influence, if only because the word on the grapevine was that, 'The Big Man or Big Fats is coming and he's a major leaguer.' People were going to try and be friendly with him and that was bound to interfere with the prison routine. People [i.e., the prison staff] are always concerned about what is going to happen on the outside and everyone knew that Scolnick had so many 'guest appearances' out there that he couldn't keep up with them.

"When they brought him here, I also recognized that there were going to be some built-in, physical problems that I had to circumvent. Years ago, we used to be hung up on the idea of blanket [prison] regulations for everybody. But it just can't work this way. If you have a diabetic, the regular prison menu might end up killing him. Consequently, when Scolnick first came, for example, he put out some complaints, that he had to have certain kinds of food, so I checked with the doctors and they confirmed that he required a special maintenance diet. And this is what he got.

"We housed him, not in General Population, but in the section we call A-one, which is a place where there are thirty-five individual cells—generally occupied by aged or other kinds of prisoners who require special attention. This is where he spent his entire time here."

Father Francis Marszalek was twenty-seven years old when he became prison priest for the institution. Scolnick arrived a year later. Father Marszalek says, "When I first saw Sylvan, he seemed to be a very impressive individual. He was on a regular hospital bed, lying on his side, laughing and telling jokes.

"Within a short period of time, I found that he totally outclassed the bulk of prisoners I was working with. He was a very impressive individual, a totally different kind of inmate and I'm not referring only to his size. Sometimes, when he was very low or depressed, I'd stay with him in his cell and we'd have long, philosophical talks.

"He became my assistant, and there's no question that he helped my efficiency on the job. Every so often, I'd get the feeling that he was intrigued by watching me run around, trying to get things done. Then, after a while, he'd walk over and say, 'Father, you are not going to get it done that way,' and tactfully suggest another procedure—which almost invariably worked."

Scolnick was asked at what point he made the decision to help the priest in his duties. He answered, "When I saw what he tried to do for the inmates. He wasn't like the minister or rabbi we had there, he really did some honest work. He was a *man* in the prison. A hundred and one percent stand-up guy.

"He knew that some of the things he tried made the authorities mad at him, but he used to do them, anyway. Not that he would ever do anything that might be considered illegal. He just made it as bearable as he could for the guys. Guys would want to know when they were going to court or why they didn't hear from their mother or wife, and he used to see what he could find out. He'd call the family to find out how the wife or the parents

281

were, or try to cement things between the husband and the wife on the outside. That's what it's all about.

"The other religious guys were all right. The rabbi used to come in and talk to me about home and things like that, but he really had nothing to do but look cute. Between you and me, most of the time he was in a hurry to get home and eat. The minister used to walk in with a great big cross and whistle around a while and then breeze. But Father Marszalek—he'd be there doing what had to be done; writing letters, seeing families, talking to judges, talking to court agencies. That's finally what got him in trouble with the guys over him."

"I guess I made too many waves," says the priest. "The first big mistake I made was with a young boy who had slashed his wrists. I was called to the hospital because they thought he was a Catholic, so I went up to anoint him. When I got there, I saw the doctor stitching the kid up—cold—no anesthetic, like he was a bag of laundry or something. So I filed a complaint with the superintendent of prisons.

"The thing was that you embarrassed all your superiors when you made a complaint. We used to have chaplain's meetings, which were very nice things, but were always completely ineffective. You might have been right on the spot when something happened, but no one seemed to want to hear about it. They'd get angry when it would seem as if I was taking the inmates' part. And the superintendent of prisons would always be embarrassed when the papers would get hold of things like near-riots, but the news of it had never reached him.

"On the other hand, the prisoners themselves would increase your frustration. A lot of the calls I made were useless because an inmate was conning me. A guy would say, 'Call my girl friend and see if she's really going to press the charges I raped her. I really didn't rape her, Father,' and I'd call and get my ear ripped off because it was true. Then I'd have to go back

282

and say, 'You son of a bitch!' and hope the next guy wouldn't con me as much. You make a certain amount of calls like that and pretty soon you're making waves.

"For a while, I used the extra secretary they had in the House of Correction to help me send out letters to the judges and lawyers about an inmate's chances or opportunities. So what happened was that the people found they'd rather come to my office instead of the social worker's. I was forever using the phones, calling here and there, tracing down records, trying to find something that might be in the files of any one of three other institutions, asking to have records transferred. Sometimes I'd have to go up to Warden Aytch's office and pull a record and if I found it blank, I'd tell the prisoner, who would immediately start pursuing the social worker.

"All this meant a great deal of extra work for the prison's administrative section. I guess everyone from the warden down, thought of me as a pain in the ass. I had a friend who was a politician who used to tell me that you don't bother things. You left things alone.

"Of course, my pastor and I had uncomfortable relations because of all this. He claimed I was acting more like a social worker than a priest and I could never convince him that I felt that's what I had to be.

"Well, one day I was called to his office and he said, 'You might as well read this, it's got your name on it,' and he threw me a letter. It said that I was banned from the institution from then on, save for emergencies and Mass on Sundays. That blow was a hard one. It happened just before Sylvan left. But up until that time, he was a remarkably good source of help for me.

"Sometimes late at night we'd be sitting out in the center of the block—he was always out of his cell—and we would be talking about things in general, and always, somewhere in the middle of the conversation, he'd try gently to steer me into more productive channels. He'd say, 'Father, I saw you helping so-and-so out. Don't waste your time. Don't spend your time with a guy who's a wrong number, when you can spend the same time helping somebody who really needs it, like so-and-so.' "

"The Father had his problems, like everybody else in prison," says Scolnick. "He needed paper to print his newspaper, so I had it removed from other areas of the prison and delivered to him. He needed slippers or something for the older men, and I used to have them sent over by the people who worked in the warehouse. If he needed stencils or stationery, I'd have it brought over from whatever prison they were in.

"Sometimes Father would ask me to help him with prisoners who were having trouble, like a couple of youngsters we were afraid were gonna get raped. So I'd have them transferred over to our block where I could keep my eye on them. After they were okay, we'd get them into another block where we felt they'd be safe because I'd have somebody there watching over them."

The priest described the rest of the population's attitude toward the Fat Man by saying, "He had a mystique about him. He was supposed to have come from some big organization which, I must say, was also the first story I had heard about him. Then when Sydney Brooks came in, the word got out that he had been brought here just to keep Sylvan company. Quite a few of the guards assured me that this was the real truth. Then, of course, Sydney added to it, himself. He'd tell the guards, 'This Big Cherry, he could buy himself three prisons. You treat him right and he'll put you on the payroll when he gets out.' "

Brooks came to the prison as a temporary occupant while he was singing for the district attorney, and then afterwards remained as a permanent member of the population. At first,

284

his continued appearances downtown kept him too busy to enter, like Scolnick, into the daily prison routine. The newspaper stories, bearing such headlines as: "Brooks Names Judges and Politicians Among His Partners in Crime," "Brooks Quizzed 4 Hours on Blaney Slaying," and "2 Detectives Shifted in Brooks Incident," were indications of his occupation with other matters than prison life.

He made one last headline before becoming just another prisoner. It read, "4 Witnesses Against Burglar Got Death Threats, DA Says," and the story reported a series of menacing phone calls received by the artist, Chickie, his wife, and two others who had testified against Brooks after the Park City West job. The wife was described as "living in sheer terror and under a 24-hour police guard."

When asked to compare the prison conduct of Brooks and Scolnick, Warden Aytch answered, "In my judgment, Brooks was much more overtly manipulative than Scolnick. Brooks had a great need to let you know he was influential. For instance, if he liked another inmate, he wouldn't hesitate to tell him, 'I know so-and-so in the DA's office. I'm going down there on Tuesday and I'll talk to him for you,' and this kind of thing made it difficult to maintain discipline.

"He would do this even insofar as my own position was concerned. On several occasions, he said to me, 'Certain people in City Hall are wondering what your qualifications are for your job. After all, you weren't a guard before you got the job here, you were a social worker. All of a sudden, you are a warden. They want to know how you're going to react if there's a riot.' He'd let me know, during a casual interview, that quite a few of his high-placed friends were concerned about my reactions.

"This, I think, is a very bold, manipulative kind of thing. Trying to get me off-balance. I never got this from Scolnick.

"We tried Brooks out on several jobs here. We tried him

285

out in the commissary and, after a while, we found fifteen cartons of cigarettes in his cell, and that he was running a business in them on the side. So we just moved him out and put him on ice for several weeks.

"After that, we tried him on another job and, pretty soon, the same thing happened. As a matter of fact, we had to try him in three or four jobs before he cooperated. He was a very manipulative kind of a person. Much more so than Scolnick.

"Of course, Sydney was much more mobile; so, in time, he became a sort of an aide for us. For example, if we had an elderly man over there that social services had not seen, it was usually Syd who came to us and said, 'This poor old guy is as nutty as a fruitcake, we had better get a place for him'; and this became a sort of a key for our staff. He helped us zero in on some problems."

"Sydney helped me, too," says Father Marszalek. "I had my office right next door to the commissary where Sydney was plying his trade. Many times, he brought me in some candy or cigarettes that I could distribute where they were needed. In fact, he warned me about a situation where I was being used, but didn't realize it. I had been carrying messages from one inmate to another on the other side, without really thinking about it. After he noticed it, he explained the problems that might be involved, and I saw where I was lucky not to have gotten jammed up. This could have landed me in some real trouble.

"Sydney was a strange man. He could be very tough with the guards and the young wise guys, but he was very tender about the old and the helpless. Some of them were incontinent, and he thought nothing of cleaning them, as gently as if he were their older brother. He had a hard exterior, but I think he was really very soft inside."

"He really is," adds Scolnick. "One time, I had pneumonia. I was really sick with a very high fever. He sat up all night, sponging me down with alcohol and giving me sips of ice water. Once or twice, I saw him have tears in his eyes. He took care of me like I was a baby until I got better. Then he started cursing me again.

"He was as arrogant as a son of a bitch. Always doing something crooked. He'd be loan-sharking cigarettes; you know, getting back two for lending 'em one, and he'd be running the business right out of the commissary. Some poor guy would come there to buy his cigarettes and Sydney would be standing there to get his off the top before the guy got any smokes for himself. He was something else, not like that nickel-and-dime creep, Herman Kutsher. That jerk stayed in solitary confinement for a couple of years because he thought that got him credit for double time!

"I know it's hard to understand how me and Sydney could pick up our friendship again after the way we had talked about each other to the cops, but that's just the way it is. Nobody on the outside can understand it, not even, I guess, some of the guards on the inside. Tommy Mitchell give me up, and I even got him a job working with the dentist in the prison hospital. But when Major Kluth came up there one day and saw me in there playing chess with him, he said to the guard on duty, 'Are you crazy? This is the guy that squealed on Scolnick. Get him out of here!' and they sent him away because they thought I might do something to him."

The prison priest commented, "It's a thing that I never understood and never wanted to get involved in. I guess there's some kind of relationship that exists between men who share jail or some hazardous occupation together that just can't be explained. But I am certain that Sylvan did not hate Sydney. In fact, I'm sure the only people he really disliked were the lawyers and the prosecutors who use individuals for their own advantage and then throw them to the dogs.

"Of course, Sylvan understood what he was getting into

the first day he went down to the DA's office. It was 'dealer time.' It was outthinking the guys you were sent there to see. Two guys could be sent down to City Hall and be the best of buddies while they were riding there in the car. But when they got there, they were pushed into two separate rooms, each worked on by a team of men who were pitting one man against the other. Then they come back here, laughing about what happened during the course of the day—yet, each knew that the other had informed on him.

"I think this is something that I shared with the inmates while I was there. Man, if I had been in the spot they were in, I'd have turned you in as fast as anybody else. This is the rule of law and life in prison.

"I don't think that anybody who was in Sylvan's shoes would have sat there and said, 'I won't talk about Sydney, even if Sydney gives me up.' The reality of it is, 'Throughout all of this, I am going to survive.'

"So you look at Brooks and Scolnick and you give them the benefit of the doubt, because you say, 'I wonder what they really went through.'

"When I think about it, I'm amazed that through it all, through all the conniving and the routines, that Sylvan survived. Do you have any idea of what it must have been like to tramp down to court and City Hall as often as he did? To go down from God-knows-what to God-knows-where, and be able to walk out again and then, maybe, go all through it again? Knowing that this is where the enemy really is. And knowing that everyone else was being subjected to the same thing.

"Man, I tell you the reality is that if it's you or me—then, buddy, it's you. Why not? This is the kind of a situation the prisoner is in. It's the only life that exists for him at that moment. So he sits there and tears you to shreds.

"I'm willing to trust and believe that another man would

288

cut his arm off for me. But he wouldn't give his life up. He might just cut off his arm, but no more. This is the fact of life for people in the spots that Brooks and Scolnick were in."

The young priest's voice trailed off, baffled and obviously disturbed by his painfully earned view of these relationships. "It's easier," he finally added, "to tell you about Sylvan's attitude in prison.

"A lot of the guards treated the inmates as if they were garbage. I don't know how many times the prisoners were told they weren't people, they were animals. But Sylvan was absolutely different from them, and the guards couldn't understand him. He never gave up his dignity.

"He seemed to know everything about everyone, and that's because he went from one to another, always keeping his private opinions to himself while playing the kind of thing that had developed in each group. He was able to accomplish things in prison that no one else could and, so, everyone thought he was a favorite son of somebody way up the line.

"I used him myself. I was busy working for the inmates and just couldn't get all the material I needed. The authorities would tell me to make a requisition of the supplies I required, and said, 'Don't worry, Father, we'll get it for you,' and then when the supplies came in, it would always be about a tenth of what I had asked for. But, if I asked Sylvan, somehow, some way, he'd get me everything that was required.

"Sylvan ran the prison because he knew how to manipulate the people who comprised it. He was the kind of an individual who knew humanity well enough to pit one group against another. And there were always groups, among the guards as well as the prisoners. There was the Irish group, the black group, the Italian group . . . all kinds, all bound by some special interest. If you looked at the roster of guards for that day, then you knew what the rules would be for that period. Every group did it

289

differently, according to what they felt they wanted. So he'd play one against the other. He had guards shifted, officers demoted, people transferred—it seemed, sometimes, almost at will. I remember, once a major came in and Sylvan was doing something that was irregular, but when the guard pointed it out, the major just said, 'Let him do what the hell he wants. I'm tired of fighting him.' "

"It wasn't as easy as Father thought," says Scolnick. "They blocked me plenty, too. I could get certain things done, but they stopped me cold on others, especially if it was for myself.

"Like, for instance, after I taught myself typing and shorthand. Ruthie brought me some books on them, and, for a while, I studied ten, twelve hours a day until I got to the point where I could handle a couple of hundred words a minute.

"So, seeing the hospital records was all fouled up, I thought I'd give them a hand. I put all their files and records in order and the doctors and nurses were really happy about it. But then, one of the majors of the guards found out about it and he sent over an order telling the medical staff that he didn't want me to be helping them there. He said I was a dangerous inmate and shouldn't have access to any of their records.

"What he thought I could do, or what he thought I had in mind, I don't know. The superintendent of nurses fought about it, but she lost. Even so, she still let me do some work in the evenings, which I enjoyed.

"Also, I had taken some Spanish in school. So I got some more books on that subject and studied them until I got to the point where I was reading and writing it pretty well. Then when they started having some trouble with the Puerto Ricans—the Spanish-speaking prisoners who didn't understand English too well—I went to the head of the social workers and volunteered to run some classes where the staff could learn some Spanish and the prisoners could learn some English. He thought it was a terrific idea, but when the same major heard about it, he knocked it down. He said I was too dangerous to be put in a position where I would be teaching or instucting inmates.

"I finally got ahold of this guy and asked him what he meant by going around saying I was too dangerous for this and that. He said, 'The fact that you never received any write-ups [for infractions of discipline] only means just how smart you are. You're just too jailwise.' And that's the way I had to leave it."

Warden Aytch explained his staff's occasional clamping down on the Fat Man's activities by saying, "Every so often, he'd give us some real problems. If he had the impression that somebody was going to do something for him, like the DA or a lawyer or a friend, and then something broke down, he would then pressure staff very much for the latitude to make the telephone calls, to get the letter in.

"Of course, we never argued with him. We saw him as being capable of manipulation. He could have manipulated certain situations much more than he did. Occasionally, we got the feeling that he was a little pushy on things, but generally, I could understand why, although staff didn't.

"There were several times when the manipulation became quite obvious. Once, an electric fan showed up in his cell. We were hard put to find out how it got there. I'm pretty sure he talked to some guy who talked to someone else and finally the fan ended up in his cell. So, if anyone on the outside had heard of it, we would have been accused of unequal treatment. There were also some complaints about the equipment he kept in his cell that he used while running the newspaper for us; pens, a stylus for the stencils, things like that. Some people could have misunderstood his possession of these things."

"It wasn't only the normal ways he ignored prison rules,"

291

said Father Francis, "some of the things he did were downright crazy. Like the time he married the two homosexuals. He had sent away to some offshoot church in Florida which, for ten dollars, licensed him as a minister. Then, with the help of Brooks, he set up the marriage ceremony and performed it. Afterwards, he sang, 'Because' as the two walked away to the cell that he and Brooks had had prepared as a bridal suite!"

"It wasn't so crazy," Scolnick pointed out. "You might laugh about it, but it was important to them. Syd and I gave them a little party. We got a load of cigarettes and candy from the commissary and we fixed up their cell with new, clean sheets from the hospital. White ones, not that muslin, and regular sized, so they wouldn't slip off the mattress. One was a black guy with a big, gold tooth, and the other was white, who was supposed to be a stone killer, only he wasn't.

"But, you know, it didn't do me any good when some guys would start saying things like, I was the guy who could get things done in the prison. I didn't enjoy that anymore, at all. Being known as a Mr. Big had never caused me nothing but grief.

"It was all bullshit, anyway. Like the time when some lawyer I knew on the outside had a client, a young kid, in there and they had put him on the same block with one of the guys from his old gang and they had murdered somebody. This lawyer was afraid the other guy was going to kill his client as soon as he could get him, to keep him from testifying. But he couldn't get him moved. So, one day, I go in to the Father's office and he tells me about it and says he's really worried about the young kid. I said, 'No problem. Where's the kid blocked and what's his name?' and I go out and, ten minutes later when I came back in, I told the Father, 'All fixed,' and that afternoon, the kid was moved to another block. Now, the lawyer thinks he's doing me a favor by telling the newspapers that if you want anything done in the prison, just talk to Big Cherry; and when that got out, I got a lot of heat from the staff for the next couple of weeks.

"But what I done wasn't very mysterious. I went to the captain who was in charge of that block, and I told him, 'Unless you want a shank in this kid's neck, you got to house him in another block. His lawyer is raising hell about keeping him near the other guy and if you don't do anything about it, he's gonna place it on record in the DA's office. When something happens to this kid, your ass is gonna be in a sling.' So he says okay and moved him. It was just common sense, but I end up with everybody getting sore at me because the papers are saying that I run the joint.

"All the time I was in prison, I never had a write-up for disciplinary action for things like sending letters out through the pipeline or anything like that. I only came close, one time, when I brought a couple of quarts of whiskey in.

"What happened was that they had me down at the City Hall checking out some things, and by the end of the day I was feeling low and depressed. You know, disheartened. So I had one of the cops go out and buy me a bottle of Vodka and a bottle of Canadian, and I taped it underneath my stomach. I got what they call an apron stomach.

"Now, when I come walking back into the prison, the whiskey in the bottles is going 'woosh, woosh,' and it sounded a lot louder to me than it probably was. When I go into the bullpen, the toughest officer in the whole jail, Lieutenant Wilson, was there. He says, 'I want him shook down,' and that was trouble.

"So I says, 'Oh, my, what am I going to do?' and I passed out like I was having a heart attack. Next thing I know, they got me on a stretcher and are taking me upstairs to the hospital, where they put me to bed. I laid down on my stomach while

293

they pulled off my pants and, as soon as they went out of the room, I took the whiskey and slipped it under my pillow. Then I laid on my back and when they came in with the doctor, I told him I felt better. He fed me some kind of medicine and I went to sleep. When I woke up, I had a guy get me a hot-water bag and we filled it with orange juice and vodka and some other guys and me had a very pleasant weekend.

"Another time, they caught me coming in with swag, but they ended up making a big joke out of it. I had been downtown testifying and the cops were taking me back home [to prison]. Ruthie had gotten a couple of bucks to me—like for lunch or if I needed something—and we passed a hoagie stand and I asked one of the cops to go in and buy me some that I could bring back to the guys. He did. He used the money to get me a shoppingbag full of twenty-five of the most magnificent Hoagies you ever saw in your whole life. They had double meat and double cheese, all in these big Italian rolls.

"Well, I never used to be searched when I came in from the outside gate. I would only be searched when I got to the bullpen, which was normal practice. But there was this one guard, his name was Geller, who was what they call an overzealous correction officer. He did his job, but he caused an awful lot of bad feelings by enjoying doing more than what his job called for.

"When I saw him at the gate, I said, 'That's trouble.' And I hold the shopping bag over to the side away from him, but he sees me carrying something, so he calls me back and says, 'What have you got there?'

"I said, 'I only have a couple of things for the guys inside, some clothes and some sandwiches,' and he says, 'Let me take it and if it's okay, I'll bring it in.'

"I said, 'Now, why are you going to do that, Geller? Why do you want to be such a nasty prick? There's nothing wrong.

294

If you want, call the guard up at the bullpen and tell him I'm bringing a package in.'

"Well, he took the Hoagies away from me and he wound up giving them to all the guards on the night shift. None of the inmates got any—all they did was hear the guards laughing amongst themselves about what Geller had pulled on me.

"So next time I seen Geller I told him, 'You'd better be one hundred percent from here on, pal, because now you're in trouble with me,' but I didn't say anything to anybody else. I just waited for the chance to nail him.

"Now, you got to know that I had a key to a refrigerator that was there on the block. It's where the doctor put the food that was on my special diet. So I waited until Geller was on the shift and, when I hear him coming, I went over and unlocked the refrigerator, and when he saw me, I acted like he had caught me at something.

"He says, 'What are you doing there?' and I answer, very guiltily, 'Nothing, nothing,' and slammed the door shut. He opens it and sees boiled chicken, canned fruit, lettuce, tomatoes, everything that's on my diet which, I know, he knows nothing about.

"He says, 'How the hell did you get all this stuff?' and I answer, 'Gee, Geller, I don't know. Maybe it was just put there for me.' Then he sends me back to my cell and I don't say anything more. I just went in and waited while he took all the food out of the refrigerator and left it on the floor—all night.

"The next morning I wrote a letter of complaint to the superintendent of prisons, saying that Officer Geller had refused to allow me the special diet that the prison doctor had prescribed for me, had let it spoil because he was overly aggressive, and that this kind of treatment was totally unnatural because I was getting to be a very sick man from the prison diet . . . and I went on from there.

295

"I made five copies of the complaint and addressed them to my attorney, the DA's office, the US attorney who was handling my case at the time, and a couple of other people. When the major of the guards comes in, because he must have heard about how Geller had put another one over on me, I said, 'Major, I'd like you to read this,' and I handed him one of the letters. He reads it and says, 'Now, what do you want to do all this for? Why make this kind of trouble?'

"I said, 'I don't want to create a problem, I just don't want Geller around because he's always looking to break my hump. I don't do anything wrong that calls for that kind of treatment. Just keep him away from me and I won't need to send out these kind of letters.'

"And that's what he done. From then on, they kept him on the outside gate and never let him work the blocks no more. They kept him on the outside and had him walk the dogs in the snow and the rain and all that. He cursed me, but he couldn't do nothing about it.

"You have to play it their way to protect yourself. But you also have to make sure nobody walked on you if you wanted to keep some self-respect. So, I used to go straight down the middle in my own way. If they didn't bother me, I didn't bother them. If I felt they didn't want to hear what I had to say, then I didn't say anything.

"I'll give an example. It's the only time I ever got mixed up in prison violence. They used to have movies on Monday and Tuesday nights. One time, they showed a picture, I think it was *Zulu* with Victor Mature. I had seen it before, and it was all about a great white hunter killing just about every black man in Africa. So I went to Lieutenant Wilson and I said, 'You're gonna have some problems with that damn movie.' But since it was me that said it, he didn't pay any attention.

"Anyway, I was bored, so I went that night. In the middle

296

of the picture, there's a scene where the hunter shoots a Zulu, right in the face, with a shotgun; and one of the inmates, a white guy named Kirby, starts laughing about it. A colored guy, sitting in front of him turns around and says, 'Kirby, if that white mother don't get killed by the end of the picture, I'm gonna kill you.'

"Well, I'm sitting alongside, but I don't say anything. I wait about five minutes and get up from the seat and walk to the back, where I tell the guard that I was tired and I was going back to the hospital.

"The ruckus breaks out as soon as the picture ends. Kirby got brained with the metal chair the colored guy had been sitting on, and another guy got killed in the general fight that this started. Guys got whacked out and cut all over the place. It turned into a hell of a riot. Later, when one of the guards told me about it, I said that they had to be stone crazy to show that picture in the first place; but, as Lieutenant Wilson had pointed out, it wasn't none of my business.

"What I learned was something I had already known on the outside; if you want to get anything done, you got to do it within their own rules. You got to maneuver within their own operation. I found out that the best gun I had going for me was to write letters.

"The example that sums it all up was that time about the pork chops. One day the cook was going through the hospital ward and I asked him what we were going to have that night for dinner. He tells me it's pork chops. 'Well, Jerry,' I said, 'that don't sound bad. Send me up a couple.' 'How many do you want?' 'Oh, maybe a few for myself and a few for the other guys.' And I give him a carton of cigarettes.

"Comes dinner time and this guy walks in with a load of pork chops that would have staggered a mule to carry. Great big commercial baking pans, piled high with pork chops. So I

297

says to the guy, 'Listen, you'd better help me get rid of all these pork chops. The captain or the major comes up here and sees all these, they'll wind up putting me in the hole for carrying swag.'

"You know, having extra food in prison gets you in trouble. They strip you down and put you in a maximum security cell for a while. And there was no way I could hide all that meat.

"But the guy says, 'Man, I can't get them pork chops back down there. The head cook is already hollering where is the goddamn pork chops. He sees me coming back down with them, and I got a problem.'

"Well, the windup is that I had another guy make at least twenty trips, giving pork chops out all over the jail. Later, when the guys are standing that night in the chow line, one guy gets just a small pork chop on his plate and he starts raising hell about it. The guy standing next to him says, 'Man, go up and see Big Cherry. He's got all the pork chops in the damned jail.'

"Well, the guards hear about it and they come up and make a big investigation. It's The Great Pork Chop Hunt; only they don't find nothing because I've already given them all out.

"Next, in comes the deputy warden, who was a major. He says, 'Listen, Scolnick, I'm going to tell you something. If I find one pork chop bone laying around this place tonight, you are in deep trouble.'

"I say, 'Why am I in trouble? Do I go down to the kitchen? You see any pork chop bones laying around here?' He looks disgusted and says, 'Come on, stop that bullshit. There ain't no swag moving through this jail unless you have something to do with it.'

"I said, 'Major, I don't understand you,' and, that night, I write a letter to the superintendent of the prisons saying I want to talk to him, and a letter to the head of the state bureau of prisons, and just about everybody else I can think of.

298

"Next day, the major comes walking in and I show him the letters. I said, 'I wrote a complaint to all these people, and I want you to read it before I mail them out.' He reads through the letter, which is about five pages, describing all the things that is wrong with the way they were running the prison, including the fact that the hospital needed painting so bad that everything was flaking off all over the beds in the wards. After he finishes it, he says, 'Scolnick, I'll make a deal with you. You rip up that letter—because none of it is necessary—and we'll see that there is enough food for you in the refrigerator and you'll have all the things, within reason, that you want. We'll even get you the goddamned paint for the hospital, if you get some of the guys to brush it on.'

"Do you see my point? In prison, they tell you you can't get meat, you can't get dessert, you can't get this and that, or nothing else. But, for cigarettes or for pressure you can get anything. In other words, it's there for the taking or the purchase, but not for the giving.

"I guess, though, prison is a lot like life. But you got to be able to step back and see it. Maybe prison wasn't all bad for me. I was able to sit there and think about what I had done with my life. I finally come to the conclusion—I must have been crazy to go on the way I did. I realized it was even a good thing that I finally got stopped. Somebody might have been killed, the way I was going on and on. I don't know where it would have ended."

"I think Sylvan became a different man in prison," Father Francis Marszalek concluded, "I remember sitting in his cell with him one night about eight o'clock. We were by ourselves, which was against the rule because he wasn't one of my inmates, he wasn't a Catholic. He was very depressed, talking about his wife, his marriage, and the effect on them that the kind of life he had led had had on the people he really loved.

"He said to me, 'Father, you may think I'm a great guy

299

and all that other kind of stuff, but I'm not. I'm a vicious man. My temper is very violent and I can be very cruel.'

"I said to him that it didn't matter, as far as I was concerned. That my view of him was that he had changed and there was enough proof of that by what he had just finished saying. I told him that I couldn't envision him ever yielding to those influences again. I knew there was a gap between us because we didn't share the same traditions, but from where I sat, I saw a man who had finally become mature."

## Chapter 16

# RELEASE, FREEDOM AND THE SILVER SHIP

*The District Attorney's office staged a surprise "Christmas Party" yesterday and the guest of honor weighed 500 pounds. The party was in the form of a court hearing for Sylvan Scolnick, criminal mastermind and one of the biggest thieves to pass through the court system. He once weighed 700 pounds.*

*Scolnick gave the DA's office guilty pleas on 18 bills of indictment dating back to 1966, and the court gave Scolnick the best present of all—his freedom.*

*The only thing that stands between Scolnick and an open prison door, is a $5000 fine and indications were that he wouldn't have much trouble raising the sum.*

—The Philadelphia *Bulletin*
December 24, 1969.

*Sylvan Scolnick is not exactly pining away in his cell at the House of Correction—he still weighs about 490 pounds—but he is getting "extremely nervous" hanging around the place, when only $5000 is barring the door.*

*Scolnick insists he can't get hold of 5 G's, which represents*

301

*a Federal fine imposed on him. . . . He may celebrate the Yuletide
on July 4th.*

—The *Philadelphia Daily News*
March 5, 1970.

The papers permitting his release from prison came through the day before Christmas 1969, and when he heard about it he yelled: "Yahoo!" so loudly that he startled the other inmates on his block.

But his delight was premature. He still had to pay the $5000 fine assessed by the federal court and, in spite of the general opinion that the Fat Man had stashed huge sums of money away before he left for prison, it was not until the following May that he could scrape up the $1000 the government finally accepted as a down payment on his freedom. The balance was paid off in small installments by the end of the following year.

There was another condition attached to his release. If he violated his probation, in any way, the Commonwealth of Pennsylvania would send him back to prison to serve out a full thirty-year term. This was the final part of the deal made between his attorney, Stanford Shmukler, and Richard Sprague.

The federal government also calculated that he owed $597,000 in undeclared and unpaid back taxes. After negotiation, this amount was reduced to $113,000. In consideration of his cooperation with federal law agencies, it was agreed that this, too, could be paid in installments, an agreement which he is meeting through current earnings.

"One of my guys met me when I walked out of the prison," he recalls. "I went over to the car and opened it up and I saw he was crying. After I sat down in the front seat, I said, 'You better lay off that stuff because you're liable to break me down. I haven't cried in twenty-five years.'

302

"Then I laid a box down on the seat between us. He says, 'What's this,' and I said, 'The key to the joint.' Just before I had left, some of the guards had gotten together and bought me a big, brass key with hearts all over it. One of the captains had presented it to me and said I could come back whenever I wanted.

"No use to say what it was like to be home with my family again. I just couldn't believe it. Just to walk over to the refrigerator again and get a glass of orange juice whenever I wanted.

"It was a treat to be in a bathroom by myself, again. In jail, the hopper don't have a seat, and there's no hot and cold running water in the cell.

"I couldn't sleep the first four or five nights because the bed was so soft and the sheets were so smooth, compared to that heavy muslin they use in prison. I couldn't even get used to the luxury of taking a shower that had mixing faucets for the water. Back there, it was two faucets—a hot one and a cold one— which you had to work like an engineer to keep from either scalding or freezing to death, depending on who was flushing a toilet or washing some socks.

"These are all small things, naturally. But they kept crowding in on me and I couldn't believe how important they were. I couldn't even get a kick out of having home-cooked food. What was important was the little things and being able to talk to my wife without a guard sitting there listening to everything we said, or being up on the witness stand or talking to the DA's and having to watch and weigh every word. It was just a tremendous, relaxed feeling and it took a while before things started to seem real to me. Then, when some people saw I was actually out, a few of them came by to pay a few bucks on account of the money I had maybe given them once, and that gave us a little cushion for a while.

"So, at first, I just took it easy. We went to the movies— drive-ins, mostly—and I started to paint. Wood prints, things

303

like that. And the biggest treat was that me and Ruth and Mom would sit and watch television together.

"Then I thought maybe I ought to do some work for the community. If I got deep enough into it, I figured, I could stop being Cherry Hill Fats, as far as everybody was concerned.

"The first thing, I got tied up with a halfway house, which was helping kids who were hooked on drugs. I laid out a fund-raising plan for them, but when they submitted it to the state for an okay, the word came back that they couldn't go into anything financial where I was mixed up in it. That killed that.

"Next, I started speaking to community groups about prison reform, which I think is one of the most important things this country has to face. I'm still doing it, but it's tough because most of the people come out to see the Fat Man, the criminal mastermind, that's on the bill. They think it's going to be a sideshow.

"Like one time, I'm addressing a group and, during my talk about how criminals need a chance to reform, I say, 'I was a thief. . . .' and a guy in the back row hollers out, 'They shouldn't be so permissive with thieves, they should chop their hands off when they steal!'

"I answered, 'That kind of thinking is why Attica happened and prison riots is going to continue to happen. The reason men die in these things is because bigots, like yourself, won't give anybody a second chance.'

"He says, 'Should I be penalized because you want to steal?' And I yelled back, 'No. You're being penalized because your son may want to steal. Are you trying to tell me you never stole anything?'

"He says, 'Right! I'm an honest man.'

"I said, 'Well, we're sitting in a house of God right now and you're lying. But you've justified what you've stolen, the same as every thief that goes to prison justifies everything crimi-

304

nal that they do. You've taken paper clips, pencils, even cheated on your income tax. You know you have. So why are you so much different from them? Because you weren't caught? No, you think because you wear a white collar, what you do is different from them because you never hurt nobody. But does it make you any less dishonest if you did it with a pencil instead of a gun? If people like you would get out when the elections come around and put in honest district attorneys and honest judges and congressmen . . . the kind of people who wouldn't be afraid to run the prisons with a little bit of humanity——'

"And then he interrupts me by saying, 'You can't say that, I'm the committeeman for my ward,' and I say, 'You mean you're a politician?' And when he answers he is, I end everything by hollering back, 'Now I know you're a thief!' "

He realized, of course, that in addition to these activities, it was now time to start earning a legitimate income. He knew that his status as an ex-convict had closed many avenues to him, but he understood and accepted this as part of his new way of life.

Irwin Paul observed, "I think Sylvan has learned that you don't beat your head against a stone wall. If he has a remedy, he'll use it. If not, what is he going to do?" The lawyer had been describing Scolnick's attitude as a businessman, but his words could be extended to cover the Fat Man's need for the kind of a career that would be approved by his probation officer.

He found it, he thought, in a franchise system. It was a company called the Silver Ship of Bargains, and it looked like a natural.

In order to understand why this venture brought him so many serious problems:

Franchising is, basically, a system in which a national company sells a local company the right to use its name, prod-

305

uct, or services and techniques. In recent years, it has attracted the fast-buck operators because they discovered that by selling off parts of their territories to subfranchise holders, there was no need for them to attend to the daily job of working at a business.

Then came the refinement of creating franchise packages; here the person who brought a territory made the purchase solely for a subsequent piecemealing off to subfranchisees. All that was needed was an idea, and it didn't matter if it involved fried chicken, cosmetics, or a quick way of filling out someone's income tax form. The only thing that was important was that the scheme could be glamorously promoted.

Obviously, many of the franchise plans are operated by honest businessmen who have perfected a product or a service and intend to take the trouble to properly train the people who buy into their systems. These systems produce a good profit for almost everyone involved. But, unfortunately, there are also a number of plans which fold as soon as the last franchise has been sold because the operators have only used the income received for a territory for themselves and for selling other territories. In this category, very little money is ever earmarked for training and then supervising a subfranchise until it has become a solid business venture.

It is difficult to police the operation of a franchise plan. Governmental agencies can never be sure if fraud is involved until after a system fails and they are given the chance to study the business records.

Scolnick swears that the Silver Ship was totally honest in concept and operation, no matter how many of his ex-associates were involved. "It was such a great idea," he says, "that there's no way anybody would ever want to make it bankrupt. It made too much money for everybody. I had some of the old guys working in it because—who else could I get? Who else wanted to be associated with me? Now it's all run by reputable business-men, but in the beginning, there just had to be George Gazzara and guys like that in it."

The idea behind the Silver Ship was simply a twist on the old advertising gimmick of a book of "two-for-one" coupons. A franchise holder would sell to the merchants in his area a space in the book which, when presented at the time of sale, would give a bonus to a customer. A dry cleaner might offer to clean three garments for his regular price for two. A bank might offer a coupon holder a checking account which involved no monthly charges for the first year. A car wash might be had for half-price when the appropriate coupon was presented.

After the franchise holder had sold out all the advertising space in his book, it was printed and placed on sale in the newsstands of his area. The book, with reason, could claim on its cover that it offered as much as $300 in values in exchange for the $10 purchase price. Obviously, a properly trained busi-nessman could build this system into a solid and sensible ven-ture.

"It first came to me," says Scolnick, "when a guy I had known around, named Morrie Reles, introduced me to Pete Adamucci. Now, Pete is a wiry little guy who's about forty, but he likes to try to look hip and young. Wears all the clothes and lets his hair hang long, all things like that. Very strong with the liquor and the dames. Loves 'em both.

"He used to work for Reuben Donnelly as a salesman, and now he's up in North Jersey, trying to operate the Silver Ship of Bargains, which was his idea, but he's doing very bad with it. Owed everybody. So, he goes to Reles, who's a guy who puts deals together for people, and asks Morrie to help him get some operating money.

"Morrie knows I'm looking for a business to get into, so he brings him down to my house one night. After he introduces

307

us, he starts to walk out. I ask him where he's going and he answers, 'I don't need to stay. If everything works out, you'll take care of me,' and he left.

"So I go over the thing with Adamucci and he'd got figures that he put together to make it look good and, after a while, I tell him, 'Let me talk to someone and come back to me in a few days.' He gives me the package of sample cards and books, and he goes.

"I studied them for a while, and got some books on franchising, which I read very carefully. As a matter of fact, I'm still studying up on the subject because there are more books being written on it than anybody'd believe. Then I call The Suit, George Gazzara, and tell him to come up to see me.

"At this time George has been working as one of the field managers in some big cosmetic outfit down in Florida. It's a phony, but he's making good money at it since he came back from his stretch in prison. The whole thing is a sales pyramid, but it hadn't busted out, yet. Anyway, George comes up and we go over the package together and, after we talked it back and forth for a while, we agree that Silver Ship can be a terrific package.

"But I told him in front that I didn't want it to be my package, it had to be his. All I would be was a consultant, getting a percentage of the take for my end. I never had the intention of being an owner or an officer or director of Silver Ship. He could talk his problems over with me, but that was all.

"I just didn't want to ever be in deals again where I could be barreled into where I had to answer for other people. I didn't want twenty guys on my shirttail, anymore. I thought about it for three years and eight months while I was in prison, and I knew I didn't want anymore to make decisions for other people. Only for myself.

"So that's what I told George in front. I said, 'If I solve

308

a problem for you, then that's that, and you pay me for it. Nothing else. I can help you, George, because I've got the ability to put a package together and I been around long enough to know how to make a business work. But it's your deal. You go with it and see what it is. You take out what's bad and replace it with what's good and make your changes until you have a real working package. The only thing, George, the deal is no good if you take over this guy's company as it stands. I made a couple of calls to people he's done business with and he always comes up NG. Everybody spoke bad about him. If you don't start a new company, you're probably going to have troubles because it looks like his old company has got nothing but debts and tax problems.' And George says the deal looks like it's for him. He knows how to do it.

"A couple of days later, Adamucci comes back and I tell him that the only way we can go into it is if we form a new company, Silver Ship, Inc., and that he has to resign as a director of the old company. He agrees, and on August 17, 1970, he, the lawyer, George and myself and some other people, got together and we started a new corporation. Then Gazzara says to Pete, 'How much do you want to make?' and Pete answers, 'forty or fifty thousand dollars a year because I think the company can earn it,' and George says, 'Okay, but it's up to you. You got a good background as a salesman and, if you train the publishees [the name given to the Silver Ship franchise holders] properly, we'll have no trouble.'

"But we did. Right off, Pete starts with the broads and the whiskey and things like that and, after a while, I had to bring him in and really chew him out. Next thing I know, he's told George Gazzara that he's quitting and that he don't have to take that kind of crap from me. Of course, I only wanted the company to be businesslike, but that's the kind of a guy Adamucci is; he just likes to dream about being a big businessman

309

he don't want the work that goes with it. So he leaves, and the next thing I hear, he's started another company based on the same deal.

"Anyway, we go on ahead. George brings in a guy he knows from New England, Bob Stennis, who puts up some front money on the deal and he becomes chairman of the board. They work out the right package, with my help, and everything is moving along good.

"Let me tell you about the package. We're different than most franchise deals because we can't pyramid. We cut up the country, so there's only a thousand franchise areas. When they are sold, that's it. The money comes in, not from selling sub-franchises, but from annual renewals. It's very simple. Silver Ship sells a territory for, say, seventy-five hundred dollars. Half of that goes to either the salesman who sold the area, or the publishee who sold it to a subpublishee. The rest of the money is used by the parent company to train the publishees and for their operating expenses.

"Only, I've got to keep a close eye on George. He just don't know about paying bills. One guy, a printer, comes around to me once and says that the company owes him ten thousand dollars. I get ahold of George and I say, 'Look, this Silver Ship is a dream. More money can be made from it legitimately than we ever thought of making the other way. So pay attention to it. Run it right. You cut off a piece for this printer out of every check that comes in, or I'm going to belt the shit out of you.'

"Well, it's hard for him to run a business. He's great in sales, but he's got no idea about administration. So, from then on, I make him sign checks in blank, which the bookkeeper uses to pay normal business expenses. I even don't let him have any credit cards in his own name. Big Murray, who's now operating a legitimate liquor store, let's us use his, and we pay him exactly what's due on the first of every month.

"The business really turned out to be wonderful. We

310

started out with a goose egg in money, and a yellow pad, and a Flair pen. Inside of no time, we built up a good company. In less than a year, somebody offered us $105,000 profit on the deal, and we turned it down because the end was nowhere in sight. Bob Stennis and George used to come back from field selling trips with their pockets full of checks from people who wanted to buy a territory. And, in every case, I would meet the customer and tell about my background. I'd say, 'I spent almost four years in prison, pal, for being a thief. But this ain't no swindle. I've never had a loser in my life, and this is gonna be the biggest winner of them all.'

"It didn't take anybody long to see that the big profit in Silver Ship was by staying legitimate. Anybody who'd bankrupt a company like that, on purpose, would have to be stone crazy.

"But, it's a lot of work. It's the one thing I didn't like about the franchise business. You got too many people not being dependent on themselves. After all, the franchise is a crutch. People could do the same thing for themselves that they pay money for to a franchise operator, but this way, if it fails, they got an excuse for flopping. That's the reason they pay for franchises. So you got to watch over them to keep them from falling on their faces. That's when this business gets to be a lot of work. You always are worrying about how the other guy is gonna do."

Some of the Silver Ship publishees did very well and some have done so poorly that they were forced to write off their purchase of the franchise as a total loss. One man, who held the rights to some areas in Eastern Pennsylvania, bitterly claims that he and his wife lost every cent they had in the world as a result of going with the project. In a conversation with a reporter, the man and his wife said that they hated Scolnick more than anyone else in the managerial group, and that they were going to devote all of their energies to seeing that "the fat thief" went back behind the bars for the rest of his life.

Another man, who had been a banker in Boston, bought

311

the rights to several New Hampshire and Massachusetts territories. He said, "I've now got three books out and I'm starting to advertise the Silver Ship on radio and television all over New England. It's a fantastic business. Now we have local community organizations like church groups and the Lions Club, and outfits like that, out selling the book for us. They get to keep three dollars out of every ten-dollar sale, and it's proving to be a real moneymaker for them. There's one parochial school that's going to use it as their prime source of making money to support the school. Everybody is a potential customer for a copy of this book, because you have to be just dumb not to buy one. There's too many values packed into it.

"I've got a partner with me in this deal. He used to run some shoe stores in Boston and now this is his main business, as well as mine. Within a couple of years, both of us expect to be making at least a hundred thousand dollars a year. If we want to keep working, there's no way we can't do it.

"I can't say enough for the help that the Silver Ship people gave me. They spent weeks up here, first selling for me, and then training my salesmen to sell like they do. I only met Sylvan Scolnick once, when we first bought in. He's a real brain. And he's a gentleman. I knew all about his past record, but everything he has said to me has been true. As long as we were willing to work, it all came about—just as he said it would. I'll take his word on anything he wants to tell me about running this business because he's been absolutely accurate, so far. All we had to do was follow his advice.

"Next year, my partner and I hope to buy some more territories. That is, if they have anything left."

This obviously satisfied publishee's version of his dealings with Silver Ship is quoted at length because his reputation in his community is good and his only ties with Silver Ship are business ones. He has no personal reasons to want to help Scolnick improve his reputation.

312

And, very shortly, the Fat Man was in need of such help. Pete Adamucci, floundering in the business that he started in competition with Silver Ship, decided that he had been unfairly frozen out of a profitable venture, and set about to recover at least a part of what he considered still belonged to him.

He sent word to Scolnick that he wanted $50,000 or he would spread the story that the Fat Man was the brains behind the deal, thus frightening away many publishee prospects. When Scolnick offered only a few dollars, "walking around money," Adamucci headed for the offices of *Philadelphia Magazine,* where Gaeton Fonzi was considering writing a story on Sylvan Scolnick's activities since leaving prison.

Adamucci's girl friend, a slender hippie named Joyce Kulpak, first followed, and then turned against him. "When I first met Pete," she said, "things weren't going so good with him. A lot of time, we had to sleep in cars because we were too broke for a hotel room. But then he heard about Sylvan and sold him on coming into the deal. I went with Pete the night he met with Gazzara and Sylvan and the lawyer, and everything looked okay. The agreement, as I remember it, was that Pete was going to get an equal share of everything that came in.

"But after a while, Pete got dissatisfied. He said Sylvan wasn't coming through with the promises he made about money. But I was there and I know that all Sylvan said was that everybody would work together and share the profit. But Pete turned this all around and, after he quit, he started to undermine the company, spreading all kinds of stories about Sylvan. I can understand why, I guess. After all, it was his company in the first place; and now other people were running it and Pete didn't have any more money in his pocket than he had before they came in.

"You see, Pete is very, very egotistical. If he had been given the respect he thought he had coming to him, he might have stayed with the company and everyone would have done

313

all right. But he was meeting head to head with Sylvan and, because he didn't get his way, he thought he was being abused.

"But I was there through it all. Sylvan always kept his word to Pete and me and he saw to it that we got a fair share of whatever there was. Pete just got too greedy too fast.

"One of the stories that Pete put around was that Sylvan had let a contract on him. Now that's very unfair. In all the times I saw Sylvan, I only saw a very nice man who was funny and very considerate. When I used to sit and talk with him, I'd forget he was fat after the first few minutes. He's so interesting and, I don't know how to say this, but also attractive. I mean, I don't know whether I would go to bed with him if he asked me, but I will say that he's the most charming guy. It's a shame he's fat. Or maybe I could turn that around and say that it's really nice that he's fat because he's so great to be with. You can look at it both ways.

"It's a shame. Pete, in his own way, is okay, too. But right now he's hiding out because he's afraid of what Sylvan might do to him because he knows that Sylvan knows about him talking to *Philadelphia Magazine.*"

Scolnick's fears of being publicly connected with the Silver Ship operations were rooted in more than business reasons. As always, with a new project, he had exhaustively studied every piece of information he could find that dealt with franchising. Very early in his investigations, he must have learned that there were many fly-by-night operators in the field and that his connection with it had to be, at the very least, considered suspect by the authorities who were supervising his status as a prisoner on probation. It is conceivable that he could have been returned to jail if they decided that he was participating in a fraudulent enterprise. He began to be terribly frightened of the forthcoming article in *Philadelphia Magazine.*

Strangely enough, he didn't concern himself over the pos-

314

sibility that some of the men who had been sent to prison as a result of his testimony might be out and looking for revenge. He said, "I'm too visible, so there's no point to worrying about it. But I never joined no brotherhood or made agreements with brotherhoods. I didn't do any lying to justify what I had done. I didn't tell any stories that buried somebody just so I could make a better deal for myself. I told the truth and that was that. They wanted to come after me, there was no way I could stop them. I haven't had any problems so far, but that doesn't mean that there isn't one laying out there, waiting for me.

"But I really was worried about Silver Ship. Here I tried my best not to be one of the owners, just a consultant, but these guys had needed help, so I stepped in. And now I could get rapped for it if anything the company did turned out sour. I was in the spot where other people had my life in their hands and I was really sweating.

"Now, at this point, I get another call from Morrie Reles, the guy who had introduced Adamucci to me. I had already paid him twelve hundred dollars for that, but now he hears, which is true, that I'm considering advising the boys to go public with Silver Ship. You know, get an underwriting. Sell stock in it to the general public. What he don't know is that I've already checked it out with a lawyer who says that my name has to be entered into the offering to the public and, if it isn't, then I could go to jail for concealing pertinent information.

"Well, that had settled it. No one was going to buy any stock where my name was in the deal, and I sure as hell wasn't going to run any risks of hiding it. I wouldn't go back to jail for something as stupid as another business deal if my life depended on it; and, now that I think of it, it probably does. So I had nixed the deal with the lawyer.

"One thing more. Morrie Reles is actually a set-up guy. He finds people to be set up for various things and he sells things,

315

like airplanes to South American rebels; and he just finished dealing off a boatload of guns to some other outfit in Central America which was trying to set up a revolution.

"So when he calls me, he says he wants twenty-five grand or he's gonna pass the word around that I'm behind Silver Ship and that not only will queer its doing business, but also there's a lot of reporters who would like to get their hands on such a story. I said, 'Well, you go ahead. Take your best shot,' and I hang up.

"A little while later, he calls back. Now he wants less dough and if I make a settlement with him (he called it a 'finder's fee' for bringing me Adamucci) then he would get off my back, as well as tell the true story that I hadn't screwed Adamucci and that I wasn't really the owner of the company. I said I'd think about it.

"After he hangs up, I call my parole officer, the U.S. attorney, the FBI, everybody right down the line, and tell 'em about it. I say I'm being shook down and wanted it on the record.

"A couple of days later, Reles shows up at the house. He agrees to take fifteen hundred dollars and call everything even. Forget about the finder's fee, forget about telling the newspapers the story, everything. So, since I got no witnesses, I give him the five hundred dollars I got in my pocket and tell him if he comes back the next night, I'll give him the rest of the money. You see, I didn't want to lose the deal [of nailing Reles on extortion], so, if he don't come back, I can't get him.

"Next morning, Gazzara, and a private detective I hired, and me go over to the FBI. They tell me it's not a strong federal case, but I should contact the local police and set him up for them. So, through my parole officer, I contact the Cherry Hill police and they come over to get my story. Most of the time, they're laughing, because they think I'm full of crap. And who comes walking in, unexpected? Morrie Reles!

316

"He pays no attention to the detectives who are sitting there and I don't bother to introduce them. He says he got a ride over to Cherry Hill so he thought that while he was here, he might as well stop and pick up the rest of the money. I tell him it's too early, that I'm borrowing the grand and that he should come back that night because I'll have it by then. And then he walks out. Now the detectives know that I've been leveling with them.

"Funny thing. He telephones me that afternoon and says he's been thinking; who was all those sleazy looking guys sitting around in my house? I said they were friends, and that satisfied him.

"That night, the two detectives show up early. We put a tape recorder under the sofa and we dust the ten hundred-dollar bills with phosphorus, and then they go into the other room.

"Reles shows up. I pass him the dough and he says, 'That's it,' and leaves. The detectives are out the door and nail him before he gets into his car. I didn't want to do it, but I had made up my mind I had to stop it somewhere."

In October 1971 the *Philadelphia Magazine* published an article, "Cherry Hill Fats Rides Again," written by Gaeton Fonzi. It described the operation of the Silver Ship of Bargains from the viewpoint of Pete Adamucci and several dissatisfied publishees. It also contained a resume of their 1964 article, "Bankruptcy for Fun and Profit," and pointed out the connection of Scolnick's old associates with his new venture. The article left the reader with a serious question of the Silver Ship's freedom from fraud.

317

# Chapter 17
## HIS ENEMIES CLOSE IN

*You can sell a ten-dollar bill to a con man for six bucks, but you can't sell it to an honest man because the honest man feels there's got to be something wrong with it. He never got anything for nothing. But a con man is always getting something for nothing, so he figures: well, it's another good deal. The easiest guy to sell is a con man because he's the biggest fool of all.*

—Sylvan Scolnick
November 1971.

He had tried every way he knew to stave off the appearance of the article, "Cherry Hill Fats Rides Again." He even called the writer, Fonzi, asking him to come to his home and hear his version of his postprison activities and to examine the books of the company, but was turned down. Fonzi evidently felt that he had all the pertinent information he needed and that another meeting with the Fat Man would only result in an attempt to charm him out of publishing the piece.

Scolnick hired Mickey Rotman, the ex-chief of the district

318

attorney's detective force, to conduct an independent investigation of the Silver Ship's affairs. Rotman, who has a reputation for honesty, reported on record that Scolnick's connection with Silver Ship was exactly what he had told everyone; that he did not own the company but served it as a consultant.

There is no question that Scolnick and the Silver Ship were both hurt when the article appeared. Three prospective publishees immediately withdrew their agreement to buy territories and the officers of the company estimated that it cost them at least another $60,000 in sales. As for Scolnick, he felt it was an unusually ominous sign when the probation authorities refused to give a preliminary indication whether his association with the company was satisfactory to them.

He decided he had nothing to lose by going on the offensive. On October 12, 1971, he called a press conference in the company's offices on nearby King's Highway in Cherry Hill, which was well attended because the assignment editors remembered that every one of his previous public appearances had resulted in a good show. And that's the way the accounts of the event were written.

The *Philadelphia Daily News*, in a story headlined: "Fats Plays Peter Pan to Win Public," began:

> Sylvan Scolnick as Peter Pan? Not so far-fetched at all. Scolnick, a/k/a Cherry Hill Fats, gave a rather credible performance yesterday that recalled the scene in Sir James Barrie's play where Peter Pan pleads with the audience to save the little fairy, Tinker Bell.
>
> "Do you believe in fairies?" beseeches Peter, "If you believe, clap your hands!"
>
> [The press conference] boiled down to a plea to the greater public, like P. Pan's; "Do you believe in Sylvan Scolnick? If you believe, clap your hands!"

319

The Camden *Courier-Post* quoted Scolnick as saying that the magazine article was based on information provided by a man [evidently referring to Adamucci] bent on destroying the company and that this was only a part of the conspiracy to put the company out of business.

In a later piece, Greg Walter of the Philadelphia *Bulletin* (who had been Fonzi's coauthor of the original "Bankruptcy for Fun and Profit" article) described Scolnick as saying, "I'm moving into an apartment in Philly. It's gonna be tough on Mom. The move. She loves this place. [But] after I started rereading all the newspaper stories and magazine pieces, I began to realize that to you guys, I'm just a stone freak. Not to my mom, not to my wife, not to the people who love me. That's what I finally figured out."

The question of whether the press conference canceled out the magazine article was not resolved for a while. Nor were there any immediate results from the indictment of Morrie Reles for extortion. The Camden *Courier-Post* quoted Scolnick as saying in court that Reles had threatened to make it look bad for him by providing information to a Philadelphia magazine about Scolnick's connection with the company. He said that Reles had told him that the information might result in the revocation of Scolnick's parole.

Reles was bound over by the court for grand jury action and was released upon the posting of $2500 bail; but this, too, apparently had no effect on the question of whether Scolnick's association with Silver Ship and the borderline characters involved in the dispute over its management was enough to send him back to prison.

It was difficult for the reporter who met him during this period to understand why the Fat Man was reacting so violently and with so much fear to "Cherry Hill Fats Rides Again."

320

After all, it appeared only in a local magazine and there already had been so much attention paid to him by the national as well as the local press.

The reporter saw Bob Stennis, slick, dark and, once, dressed in a snakeskin jumpsuit. He met obvious con merchants like George Gazzara and Big Murray and, above all, there was Scolnick; eternally talking, charming, maneuvering, and there was no apparent reason why people like these would worry so much over one more public examination of their activities.

One incident seemed particularly revealing; a salesman for the company had told him that he was having trouble with the transmission in his car and Scolnick sent him to a garage operator whom he knew. A half hour later, the mechanic called back and said that the repair job would cost at least $300 and that the car wasn't worth putting that much into it. There wasn't even a beat in the conversation before Scolnick answered, "Okay. I'm not going to be responsible for that guy's bills. Stuff it with sawdust so it'll run for a couple of weeks more and give him a bill for three hundred twenty-four dollars. Mark it 'paid' and tell him I took care of it." Then he returned to the reporter and said, "Now the bum is obligated to me."

This naked manipulation struck the reporter as ugly. But later, he met the salesman who owned the car and he was obviously the kind of man whom any employer would keep on a tight rein.

A month went by while the reporter stayed at Scolnick's side through every business conversation and every meeting. He began to know the man and, sometimes during their long conversations, found that his respect for the Fat Man's total lack of hypocrisy was ripening into affection.

Scolnick sensed this. "Look," he said, "you're starting to like me as a friend. Don't let that interfere with what you write."

321

"It won't. Whatever comes out will be exactly what you say and what people say about you. That includes your enemies as well as your friends."

"Well, I know you're gonna be honest. I been watching you. I met your wife and I know two people like you wouldn't be capable of a hatchet job. You're wonderful people, but your hearts are too big."

The reporter laughed. "Sylvan, you're trying to back me into a corner where I've got to be a saint. You're using reverse English on me, but it won't work."

"No," he answered, "I've got you. You're gonna have to be perfect in spite of yourself."

It worked. In spite of all his professional instincts, the reporter found himself caring very much whether Big Cherry went back to prison. Because such a decision could be conceivably based on an authoritarian whim, the reporter went back to the people close to Scolnick for their own estimates of the probability of his being returned to jail to serve out the rest of the thirty-year term.

The district attorney, Richard Sprague, said, "Would I be surprised if he ran afoul of the law, again? Well, he certainly has done his damnedest to convince me that he would never do anything that would bring him back here and, in my heart, I hope he meant it. But I haven't been able to reach any absolute conviction about the matter. I don't know. I prefer to give him the benefit of the doubt. I really want to believe that he meant everything he told me. But I can't help wondering about the contacts he has with people who were involved in criminality. I don't know whether or not he can keep himself separated from them, or whether one little thing will lead to another. I recognize that even if I assume that he means everything that he has told me, his relationships with people like these might be sufficient, anyway, to put him back in jail."

322

At this point, one of the assistant district attorneys came in and said that Mrs. Kutsher [wife of the burglar who was convicted with Sydney Brooks] was outside and was begging to see him. Sprague looked uncomfortable but finally said, 'Does she know what's wrong with her?"

When the other man answered that he thought so, Sprague shrugged and said, "Okay, let her come in." To the reporter, he said, "You can stay. I want you to see what judgments like you're asking me to make can be."

It was obvious from the moment that Mrs. Kutsher walked into the room that she was very aware of what was wrong with her: She had been told that she had cancer. She was in her midthirties but neither her platinum hair nor elaborate makeup detracted attention from the awful fear that possessed her.

She began her plea immediately. "Mr. Sprague, isn't there some way that Herman's bail could be set lower? Just so he can be free for a while?" She was asking that her husband be allowed to remain with her until the illness had run its course.

Sprague's face tightened. "I'd like to. But I've given him too many breaks in the past. Every time he's gotten out, he's gone crazy with burglaries and arsons. He's no good. He uses everybody. Right now, he's probably using your condition for his purposes."

She said, "We've only been married a year. He's different now. Everybody says so. I swear he was down in Atlantic City with me when that burglary happened that he's supposed to have done. Why can't I testify to this? Why do we have to wait for the hearings before I can tell them?" She burst into tears. Not because she wanted the effect, but because she had no way of controlling her tragedy.

Evidently Sprague's stony reception of her had been only his attempt at a defense against the utterly personal plea he

323

knew she would make. "Look," he said gently, "you don't have to worry. If you can prove to us that he's not guilty, we won't have to go to a hearing on it. This Saturday, let's bring everybody in. You bring your lawyers and I'll get Herman down from prison and we'll discuss it."

By now she was crying so hard that she couldn't use the words to thank him. The other assistant took her from the room. It was obvious that Sprague was going to try and get one last assurance that Kutsher would live up to a deal if one was extended to him.

After she was gone, the reporter said, "I wouldn't have your job for anything in the world."

"It's tough," he answered, "but you can't get emotionally involved with these people. You can't ever forget that your first responsibility is to the community and nothing ought to ever interfere with that responsibility. Here, maybe, the situation is such that Kutsher will stay straight if we give him a break. Maybe his wife is right about him having changed since their marriage.

"But this is the kind of trouble that I have in answering your question about whether Scolnick will ever be back. I'll say it to you, and I hope you'll repeat it to him; this office has jurisdiction over him for the next thirty years. We brought Sydney Brooks back from Rhodesia and we'll get Scolnick, wherever he is, if he goes wrong. We'll bring him back here no matter where he's moved to.

"I'm trying to impress you with the fact that *if he does anything at all wrong, he comes back!* I like him as well as you do, but that will have absolutely nothing to do with the fact that if he violates his probation in any way, he's going to spend the rest of his life in prison!"

The reporter left City Hall, but instead of heading for his next appointment, he sat on one of the benches on the parkway

324

outside the building, wondering whether his own frame of reference had become so warped by his affection for the Fat Man that he had lost some of the objectivity he needed for the project. His own conviction was that Scolnick would go back to prison, not because he would ever again knowingly enter into an unlawful scheme, but because his ego drive would tempt him to respond to the inevitable plea from anyone of his former friends; "Syl, you just gotta show me the way out of this spot I'm in."

"I don't know whether he'll make the slip that will send him back," said his lawyer, Stanford Shmukler, "but I'm sure that if he does return to prison, it will drive him crazy. He won't be able to stand it. No matter how long his body stays alive, a man like Sylvan is dead without hope. And he won't have any hope. He's shot his wad. He already used up everything he knew to get his deal, and he's got nothing left to deal with. If he falls back again, I don't think there is any chance of his coming up with anything significant that would get him out another time."

Warden Aytch said, "We have a prisoner here who's been in and out at least ten times. One time I brought him in to talk. I said, 'Look at me, I'm a black man and I'm the warden of this place. You've got so much brains and ability, you could make it, too.'

"He answered, 'It sounds good, but you gotta be able to prove it. When I get out there, I got a big Cadillac, money in my pocket, and I can get anything I want because I got the connections. Now you tell me if you mean it when you say I can get the same thing if I go to school and learn a trade.'

"What could I say to the guy? I couldn't promise anything besides the fact that he could stop living his life on the installment plan—the term they use here for a man who's in and out of jail.

325

"I have to give you the same answer about Scolnick. It all depends, I guess, on whether his old patterns and wants are stronger than his fear of prison life."

"I don't think Scolnick would ever want to experience prison life again," said Father Francis Marszalek. "He's older now and I think he feels that he could never survive another prison term. That's a complete deterrent, as far as I'm concerned. It totally changed him."

His probation officer, Eugene Kelly, said, "I regularly counsel with him and try to be aware of his activities. But I have to take the man on what he tells me; but there are certain things that he does, or people that he's in contact with that I don't particularly agree with.

"He'll be all right only so long as he keeps within the guidelines set down by the board of parole. We have to try and get through to him that ethical behavior is not only sensible, it's also necessary. I'm successful in impressing that point on some of my cases, and in others, I'm not."

Kelly did not seem too certain in which category Scolnick belonged so he was asked whether there were any flags which would indicate the path that an ex-convict might be traveling.

"Well, they are usually unemployed or have a pattern of unemployment. This is particularly true of professional gamblers and burglars. It's also important if they indicate that they think they are important because of who they are. So when they encounter someone writing a story about them, they tend to ignore the damage they have done to other people and make certain rationalizations such as, 'Everybody has larceny in their hearts.'

"I'd say that one of Scolnick's chief problems is distinguishing, as a businessman, what is ethical and what is not. As a parole officer, I have to try and help him make that distinction. All businessmen have the problem of establishing that they are ethical, but, in his case, it's an acute one.

326

"If he gets back in trouble, I think it might probably be by mistake. His problem is with his thought processes. This idea of his old friends returning him into the wrong channels is covered by a theory that's known as differential associations. All that means is, for example, suppose a group of businessmen get together and decide to fix prices in their industry.

"Although this is against the law, they don't think of themselves as criminals. They belong to the same clubs, know the same people, have similar living patterns and no one they know would think that their action in price-fixing was reprehensible. It's just good business. Now, it may be that Mr. Scolnick would fall into the same error when he is with his friends.

"My problem with him is in getting a list of his friends and, in the cases where I do know who they are, trying to find out if they have legal or ethical standards. I have to be sure that he can, within reason, have faith or trust in these friends. I have to be sure that he doesn't misinterpret the standards he must live by."

His friends are almost unanimous in their conviction that Scolnick is too smart to ever do anything that would send him back to prison. But one of them said, "The only trouble, though, is that Syl is like an old gunfighter with a big reputation. Some smart DA, or reporter, or some politician trying to grab newspaper space for himself, is going to try and get him in order to help their own reputation."

It is clear to anyone who spends time with Scolnick that he doesn't willingly forego old friendships. He has found the fellowship with them that has been denied him elsewhere because of his weight and appearance and lack of social or cultural standing. His old friends accept him because he is bigger and smarter than they are. They have all lived better than they deserved because he showed them how.

Most of them are immature individuals who find a measure of superiority in their own theories that the rest of the

327

world is inhabited by squares. Scolnick doesn't totally reject them because they are almost the only group with which he has had a community of interest. He feels he needs their admiration and respect. Sometimes he thinks he's reached this bond with the law enforcement officers with whom he has worked, but in his "down" periods, he realizes that they will never consider him anything but an implement.

He gets depressed too easily. There are times when he furiously resents Stanford Shmukler because he thinks the lawyer is "only a crepe hanger." This generally happens after Shmukler punctures some bright, new balloon of a business scheme by pointing out that some people might consider parts of it as possibly unethical. He construes this advice as a reminder that he is an ex-jailbird. "The guy always brings me down," he says. "He's always throwing cold water on me and it's tough for me to be around guys like that. Especially when I know how bad I need him to do just what he does."

One man, a dissatisfied franchise purchaser, refused to meet with the reporter. He said over the telephone, "My lawyer doesn't want me to talk to anybody about Scolnick because we're bringing suit against him. I'm going to destroy him and I'm going to destroy his company for what they did to me. I don't care if it takes me the rest of my life, I'm going to see that he goes back behind the bars where he belongs.

"I can prove that he framed that guy who he had arrested because he said he was trying to blackmail him. I tell you, he's the most evil man I've ever met. When I told him that his lies had cost my wife and me and a friend all of our savings, he only laughed and said, 'You can't do anything to me. I own this part of the country.'

"I've been in sales all my life and when that fat thief thinks he can slough me off, he's dead wrong. I'm going to get his parole revoked if it's the last thing I ever do, I don't care if I have to go to every federal authority in the East to get it done!"

The United States attorney in Newark, New Jersey, subpoenaed the company's books after the *Philadelphia Magazine* article appeared. Scolnick's secretary called one of the investigators in the office to make a date for the delivery of the documents. The man said, "Will Big Cherry be bringing them up? I can't wait to get into the arena and match wits with him."

That night the reporter sat in the living room in Cherry Hill, talking with Scolnick, his mother and his wife. Scolnick was angry. "They made me Cherry Hill Fats and the criminal mastermind," he said. "The newspapers and the people create you and make you into what they want to think you are. Then they believe what they first told you.

"But I'm no criminal mastermind. I was a crook and now I'm trying to be straight. But they don't want me to. They don't want the bubble broken. Last week, I was supposed to talk to some lodge and they sent me a window card they had made up to advertise it. It said something about my weight and that I was the big, criminal mastermind and all that. They was advertising a freak, not that I had anything to say about prison reform that might be worth listening to!"

"Sylvan," interrupted the reporter, "I wish you'd listen to me. You're in trouble and no amount of claiming that everyone made you what you are is going to change it. You're surrounded by people who want to see you back in prison and if you keep on, they're going to get their way.

"You told me that your parole officer, Kelly, is a fine man, a very nice man. He may be. But you haven't charmed him one damned bit. He plays it straight down the line and if he's ever convinced that you are crossing over the line, even a little bit, he's going to recommend that you go back to prison. He doesn't see himself as your friend. He sees himself as your probation officer.

329

"I talked with Alan Halpern, the editor of *Philadelphia Magazine*. I've known Alan for twenty years and he's about as fair as a man can be. He doesn't see Fonzi as you do: an arrogant guy who appointed himself as an avenging angel. He sees Gaeton as a reporter who wouldn't write anything that he wasn't honestly convinced was true. There's a hell of a lot of other people in the community who feel the same way about Gaeton. Some of them are law officers.

"These guys have no affection for you, but they really aren't your worst enemies. That description only fits guys like George Gazzara and the two Murrays and all the rest of your old friends who keep coming back to you.

"There's not one law officer who thinks those guys are healthy for you. They are going to sink you, Sylvan. You can't afford to see them, be with them. You can't ever consider bringing them into some new business with you.

"Forgive me," the reporter said, conscious that he was in an area where he had absolutely no professional right to be, "but you shouldn't have the slightest trace of a connection with Silver Ship. It's a borderline kind of a business and it's full of borderline people. I know you say you're only a consultant, but even that is too damned much. You just can't afford to have anything to do with it. The law of averages is against you. There's just bound to be a certain percentage of unsuccessful franchisees and, because you're you, they are going to say that you conned them into the deal."

As the reporter spoke, Scolnick's face first became blank and controlled and then, finally, desperately worried. "What am I going to do? I tried to get away from them."

"It isn't enough. It's none of my business, but I guess that if it were me, I'd have a completely formal meeting, witnessed by someone whose word is absolutely good, that you have given back any interest that you might still have in the deal."

330

He lost no time in fighting the idea. "I'll get Shmukler. No, he's represented me in too many criminal cases. Better, I'll get Alan Davis. He used to be an assistant DA while I was testifying. Everybody knows he's absolutely straight. I'll have Alan at the meeting. Give me the phone."

As he began to dial, his wife leaned toward the reporter. "By telling him this," she said, "you proved that you're his friend."

"Hullo, Alan?" he said, almost shouting into the phone. "Alan, you got to help me. You got to be my front. I'm going to meet with George Gazzara and Bob Stennis this Sunday, Alan, and I'm going to get a paper signed by them that I have no part in the business, that it's all theirs and I got nothing more to do with it.

"Please, Alan. You got to be my front. You got to be there, Alan, to be like a guarantee that I'm totally out of the deal. Six months from now when they get in trouble, you got to be my witness that I had nothing to do with it."

He listened, brooding, and glanced over to his wife and mother. "He says," he told them, "that he can't because he's too close to Dick Sprague and it would look like I'm using him as a front."

Back into the phone, he said, "I *am* using you as a front, Alan, but you are proving you are my friend if you do it. Remember, you said you'd help me stay straight."

He listened some more and then said, "Then how about somebody in your office? Everybody knows you're in one of the most respectable offices in town. They wouldn't do nothing wrong for nobody."

The lawyer spoke at length in return while Scolnick's face became more Buddha-like with almost every passing second. His voice was soft and sad as he finally said, "All right, Alan.

I understand. That's what I'll do. Thanks, anyway, Alan," and hung up.

He turned and said, "Alan says he just can't do it. It just wouldn't be fair to his friends in the DA's office. He told me that Shmukler would be okay to witness it, that everyone accepts it when he gives his word."

The two women did not answer. They were sitting forward in their chairs, anxiously studying the man they both loved. Their faces seemed gray, even in the brightly lit living room.

# Chapter 18

# THE EPILOGUE

On the Sunday following the conversation with Alan Davis, Scolnick met with Gazzara and Stennis and transferred to them every vestige of the claim he had upon affairs of the Silver Ship of Bargains. His contract as a consultant to the company was also terminated at that meeting.

A month later, on the night of November 24, 1971, I received a phone call from Sylvan Scolnick. He was crying so uncontrollably that, at first, I could not understand what he was saying.

"Mom just died," he said. "She died an hour and a half ago, alone, in her car. She was out driving to get something and she had some kind of a seizure and although she got into a drive-in restaurant, it was too late. She died there, all alone.

"She was all my strength. When I was a kid or even after I was a man, she'd say, 'It's always darkest just before daylight,' and then I'd be able to go to sleep. I even did this in prison. It was the thought of her that made me able to keep on going.

"She was such a great woman, but she never had a happy day in her life from me. I realize it now. I never gave her anything but aggravation.

333

"All her life she struggled so hard. And now when she could live and laugh a little bit, it's too late. I could have done so much more for her. Given her so much more pleasure. I didn't have to build this monstrosity of a house. Even if I had just lost some of the weight, I could have been driving her tonight and then she wouldn't have been so alone.

"All this time I thought I was such a big man. But all the time, I was just a clown dancing on her grave."